남북한 유엔 가입

결의안 채택 및 대응 2

남북한 유엔 가입

결의안 채택 및 대응 2

한국학술정보

| 머리말

유엔 가입은 대한민국 정부 수립 이후 중요한 숙제 중 하나였다. 한국은 1949년을 시작으로 여러 차례 유엔 가입을 시도했으나, 상임이사국인 소련의 거부권 행사에 번번이 부결되고 말았다. 북한도 마찬가지로, 1949년부터 유엔 가입을 시도했으나 상임이사국들의 반대에 매번 가로막혔다. 서로가 한반도의 유일한 합법 정부라 주장하는 당시 남북한은 어디까지나 상대측을 배제하고 단독으로 유엔에 가입하려 했으며, 이는 국제적인 냉전 체제와 맞물려 어느 쪽도 원하는 바를 성취하지 못하게 만들었다. 하지만 1980년대를 지나며 냉전 체제가 이완되면서 변화가 생긴다. 한국은 북방 정책을 통해 국제적 여건을 조성하고, 남북한 고위급 회담 등에서 남북한 유엔 동시 가입 등을 강력히 설득한다. 이런 외교적 노력이 1991년 열매를 맺어, 제46차 유엔총회를 통해 한국과 북한은 유엔 회원국이 될 수 있었다.

본 총서는 외교부에서 작성하여 30여 년간 유지한 남북한 유엔 가입 관련 자료를 담고 있다. 한국의 유엔 가입 촉구를 위한 총회결의한 추진 검토, 세계 각국을 대상으로 한 지지 교섭 과정, 국내외 실무 절차 진행, 채택 과정 및 향후 대응, 관련 홍보 및 언론 보도까지 총 16권으로 구성되었다. 전체 분량은 약 8천 쪽에 이른다.

2024년 3월

한국학술정보(주)

| 일러두기

· 본 총서에 실린 자료는 2022년 4월과 2023년 4월에 각각 공개한 외교문서 4,827권, 76만 여 쪽 가운데 일부를 발췌한 것이다.

· 각 권의 제목과 순서는 공개된 원본을 최대한 반영하였으나, 주제에 따라 일부는 적절히 변경하였다.

· 원본 자료는 A4 판형에 맞게 축소하거나 원본 비율을 유지한 채 A4 페이지 안에 삽입하였다. 또한 현재 시점에선 공개되지 않아 '공란'이란 표기만 있는 페이지 역시 그대로 실었다.

· 외교부가 공개한 문서 각 권의 첫 페이지에는 '정리 보존 문서 목록'이란 이름으로 기록물 종류, 일자, 명칭, 간단한 내용 등의 정보가 수록되어 있으며, 이를 기준으로 0001번부터 번호가 매겨져 있다. 이는 삭제하지 않고 총서에 그대로 수록하였다.

· 보고서 내용에 관한 더 자세한 정보가 필요하다면, 외교부가 온라인상에 제공하는 『대한민국 외교사료요약집』 1991년과 1992년 자료를 참조할 수 있다.

| 차례

정 리 보 존 문 서 목 록					
기록물종류	일반공문서철	등록번호	2020090038	등록일자	2020-09-08
분류번호	731.12	국가코드		보존기간	영구
명 칭	남북한 유엔가입, 1991.9.17. 전41권				
생 산 과	국제연합1과	생산년도	1990~1991	담당그룹	
권 차 명	V.33 유엔가입 축하메시지				
내용목차	* 대통령 및 장관 앞 각국의 축하메시지 접수 및 답신				

0001

THE REPRESENTATIVE
OF THE
UNITED STATES OF AMERICA
TO THE
UNITED NATIONS

September 12, 1991

Dear Mr. Minister:

It was especially pleasant to meet with you again during my recent visit to Korea. I thank you for having received me in the Foreign Ministry, for the excellent talks which we held there, and for the opportunity to review with you a number of issues of current importance to both of our governments here at the United Nations.

It was especially pleasant being with you as well at the marvelous luncheon given for us at the Blue House by President Roh Tae-Woo.

You and all Koreans can take considerable pride in the enormous accomplishment you have made to ensure your admission to the United Nations which will go forward now on the 17th of September. We join all others in congratulating you on this significantly important success.

I look forward to seeing you here in New York during your coming visit and send again my deepest thanks for your many kindnesses during my visit and for the opportunity to meet with you.

Sincerely,

Thomas R. Pickering

His Excellency
Lee Sang-Ock,
Minister of Foreign Affairs,
Seoul, Korea.

0002

THE REPRESENTATIVE OF THE UNITED STATES
OF AMERICA TO THE UNITED NATIONS
799 UNITED NATIONS PLAZA
NEW YORK, NEW YORK 10017

주한미국대사관
서울특별시 종로구 세종로 82번지
110-050

26. 9. 91
GOVT. BLDG. KOREA
대한민국우
≈06.50

His Excellency
Lee Sang-Ock
Minister of Foreign Affairs
Seoul, Korea

0003

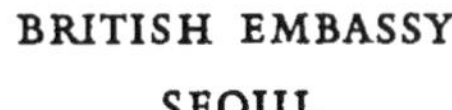

BRITISH EMBASSY
SEOUL

17 September 1991

HE Lee Sang-ock
Minister of Foreign Affairs
Seoul

My Dear Minister,

I have been instructed by the Rt Hon Douglas Hurd CBE MP, Secretary of State for Foreign and Commonwealth Affairs, to pass on the following message:

> "Dear Colleague
>
> I should like to extend my warmest congratulations to you and the Korean Government upon the entry of the Republic of Korea to membership of the United Nations on 17 September. I know that this is an event of the greatest significance for the Korean Government and people, the fruit of many years' patient diplomacy and hard work. The admission of both Koreas marks a further important step in strengthening the role of the United Nations as an instrument of peace and security and in matching the aspirations of its membership towards universality.
>
> The United Kingdom was glad to have played a small part in helping you to achieve this long-sought goal and I am confident that our relationship, both bilaterally and at the United Nations, will continue to flourish.
>
> I hope that the admission of both Koreas will now contribute to a more productive dialogue between North and South and that the high-level talks scheduled for the end of October will go ahead as planned. It is the hope of all the friends of Korea that a momentum can now be maintained which will lead in the fullness of time towards your ultimate goal of the peaceful reunification of the Korean peninsula."

I avail myself of this opportunity to renew to Your Excellency the assurance of my highest consideration.

Yours sincerely,

Peter Longworth

P Longworth
Chargé d'Affaires a.i

0004

SC/91/315

PERMANENT MISSION OF JAPAN
TO THE UNITED NATIONS
NEW YORK

17 September 1991

Excellency,

I have the honour to forward the enclosed message from H.E. Mr. Taro Nakayama, Minister for Foreign Affairs of Japan, congratulating you on the admission of your country to the United Nations.

May I take this opportunity to express my own congratulations to you on this auspicious occasion.

Accept, Excellency, the assurances of my highest consideration.

Yoshio Hatano
Ambassador Extraordinary
and Plenipotentiary
Permanent Representative of
Japan to the United Nations

H.E. Mr. LEE Sang-Ock
Minister for Foreign Affairs
The Republic of Korea

0005

September 17, 1991

Excellency,

I would like to extend my heartfelt congratulations to Your Excellency on the simultaneous admission of South and North Koreas to the United Nations membership. I also wish to express my deepest respect for the unsparing efforts which Your Excellency has made to achieve this long-pending objective. I sincerely hope that this historical event would be conducive to relieving the tension in the Korean Penisula through the South-North dialogue, and could ultimately lead to the peaceful unification of the Korean Peninsula.

The recent exchange of visits between Prime Minister Kaifu and President Roh has paved the way for developing global and future-oriented partnership between Japan and the Republic of Korea. In this context, it is very important that our two countries will henceforth establish close and cooperative relations in the United Nations, and thereby will contribute jointly to the settlement of various international issues.

I am looking forward to seeing Your Excellency soon in New York.

Yours sincerely,

Taro Nakayama
Minister for Foreign Affairs,
Japan

H.E. Mr. LEE Sang-Ock
Minister for Foreign Affairs
The Republic of Korea

0006

FAX TRANSMISSION

DATE : September 17, 1991

TO : His Excellency Sang-Ock Lee
Minister of Foreign Affairs
Republic of Korea

FAX NO. : (212)371-8873

FROM : LES BROWN
Director, Fellows Program

FAX NO. : (617) 496-5642

PHONE NO.: (617) 495-2112

Total number of pages: 2
(including cover sheet)

Comments : PLEASE NOTIFY IF UNABLE TO DELIVER

Center for International Affairs
Fellows Program
Harvard University

0007

TOTAL P.01

The Center for International Affairs

Harvard University

1737 Cambridge Street, Cambridge MA 02138
Telephone (617) 495-0539
Facsimile (617) 495-8292

Joseph S. Nye, Jr.
Director

September 16, 1991

His Excellency Sang-Ock Lee
Minister of Foreign Affairs
Republic of Korea

Dear Mr. Minister,

I am writing to congratulate you on the occasion of the accession of the Republic of Korea to Permanent Membership in the United Nations. Given the warm collaborative relationship that our two countries have enjoyed for over four decades, it is a source of great satisfaction to me and, indeed, all Americans to see this successful outcome of the campaign that you and your predecessors have conducted so ably over many years.

You will agree, I think, that this is a very critical period for the UN and that if international institutions are to play the role that global developments in security, environment, health, development and trade increasingly demand, then the UN will have to be a key player. In this respect, the addition of the Republic of Korea as a voting member of the UN family is greatly to be welcomed.

As you may know, the first Korean to have joined the Fellows Program at the Center for International Affairs, was your former Prime Minister Chung Il Kwon, in 1960. Since that time we have enjoyed a steady stream of diplomats from your ministry, including one of your predecessors, Lee Won-Kyung. In microcosm, Harvard's close relations with your ministry have paralleled the relations of our respective countries and I look forward to the next thirty years of productive collaboration at both levels.

Sincerely,

JSNye

0008

TOTAL P.01

원 본

외 무 부

종 별 :

번 호 : COW-0398 일 시 : 91 0917 1600

수 신 : 장 관(연일,미중)

발 신 : 주 코스타리카 대사

제 목 : 아국유엔가입

주재국 CASTRO 외무차관은 금 17일 본직에게 아국의 유엔 가입을 진심으로 축하함을 우선전화로 알려왔음.끝.

(대사 김창근-국장)

국기국 1차보 미주국 외정실 안기부

PAGE 1

91.09.18 10:02 WG

외신 1과 통제관

0003

원 본

외 무 부

종 별 :

번 호 : SLW-0738 일 시 : 91 0918 1800

수 신 : 장 관(국연,아프일)

발 신 : 주 세네갈 대사

제 목 : 유엔가입 축하

주재국 ANDRE SONKO 문교장관은 9.18.본직에게 한국의 유엔가입 축하전화하여 왔음.끝.

(대사 허 승-국장)

국기국 1차보 중아국 외정실 분석관 안기부

PAGE 1

91.09.19 09:35 WG

외신 1과 통제관

0010

DUTA BESAR REPUBLIK INDONESIA

(AMBASSADOR OF THE REPUBLIC OF INDONESIA)

YOUIDO-DONG, YOUNGDEUNGPO-KU.

S E O U L

His Excellency Lee Sang Ock
Minister of Foreign Affairs
Republic of Korea
S E O U L

0011

AMBASSADOR OF THE REPUBLIC OF INDONESIA SEOUL

Seoul, 18 September 1991

His Excellency Lee Sang Ock
Minister of Foreign Affairs
Republic of Korea
Seoul

Excellency,

On behalf of the Heads of the ASEAN Missions in Seoul, I would like to extend our hearty congratulations to the Republic of Korea and your people for having become a member of the United Nations, as anticipated by your people for over 40 years.

Special felicitations to the Government of the Republic of Korea who has accomplished the historic entry to the United Nations, due mainly to the initiative of your country. It is our sincere hope that the admission to the United Nations of your two divided countries truly serve for the realization of eventual peaceful reunification. We are very sure that the Republic of Korea further will enhance her contribution to the peace and prosperity of our international community.

Please allow me to avail myself of this opportunity to renew to Your Excellency the assurances of my highest consideration.

KEDUTAAN BESAR REPUBLIK INDONESIA SEOUL

RUDOLF KASENDA
Ambassador of the Republic of Indonesia
Chairman of the ASEAN Committee in Seoul (ACS)

0012

관리번호	91-5014

외 무 부

1

종 별 :

번 호 : NMW-0756 일 시 : 91 0918 1220

수 신 : 장관(아프이,연일)

발 신 : 주 나미비아 대사

제 목 : 남아공외상의 유엔가입축전

1. 남아공외무부는 아국의 유엔가입과 관련, BOTHA 외무장관명의의 장관앞 축전을 아래와 같이 발송했다고 알려왔기 보고함.

18 SEP.1991

HIS EXCELLENCY KLEE SANG-OK

MIN.OF FOREIGN AFFS.KF THE REP.OF KOREA

SEOUL

REPUBLIC OF KOREA

YOUR EXCELLENCY

IT IS WITH MUCH INTREST THAT THE REPUBLIC OF SOUTH AFRICAHAS FOLLOWED THE DIPLOMATIC AND ECONOMIC PROGRESS OF THE REPUBLIC OF KOREA.THE ADMISSION ON 17 SEP. 1991 OF YOUR EXCELLENCY'S COUNTRY AS A MEMBER OF THE U.N. IS AN IMPORTANT MILESTONE AND I EXTENDED MY CONGRETULATIONS TO YOU WITH THE ACHIEVEMENT.

ON BEHALF OF THE GOVERNMENT OF THE REP.OF SOUTH AFRICA I WISH YOU AND YOUR COUNTRY EVERYTHING OF THE BEST IN YOUR ENDEAVOURS AND WE LOOK FORWARDTO IMPROVING THE RELATIONS BETWEEN OUR TWO COUNTRIES.

PLEASE ACCEPT, YOUR EXCELLENCY, THE ASSURANCES OF MY HIGHEST CONSIDERATION.

SIGNED

R.F.BOTHA

MINISTER OF FOREIGN AFFAIRS OF THE REP.OF SOUTH AFRICA

2. 상기 축전에대해 축전접수를 확인하고 사의를 표하면서 양국관계가 점진적으로 발전되기를 희망한다는 내용의 회신을 발송하는것이 좋을것으로 사료되어건의함. 끝.

중아국 장관 차관 1차보 국기국 청와대 안기부

PAGE 1

91.09.18 22:17

외신 2과 통제관 CD

0013

(대사 송학원-국장)

예고: 91. 12. 31. 일반

PAGE 2

0014

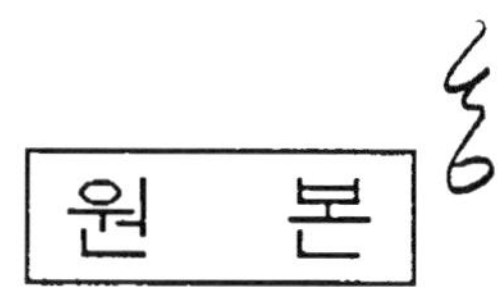

관리번호	91-1113

외 무 부

종 별 : 지 급

번 호 : UNW-2823　　　　일 시 : 91 0918 2400

수 신 : 장관대리(연일,서구일)

발 신 : 주 유엔 대사

제 목 : 영국외상 축하메세지

1. 주유엔 영국대사는 금 9.18 아국의 유엔가입을 축하하는 HURD 외상의 이상옥 장관님앞 메세지를 별첨과같이 송부해옴.

2. 또한 주유엔 남아공 대사가 금일 송부해온 BOTHA 외상의 축하메세지도 별첨보고함.

3. 동 메세지를 장관님께 기 보고 조치하였음.

첨부:상기 메세지:UNW(F)-541 끝

(대사 노창희-차관)

예고:91.12.31. 까지 문에 의거 일반문서로 재분류됨

국기국　장관　차관　구주국

PAGE 1

91.09.19　13:15

외신 2과　통제관 BS

0015

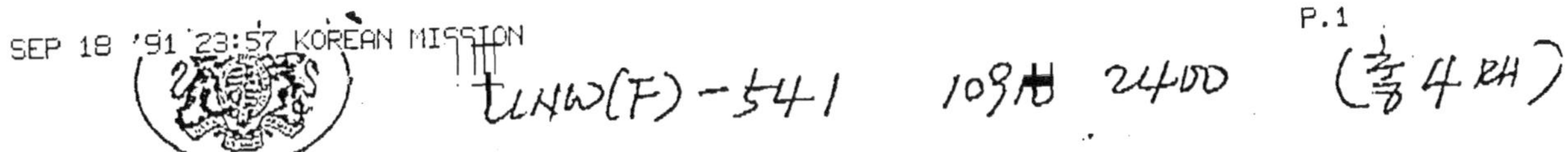

Message from the Rt Hon Douglas Hurd to Mr Lee Sang-Ock

Dear Colleague

I should like to extend my warmest congratulations to you and the Korean Government upon the entry of the Republic of Korea to membership of the United Nations on 17 September. I know that this is an event of the greatest significance for the Korean Government and people, the fruit of many years patient diplomacy and hard work. The admission of both Koreas marks a further important step in strengthening the role of the United Nations as an instrument of peace and security and in matching the aspirations of its membership towards universality.

The United Kingdom was glad to have played a small part in helping you to achieve this long-sought goal and I am confident that our relationship, both bilaterally and at the United Nations, will continue to flourish.

I hope that the admission of both Koreas will now contribute to a more productive dialogue between North and South and that the high-level talks scheduled for the end of October will go ahead as planned. It is the hope of all the friends of Korea that a momentum can now be maintained which will lead in the fullness of time towards your ultimate goal of the peaceful reunification of the Korean peninsula.

4-1

0016

UNITED KINGDOM MISSION
TO THE UNITED NATIONS
845 THIRD AVENUE
NEW YORK, N.Y. 10022

FROM THE PERMANENT REPRESENTATIVE

18 September 1991

H E Mr Chang Hee Roe
Permanent Mission of the Republic
of Korea to the UN
866 UN Plaze, Suite 300
New York, NY 10017

Dear Ambassador,

I have been asked to pass the enclosed message from the Secretary of State for Foreign and Commonwealth Affairs, the Rt Hon Douglas Hurd, to Mr Lee Sang-Ock, who is visiting New York.

Yours sincerely

David Hannay

D H A Hannay

4-2

0017

THE PERMANENT REPRESENTATIVE OF SOUTH AFRICA
TO THE UNITED NATIONS
333 EAST 38TH STREET 9TH FLOOR
NEW YORK, N.Y. 10016
(212) 213-5583

9/1
9/1/2/1

17 September 1991

Your Excellency

Allow me to express my personal congratulations to you on the Republic of Korea being accepted as a new member of the United Nations.

I have the honour to enclose for your information the content of a letter from the South African Minister of Foreign Affairs, which is being transmitted to His Excellency Lee Sang-ok, Minister of Foreign Affairs of the Republic of Korea. This letter is being transmitted through the office of the South African Consul-General in Tokyo, to your Embassy there. The letter reads as follows:

"Your Excellency,

It is with much interest that the Republic of South Africa has followed the diplomatic and economic progress of the Republic of Korea. The admission on 17 September 1991 of Your Excellency's country as a member of the United Nations is an important milestone and I extend my congratulations to you with the achievement.

On behalf of the Government of the Republic of South Africa I wish you and your country everything of the best in your endeavours and we look forward to improving the relations between our countries.

Please accept, Your Excellency, the assurance of my highest consideration.

Signed
R F Botha
Minister of Foreign Affairs
of the Republic of South Africa"

4-3

0018

- 2 -

Excellency, I wish to associate myself with the sentiments expressed in the above letter. Having only just arrived at the United Nations, I look forward to meeting you and congratulating you in person in due course.

Please accept, Your Excellency, the assurances of my highest consideration.

VRWSteward.

V R W Steward
Ambassador
Permanent Representative

H.E. Mr Chang Hee Roe
Permanent Mission of the Republic
of Korea to the United Nations
866 United Nations Plaza, Suite 300
NEW YORK, N.Y. 10017

4-4

0013

Ambassador of Hungary

1991. 9. 18.

서 울

대한민국 이 상 옥 외무장관님

뉴 욕

존경하는 장관님,

저는 대한민국이 161번째 유엔 회원국이 되었다는 기쁜 소식을 접하고 따뜻한 축하의 말씀을 보내는 바입니다.

한국 시간으로 1991년 9월 18일 새벽, 한국 TV 생방송을 통하여 유엔가입 결의안 통과 후 이상옥 외무장관님이 총회에서 행하신 연설과 태극기 게양식을 직접 시청하면서 이 역사적인 순간에 받은 깊은 감동을 본인은 잊을 수 가 없을 것입니다. 유엔 가입은 대한민국이 수 십여년동안 공들여온 꾸준한 외교노력의 결실이라고 봅니다. 저는 유엔 가입을 계기로 남북간에 새로운 대화와 평화적 재결합 실현, 그리고 인적·물적 교류의 마당이 마련됨과 동시에 남북한 상호 신뢰구축에 새로운 장이 열릴 것을 희망합니다.

대한민국의 무궁한 발전을 빌며 한국의 뜻깊은 명절 한가위를 맞이하여 장관님께서 즐겁고 평안하시기를 기원합니다.

샨도르 애뜨래

0020

RICHARD V. ALLEN
905 SIXTEENTH STREET, N.W.
WASHINGTON, D.C. 20006

TELEPHONE (202) 737-2824

VIA FACSIMILE FROM WASHINGTON, D.C.

September 18, 1991

Dear Mr. Minister:

Thank you so much for seeing me last week and for the enjoyable conversation. It is always a pleasure to share views with you, especially at this important time in Korean history.

Which leads me to offer my sincere congratulations to you as a new member of the United Nations. It is an honor you fully deserve and I and your many other American friends are delighted with this development.

Again, it was a pleasure seeing you.

Warmest regards,

Sincerely,

Dick

Richard V. Allen

The Honorable Lee Sang Ock
Minister of Foreign Affairs
The Republic of Korea
Seoul, Korea

0021

1991.9.18.
국제기구국

1. 일본수상 및 외상, 유엔가입축하 메세지 발송

   o 주한 일본대사관은 9.18. 유엔가입을 축하하는 가이후 수상의 대통령 앞 전문 멧세지와 장관님 앞 나카야마 외상의 전문 메세지를 공한 첨부 전달해 옴.

2. IAEA 이사 임명

   o 금번 제35차 IAEA 총회(9.16-20)에서의 아국의 IAEA 이사국 진출에 대비하여 이장춘 주오스트리아 대사를 아국 이사로 결정, 주오지리 대사관에 통보(9.23. 신임 이사회참석 대비)

공람 91년 9월 18일	담 당	과 장	국 장
	(서명)	(서명)	代 (서명)

0022

EMBASSY OF JAPAN
SEOUL

No. P-449

NOTE VERBALE

The Embassy of Japan presents its compliments to the Ministry of Foreign Affairs and has the honour to enclose a message from Minister for Foreign Affairs Taro Nakayama to His Excellency Minister of Foreign Affairs Sang-Ock Lee.

The Embassy of Japan avails itself of this opportunity to renew to the Ministry of Foreign Affairs the assurances of its highest consideration.

Enclosure : as stated

Seoul, September 18, 1991

0023

September 17, 1991

Excellency,

I would like to extend my heartfelt congratulations to Your Excellency on the simultaneous admission of South and North Koreas to the United Nations membership. I also wish to express my deepest respect for unsparing efforts which Your Excellency has made to achieve this long-pending objective. I sincerely hope that this historical event would be conducive to relieving the tension in the Korean Peninsula through the South-North dialogue, and could ultimately lead to the peaceful unification of the Korean Peninsula.

The recent exchange of visits between Prime Minister Kaifu and President Roh has paved the way for developing global and future-oriented partnership between Japan and the R.O.K.. In this context, it is very important that our two countries will henceforth establish close and cooperative relations in the United Nations, and thereby will contribute jointly to the settlement of various international issues.

I am Looking forward to seeing Your Excellency soon at New York.

Yours sincerely,

Taro Nakayama
Minisiter for Foreign Affairs,
Japan

H.E. LEE Sang-Ock
Minister of Foreign Affairs
The Republic of Korea

0024

원 본

외 무 부

종 별 :

번 호 : OSW-0620 일 시 : 91 0919 1740

수 신 : 장관(연일,아일)

발 신 : 주오사카총영사

제 목 : 유엔가입 축전

아래 인사들이 아국의 유엔가입에 대한 축전을 본직 앞으로 보내왔음.

아래

1.오사카시장(니시오 마사야)

2.관서 경제인연합회 전무이사(하루야스 오수미).끝

(총영사 박노수)

국기국 아주국

PAGE 1

91.09.20 02:58 DW

외신 1과 통제관

0025

관리 번호	91 —1106

분류번호	보존기간

발 신 전 보

번 호 : WUS-4319 910919 1000 DQ 별 :

수 신 : 주 미 대사. 총영사 (사본 : 주유엔대사) WUN-3027

발 신 : 장 관 (연일)

제 목 : 차관명의 메세지 송부

9.18. 우리의 유엔가입과 관련 차관명의의 Bolton 국제기구담당 차관보 앞 메세지를 별첨 타전하니 동 차관보에게 전달하고, 결과 보고바람.

첨부 : 상기 메세지 1부. 끝.

(국기국장대리 금정호)

1991.12.31.에 예고문에 의거 일반문서로 재분류됨

보안 통제	

앙 고 재	91년 9월 19일	유엔1과	기안자 성명		과 장	심의관	국 장		차 관	장 관
							전결			

외신과통제

0026

(DRAFT)

18 September 1991

Dear Mr. Bolton,

On this special day of my country's admission to the United Nations, I am writing to say how much we appreciate your cooperation and assistance in our efforts to attain UN membership.

The firm commitment of your Government to our joint campaign from the initial stage throughout to its final realization was essential to today's success. Particularly, your personal interest and encouragement as well as professional advice was very much helpful.

Hoping that you will continue to help us at the UN, I wish you all the best.

With my warmest regards.

Yours sincerely,

YOO Chong Ha
Vice Minister of
Foreign Affairs

Mr. John Bolton
Assistant Secretary of State
for International Organization Affairs

0027

(DRAFT)

18 September 1991

Dear Mr. Bolton,

On this special day of my country's admission to the United Nations, I am writing to say how much we ~~have~~ appreciated your cooperation and assistance in our efforts to attain UN membership.

The firm commitment of your Government to our joint campaign from the initial stage throughout to its final realization was essential to today's success. Particularly, your personal interest and encouragement ~~attention~~ as well as professional advice ~~is highly appreciated~~ was very much helpful.

Hoping that you will continue to help us at the UN, ~~our paths may cross again before too long,~~ I wish you all the best. ~~continued success and good luck for the furure.~~

With my warmest regards.

Yours sincerely,

YOO Chong Ha
Vice Minister of
Foreign Affairs

Mr. John Bolton
Assistant Secretary of State
for International Organization Affairs

0028

46017

기안용지

분류기호 문서번호	연일 2031 -	(전화 :)	시행상 특별취급	
보존기간	영구·준영구. 10. 5. 3. 1	장		관
수신처 보존기간				
시행일자	1991.9.19.			

보조기관			협조기관		문서통제
	국장	전결			1991. 9. 19 통제관
	심의관				
	과장				
기안책임자		송영완			발송인

경유		발신명의		1991. 9. 19 외무부
수신	대통령 비서실장			
참조	의전수석 비서관			

제목 일본 카이후 수상 축전

91.9.18. 주한 일본대사관은 우리의 유엔가입에 관한 일본 카이후 수상의 대통령각하 앞 축전을 송부하여 왔는 바, 동 축전 및 번역문을 별첨 송부합니다.

첨부 : 일본수상 축전 및 번역문 각 1부. 끝.

0023

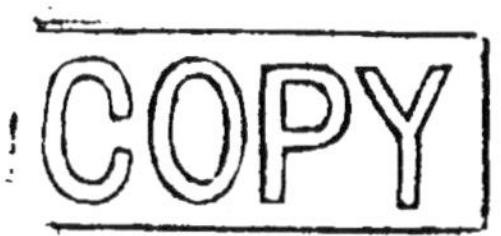

EMBASSY OF JAPAN
SEOUL

No. P-448

NOTE VERBALE

The Embassy of Japan presents its compliments to the Ministry of Foreign Affairs and has the honour to request the Ministry to transmit a message attached herewith from Prime Minister Toshiki Kaifu to His Excellency President Roh Tae-Woo.

The Embassy of Japan avails itself of this opportunity to renew to the Ministry of Foreign Affairs the assurances of its highest consideration.

Enclosure : as stated

Seoul, September 18, 1991

0030

(번역문)

盧泰愚 大統領閣下：

이번의 제46차 유엔총회에서 남북한의 유엔가입결의가 채택된것에 대하여 진심으로 축의를 표하고자 합니다.

귀국의 오랜 숙원이었던 남북유엔동시가입이 실현된것은 바로 각하의 탁월한 지도력 덕택이며 한국외교의 큰 성과로서 역사에 오래 기록될 것입니다. 저는 이를 계기로 남북대화를 통해 한반도의 긴장완화가 더욱 진전되어 평화적 통일로 연결되기를 강력히 기대하는 바입니다.

또, 올해 1월 귀국방문시의 정상회담에 있어서 각하와의 사이에 세계적시야에 입각한 미래지향적인 새로운 일한관계를 구축해 나가기를 확인하였습니다만, 앞으로는 유엔무대에 있어서도 국제사회가 안고있는 여러 문제의 해결에 함께 공헌하기 위하여 각하와 긴밀한 연계와 협력을 도모하고자 생각합니다.

각하의 건승하심과 귀국의 가일층의 발전을 바라는 바입니다.

1991년9월18일
日本國 内閣總理大臣
海部 俊樹

0031

盧泰愚大統領閣下：

今般、第４６回国連総会において、南北朝鮮の国連加盟承認決議が採択されたことに対し、心からの祝意を表したいと思います。貴国の長年の宿願であった南北国連同時加盟が実現したことは、まさに閣下の卓越した指導力の賜物であり、韓国外交の大きな成果として長く歴史に記録されることとなるでしょう。私は、これを契機として、南北対話を通じ朝鮮半島の緊張緩和が一層進み、その平和的統一につながることを強く期待いたします。

また、本年１月の貴国訪問の際の首脳会談において、閣下との間で、世界的視野に立った、未来志向的な新しい日韓関係を構築していくことを確認いたしましたが、今後は、国連の舞台においても、国際社会の抱える様々な問題の解決に共に貢献するため、閣下と緊密な連携と協力を図って行きたいと考えております。

閣下のご健勝と貴国の更なる発展をお祈り申し上げます。

１９９１年9月１８日

日本国　内閣総理大臣

海部　俊樹

0032

3041

69/66 SEOUL 7839 1150 19TH

한국통신
1991. 9. 19
서울전신국

H. E. MR. LEE SANG-OCK

MINISTER OF FOREIGN AFFAIRS OF

REPUBLIC OF KOREA.

YOUR EXCELLENCY.

I CONGRATULATE YOU FOR THE EFFORTS DEPLOYED IN ORDER TO ACCOMPLISH THIS HISTORICAL EVENT WHICH IS THE ADMISSION OF BOTH KOREAS AS FULL MEMBERS OF THE U.N. HOPING THAT THIS WOULD BE A POSITIVE STEP TOWARDS THEIR BETTER UNDERSTANDING AND FUTURE REUNIFICATION.

SINCERELY YOURS
MOHAMED AMIN CHOLKAMY
CONSOL GENERAL OF EGYPT

0033

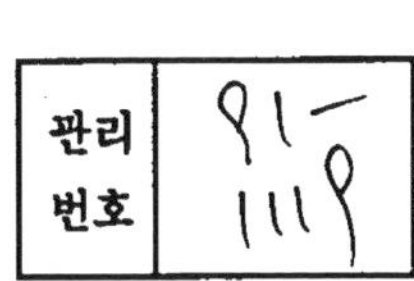

원 본

외 무 부

종 별 : 지 급

번 호 : MXW-1382 일 시 : 91 0919 1200

수 신 : 장 관(국연,미중, 주유엔대표부 및 시애틀총영사관경유-중계필)

발 신 : 주 멕시코대사

제 목 : 유엔가입 축전

아국의 유엔가입관련, 주재국 외무성으로 부터 접수한 장관님 앞 SOLANA 외상의 축전(9.18 자) 를 아래보고함.

- 아래-

이상옥 외무장관 각하

한국의 유엔 가입은 멕시코 정부의 큰 기쁨이며 또한, 세계의 보편주의 원칙 및 동남아 정세안정에 기여할 것임.

금번 노대통령 각하의 방멕은 역사적 유엔가입 직후 첫번째 방문국으로 더욱 경사스러운 일임.

각하를 곧 뵙게 되어 기쁘게 생각하며 경의를 표함.

SOLANA 외상

(대사 이복형-국장)

예고:91.12.31. 까지 일반문에 의거 일반문서로 재분류됨

국기국 장관 차관 미주국 중계

PAGE 1

91.09.20 07:18

외신 2과 통제관 BS

0034

AUSTRALIAN EMBASSY SEOUL

REF: 19 September 1991

H.E. Mr Lee Sang-Ock
Minister for Foreign Affairs
Republic of Korea
SEOUL

Your Excellency,

I have the honour to convey the following message from the Acting Foreign Minister of Australia, the Honourable Neal Blewett, MP, on the occasion of Korea's admission to the United Nations.

Begins

Dear Mr Lee,

I am writing to congratulate you on the admission of your country to the United Nations. Australia has been a staunch advocate of the ROK's admission to the UN and co-sponsored the General Assembly Resolution on the admission of the ROK and the DPRK. I am therefore delighted with this result, which will allow your country to assume its rightful role and responsibility in international affairs. You will recall that when Senator Evans wrote to you in April, he indicated that Australia would support either separate or simultaneous admission to the UN by the ROK and the DPRK in line with our support for the principle of universal UN membership. Australia is therefore also pleased to welcome the DPRK to the United Nations. I believe the simultaneous entry of both Koreas into the UN will assist the process of Korean reconciliation as well as contributing to an improved security environment in the Asia Pacific region. I am confident our close bilateral relationship and cooperation on international and regional issues can only be strengthened by your country's admission to the UN.

I wish you and your nation every success.

Yours sincerely,

NEAL BLEWETT"

Ends

...2

TELEPHONE 7306491 FAX. 7229264 TELEX 23663 K. P. O. BOX 562 SEOUL

0035

May I add to Dr Blewett's words my own sincere congratulations and my assurances of the continued full cooperation of this Embassy in working to strengthen relations between Korea and Australia.

Yours sincerely,

(Andrew Mullin)
Charge d'Affaires a.i.

0036

ㄴㄴㄴㄴ

유엔가입 축전
(WHO regional director)

NNNN

⊘
↑ WOIMUBU K24651
↓ 221012 GONGK CN
KKKKK

배부처	장관실	차관실	一차보	二차보	기획실	외정실	분석관	외전장	아주국	미주국	구주국	중아국	국기국	경제국	통상국	문협국	영교국	총무과	감사관	공보관	외연원	청와대	총리실	안기부	공보처
													o												

↓ ⊘
↑ WOIMUBU K24651

↓ THE HONOURABLE LEE SANG-OCK
MINISTER OF FOREIGN AFFAIRS
WOIMUBU SEOUL

1979 THE WORLD HEALTH ORGANIZATION REGIONAL OFFICE FOR THE WESTERN PACIFIC WISHES TO EXTEND ITS CONGRATULATIONS TO THE REPUBLIC OF KOREA ON ITS WELL-DESERVED ADMISSION TO THE UNITED NATIONS. WE TRUST THAT THIS NEW DEVELOPMENT WILL CONTRIBUTE TO AN EVEN MORE ACTIVE ROLE FOR YOUR GOVERNMENT IN INTERNATIONAL AFFAIRS AND TO FURTHER STRENGTHENING OF THE CLOSE COLLABORATION EXISTING BETWEEN YOUR GOVERNMENT AND THE WORLD HEALTH ORGANIZATION IN THIS REGION

DR SANG TAE HAN
REGIONAL DIRECTOR
WHO REGIONAL OFFICE
FOR THE WESTERN PACIFIC
MANILA

20/9/91/M
NNNNNN⊘
↑ WOIMUBU K24651
↓ 27652 WHO PH
.....

REPLY(75)OR(722 FROM USA)27652 WHO PH

0037

NO. 276

The Embassy of Brunei Darussalam presents its compliments to the Ministry of Foreign Affairs of the Republic of Korea and has the honour to convey the following message from His Royal Highness Prince Mohamed Bolkiah, Minister of Foreign Affairs of Brunei Darussalam to His Excellency Mr Lee Sang Ock, Minister of Foreign Affairs of the Republic of Korea.

YOUR EXCELLENCY,

I WOULD LIKE TO EXTEND MY WARM CONGRATULATIONS TO YOU, THE GOVERNMENT AND THE PEOPLE OF THE REPUBLIC OF KOREA ON THE AUSPICIOUS OCCASION OF THE ADMISSION OF THE REPUBLIC OF KOREA AS A MEMBER OF THE UNITED NATIONS.

I AM CONFIDENT THAT THE CLOSE COOPERATION BETWEEN BRUNEI DARUSSALAM AND THE REPUBLIC OF KOREA WILL BE FURTHER PROMOTED BILATERALLY AND WITHIN THE FRAMEWORK OF THE UNITED NATIONS.

PLEASE ACCEPT, YOUR EXCELLENCY, THE ASSURANCES OF MY HIGHEST CONSIDERATION.

PRINCE MOHAMED BOLKIAH

The Embassy of Brunei Darussalam avails itself of this opportunity to renew to the Ministry of Foreign Affairs of the Republic of Korea the assurances of its highest consideration.

MINISTRY OF FOREIGN AFFAIRS
77-6 SEJONGNO
CHONGNOKU
SEOUL

REF: KBROK: 23:1/1

DATE: 20 September 1991

0038

원 본

외 무 부

종 별 :

번 호 : FUW-0377 일 시 : 91 0921 1200

수 신 : 장관(국연)

발 신 : 주후쿠오카총영사

제 목 : 유엔가입 축전 접수

키타 규슈시장 스에요시 고우이찌는 9.20 아국의 유엔가입과 관련,축하및 금후 국제사회에서의 아국의 기여를 기원하는 축문을 보내왔음을 보고함 끝.

(총영사-국장)

국기국

PAGE 1

91.09.21 21:11 DQ

외신 1과 통제관

0033

EMBASSY OF THE REPUBLIC OF CHINA
SEOUL, KOREA

September 21, 1991

His Excellency Yoo Chong Ha
Acting Minister
Ministry of Foreign Affairs of
the Republic of Korea
77-6, Sejong-ro, Chongro-ku
Seoul, Korea

Excellency,

I have the honor, upon instructions, to transmit to Your Excellency the following telegraphic message addressed to His Excellency Roh Tae Woo, President of the Republic of Korea, from His Excellency Lee Teng-hui, President of the Republic of China, expressing his warmest congratulations on the occasion of the Republic of Korea's entry into the United Nations, which reads as follows:

"HIS EXCELLENCY PRESIDENT ROH TAE WOO
SEOUL, REPUBLIC OF KOREA
I WISH TO EXTEND TO YOU MY SINCERE CONGRATULATIONS ON THE OCCASION OF THE REPUBLIC OF KOREA'S ENTRY INTO THE UNITED NATIONS STOP PLEASE ACCEPT MY BEST WISHES FOR THE SUCCESS OF YOUR GREAT COUNTRY STOP
LEE TENG-HUI, PRESIDENT OF THE REPUBLIC OF CHINA"

I should be much obliged if Your Excellency would be kind enough to convey the above message to its highest destination at your earliest convenience.

Please accept, Excellency, the renewed assurances of my highest consideration.

Charles Shu-chi King
Ambassador

0040

외 무 부

종 별 :

번 호 : TNW-0361 일 시 : 91 0922

수 신 : 장 관(중동이, 연일)

발 신 : 주 튜니지아 대사

제 목 : 주재국 대통령 축전

주재국 외무부 아주 국장에 의하면 BEN ALI대통령은 9. 21 남북한 대통령에게 각각 국련가입을 축하하는 축전을 발송하였으며, 동축전에서 남북한의 국련 가입은 세계평화에 기여할 것이며, 남북한 통일에 도움을 줄 것이라고 하였다함. 끝.

(대사 변정현-국장)

중아국 국기국

PAGE 1

91.09.21 21:21 DQ

외신 1과 통제관

0041

Minister for Trade and Overseas Deve[illegible]ent
and Acting Minister for Foreign
Affairs and Trade

Parliament House
CANBERRA ACT 2600

23 SEP 1991

His Excellency Lee Sang-Ock
Minister of Foreign Affairs
Republic of Korea

Dear Mr Lee

I am writing to congratulate you on the admission of your country to the United Nations. Australia has been a staunch advocate of the ROK's admission to the UN and co-sponsored the General Assembly resolution on the admission of the ROK and the DPRK. I am therefore delighted with this result, which will allow your country to assume its rightful role and responsibility in international affairs.

You will recall that when Senator Evans wrote to you in April, he indicated that Australia would support either separate or simultaneous admission to the UN by the ROK and the DPRK in line with our support for the principle of universal UN membership. Australia is therefore also pleased to welcome the DPRK to the United Nations.

I believe the simultaneous entry of both Koreas into the UN will assist the process of Korean reconciliation as well as contributing to an improved security environment in the Asia Pacific region.

I am confident our close bilateral relationship and cooperation on international and regional issues can only be strengthened by your country's admission to the UN.

I wish you and your nation every success.

Yours sincerely

NEAL BLEWETT

0042

EMBASSY OF ROMANIA
SEOUL
No. 565

The Embassy of Romania presents its compliments to the Ministry of Foreign Affairs of the Republic of Korea and has the honour to convey enclosed a message of congratulation addressed by H. E. Mr. ADRIAN NASTASE, Minister of Foreign Affairs of Romania, to H. E. Mr. LEE SANG OCK, Minister of Foreign Affairs of the Republic of Korea, on the occasion of the admission of the Republic of Korea to the United Nations Organization.

The Embassy of Romania avails itself of this opportunity to renew to the Ministry of Foreign Affairs of the Republic of Korea the assurances of its highest consideration.

ROMANIA - SEUL - AMBASADA

Seoul, September 24, 1991

To the Ministry of Foreign Affairs
of the Republic of Korea

Seoul

0043

HIS EXCELLENCY
MR LEE SANG OCK
MINISTER OF FOREIGN AFFAIRS
OF THE REPUBLIC OF KOREA

Seoul

I am very pleased to express to you my sincere congratulations on the occasion of the admission on the Republic of Korea to the United Nations Organization.

I am confident that, by direct participation to the activity of the United Nations Organization, the Republic of Korea could bring its own contribution, in consensus with the efforts of the international community, to the promotion of the noble ideas of cooperation, security and peace, to the settlement of fundamental issues the mankind is confronted with.

At the same time, we sincerely hope that the constructive participation of the Republic of Korea and of the Democratic People's Republic of Korea to the activities of the world organization will represent a new and positive factor in the inter-Korean relations aimed to promote the approaching and the national reconciliation, in order to achive the desideratum of the Korean nation - the reunification of the country.

Being convinced that the relations between our countries will be extended and developed, both in the bilateral fields and in the international arena, please accept, your Excellency, my best whishes for your good health and succes in your activity.

ADRIAN NASTASE
MINISTER OF FOREIGN AFFAIRS
OF ROMANIA

0044

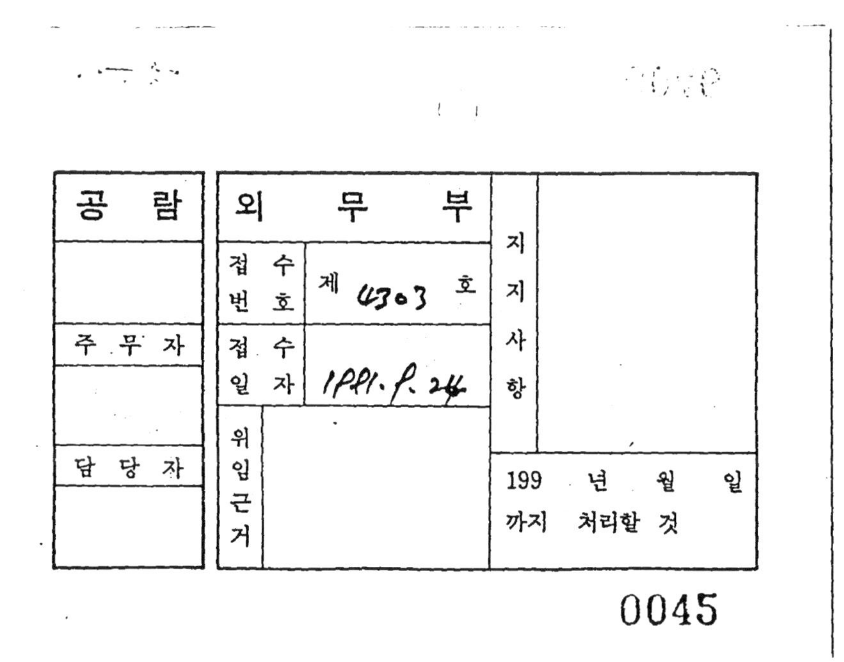

공 람	외 무 부		지 지 사 항	
	접수 번호	제 4303 호		
주 무 자	접수 일자	1991. 9. 24.		
	위임근거		199 년 월 일 까지 처리할 것	
담 당 자				

0045

0042

배 부 처

장관실 ✓

기 획 실		아 주 국		국제기구 조 약 국		영 교 국	
정 책 실		미 주 국		국 제 경 제 국		총 무 과	
의 전 실		구 주 국		통 상 국		감사관실	
특 전 실		중 아 국		문 화 협 력 국		여 권 과	

0046

Embassy of the
Mongolian People's Republic

Сеул, I99I оны 9 дүгээр сарын 18 өдөр.

Эрхэмсэг Ноён сайд аа,

Бүгд Найрамдах Солонгос Улс НҮБ-д элссэнтэй холбогдуулан Танд чин сэтгэлийн баяр хүргэе.

БНСУ олон улсын харилцааны субъектын хувьд хамтын нийгэмлэгт зохих ёсны байр суудлаа эзлэсэн нь олон улсын харилцаанд нэгэнт эхлэсэн шинэ хандлагыг тусгасан БНСУ-ын гадаад бодлогын томоохон амжилт гэж үзэж байна.

Бий болж буй өнөөгийн шинэ нөхцөл байдалд Солонгосын хойгд өнө бат энх тайвныг хангах, эх орноо нэгтгэхэд чиглэсэн Таны үйлсэд их амжилт ерөөе.

БНМАУ-ын ЭЛЧИН САЙД

ПЭРЭНЛЭЙН ҮРЖИНЛХҮНДЭВ.

БНСУ-ын ГЯЯ-ны
САЙД ЭРХЭМСЭГ НОЁН
ЛИ САН ОК ТАНАА

0047

Embassy of the
Mongolian People's Republic

서울 1991년9월18일

가장 존경하는 장관님,

저는 대한민국이 유엔에 가입한데 대하여 장관님께 진심으로 축하를 드립니다.

대한민국이 국제관계의 한 일원으로서 공동체에 자기 합법적인 자리를 차지하게 된것은 현 국제관계의 새로운 추세를 반영한 대한민국의 대외정책의 커다란 성과라고 저는 봅니다.

새로 조성된 현시기에 한반도의 항구적인 평화와 통일을 위한 장관님의 고귀한 위업에 보다 큰성과가 있기를 진심으로 축원 합니다.

주한 몽골 대사

바우르진루훈대브

대한민국 외무부
이 상 옥 장관님

0048

Ambassador of India
Seoul

No.SEO/123/1/88 September 25, 1991

Excellency,

I have the honour to enclose herewith a message from Mr. Eduardo Falerio, Minister of State for External Affairs of India, addressed to His Excellency Mr. Lee Sang-ock, Minister of Foreign Affairs, Republic of Korea. I would be grateful if the message is transmitted to its high destination.

Please accept, Excellency, the assurances of my highest consideration.

(L.T. Pudaite)

His Excellency Mr. Chang Sun-sup,
Chief of Protocol,
Ministry of Foreign Affairs,
Republic of Korea,
Seoul.

0043

TEXT OF THE MESSAGE

Excellency,

Please accept my sincere felicitations on admission of the Republic of Korea as a member of the United Nations Organisation.

India has consistently supported the aspirations of the Korean people to actively contribute towards the realisation of the purposes and principles of the United Nations through representation in this world body.

It is our sincere hope that entry of the Republic of Korea and the Democratic People's Republic of Korea into the United Nations will further promote the process of peaceful dialogue and reduction of tensions in the Korean peninsula.

With my good wishes for your personal well-being and happiness and the prosperity of the friendly people of the Republic of Korea.

(Eduardo Falerio)

H.E. Mr. Lee Sang-ock,
Minister of Foreign Affairs,
Republic of Korea,
Seoul.

0050

T E L E X

SEPTIEMBRE 25.1991.

AL
EXCELENTISIMO SEÑOR
SANG-OCK LEE
MINISTRO DE RELACIONES EXTERIORES DE LA REPUBLICA DE COREA
S E U L

CON MOTIVO DEL INGRESO DE LA REPUBLICA DE COREA COMO ESTADO MIEMBRO DE LA ORGANIZACION DE LAS NACIONES UNIDAS, HAGO LLEGAR A VUESTRA EXCELENCIA MIS MAS AFECTUOSAS FELICITACIONES.

JUNTO CON HACER PROPICIA LA OPORTUNIDAD PARA FORMULAR VOTOS POR VUESTRA VENTURA PERSONAL Y POR EL ESTRECHAMIENTO DE LAS RELACIONES ENTRE NUESTROS DOS PAISES, REITEROLE LAS SEGURIDADES DE MI MAS ALTA Y DISTINGUIDA CONSIDERACION.

ENRIQUE SILVA CIMMA
MINISTRO DE RELACIONES EXTERIORES
DE LA REPUBLICA DE CHILE

0051

EMBAJADA DE CHILE SEUL, COREA

No.38/91

The Embassy of Chile presents its compliments to the Ministry of Foreign Affairs and has the honour to attache herewith a telex that the Minister of Foreign Affairs of Chile H.E.Mr.Enrique Silva is sending to the Minister of Foreign Affairs of Korea, H.E.Mr.Lee Sang-Ock.

The Embassy of Chile will thank the Ministry of Foreign Affairs to hand over the message enclosed to its high addressee.

The Embassy of Chile avails itself of this opportunity to renew to the Ministry of Foreign Affairs the assurances of its highest consideration.

Seoul, September 26, 1991.

0052

외 무 부

종 별 :

번 호 : JAW-5486 일 시 : 91 0925 1500

수 신 : 장 관(아프이, 연일)

발 신 : 주 일 대사(일정)

제 목 : 유엔가입

당지 남아공 총영사관은 아국의 유엔가입에대한 BOTHA 외상의 아래 축전을 당관에 전달해 왔음.

' HIS EXCELLENCY LEE SANG-OK

MINISTER OF FOREIGN AFFAIRS OF

THE REPUBLIC OF KOREA

SEOUL

REPUBLIC OF KOREA

YOUR EXCELLENCY

IT IS WITH MUCH INTEREST THAT THE REPUBLIC OF SOUTH AFRICA HAS FOLLOWED THE DIPLOMATIC AND ECONOMIC PROGRESS OF THE REPUBLIC OF KOREA. THE ADMISSION ON 17 SEPTEMBER 1991 OF YOUR EXCELLENCY'S COUNTRY AS A MEMBER OF THE UNITED NATIONS IS AN IMPORTANT MILESTONE AND I EXTEND MY CONGRALATIONS TO YOU WITH THE ACHIEVEMENT.

ON BEHALF OF THE GOVERNMENT OF THE REPUBLIC OF SOUTH AFRICA I WISH YOU AND YOUR COUNTRY EVERYTHING OF THE BEST IN YOUR ENDEAVOURS AND WE LOOK FORWARD TO IMPROVING THE RELATIONS BETWEEN OUR COUNTRIES.

PLEASE ACCEPT, YOUR EXCELLENCY, THE ASSURANCE OF MY HIGHEST CONSIDERATION.

SIGNED

R F BOTHA

MINISTER OF FOREIGN AFFAIRS OF THE REPUBLIC OF SOUTH AFRICA

PRETOIA

17 SEPTEMBER 1991' 끝

중아국 1차보 아주국 국기국 외정실 분석관 청와대 안기부

PAGE 1

91.09.25 16:07 WG

외신 1과 통제관

0053

1991. 9. 25. 산티아고

이 상 옥

대한민국 외무부장관 각하

본인은 대한민국이 UN 회원국으로 정식가입하게 된 것에 대해 각하께 진심으로 축하를 드립니다.

각하의 건안을 축원드리며 한.칠레 양국관계가 더욱 긴밀해지기를 기원하면서 본인 최대의 경의와 안부를 전합니다.

엔리께 실바 시마

칠레공화국 외무부장관

0054

SANTIAGO, 25 DE SEPTEMBRE DE 1991.

AL
EXCELENTISIMO SENOR
SANG-OCK LEE
MINISTRO DE RELACIONES EXTERIORES DE LA REPUBLICA DE COREA
SEUL

TELEX OFICIAL NR.256

CON MOTIVO DEL INGRESO DE LA REPUBLICA DE COREA COMO ESTADO MIEMBRE DE LA ORGANIZACION DE LAS NACIONES UNIDAS, HAGO LLEGAR A VUESTRA EXCELENCIA MIS MAS AFECTUOSAS FELICITACIONES.

JUNTO CON HACER PROPICIA LA OPORTUNIDAD PARA FORMULAR VOTOS POR VUESTRA VENTURA PERSONAL Y POR EL ESTRECHAMIENTO DE LAS RELRCIONES ENTRE NUESTROS DOS PAISES, REITEROLE LAS SEGURIDADES DE MI MAS ALTA Y DISTINGUIDA CONSIDERACION.

ENRIQUE SILVA CIMMA
MINISTRO DE RELACIONES EXTERIORES
DE LA REPUBLICA DE CHILE

0055

0
WOIMUBU K24653
340271 CHILE CK0
WOIMUBU K24653

배부처	장관실	차관실	一차보	二차보	기획실	외정실	분석관	외전장	아주국	미주국	구주국	중아국	국기국	경제국	통상국	문협국	영교국	총무과	감사관	공보관	외연원	청와대	총리실	안기부	공보처
								O		/															

AL
EXCELENTISIMO SENOR
SANG-OCK-LEE
MINISTRO DE RELACIONES EXTERIORES DE LA REPUBLICA DE COREA
S E U L

TELEX OFICIAL NR.258

CON MOTIVO DEL INGRESO DE LA REPUBLICA DE COREA COMO ESTADO MIEMBRO DE LA ORGANIZACION DE LAS NACIONES UNIDAS, HAGO LLEGAR A VUESTRA EXCELENCIA MIS MAS AFECTUOSAS FELICITACIONES.

JUNTO CON HACER PROPICIA LA OPORTUNIDAD PARA FORMULAR VOTOS POR VUESTRA VENTURA PERSONAL Y POR EL ESTRECHAMIENTO DE LAS RELACIONES ENTRE NUESTROS DOS PAISES, REITEROLE LAS SEGURIDADES DE MI MAS ALTA Y DISTINGUIDA CONSIDERACION.

ENRIQUE SILVA CIMMA
MINISTRO DE RELACIONES EXTERIORES
DE LA REPUBLICA DE CHILE..

SANTIAGO, 25 DE SEPTIEMBRE DE 1991.-
TTTT

0056

FOREIGN AFFAIRS AND TRADE

MEMORANDUM

DATE: 26/9/91

INFORMATION:	In Reply quote:	Registry code: 310139
	TO: SEOUL	
	REF:	TO FILE:
	FM: CANBERRA	
	FM FILE: 3127/9/1	PSN:

CLASSIFICATION: UNCLASSIFIED

SUBJECT: ROK UN ADMISSION - CONGRATULATORY MESSAGE

The amended congratulatory letter from Dr Blewett to Korean Foreign Minister, Lee Sang-Ock on the ROK's admission to the UN (telecon McCarter/Mullin of 18 September refers) is attached.

2. Please arrange for it to be forwarded to the Minister as soon as possible.

M.M. Emberson

Matilda Emberson
Korea Section

0057

PERMANENT MISSION OF THE COMMONWEALTH OF DOMINICA

TO THE UNITED NATIONS (GENEVA)

Geneva, September 26,1991

His Excellency Mr Lee Sang-ock
Minister for foreign Affairs
Government Headquarters
Seoul
Republic of Korea

Dear Mr Minister,

I wish to congratulate you for conducting a superb foreign-policy,and I wish to express to you as well to the Government and people of the Republic of Korea my Government and my personal sincere welcome to the United Nations membership.

May I wish you continue success on behalf of the people and the Government of the Republic of Korea.

Yours sincerely,

Hugo Lodrini
Ambassador
Permanent Observer
of the ACP-EEC Joint Assembly
to UNCTAD

9, AVENUE EUGÈNE PITTARD - CH-1206 GENEVA - TELEPHONE (022) 7.89.04.42 0058

주 파 키 스 탄 대 사 관

주파(정)760 -235　　1991. 9. 26.

수신　외무부장관

참조　아주국장, 국제기구국장

제목　아국 유엔가입 축하

연 : 주파(정)760 - 223

1. Wasim Sajjad 주재국 상원의장은 아국의 유엔가입을 축하하는 서한(9.21자)을 박준규 국회의장에게 발송한바, 동 서한 사본 별첨 송부합니다.
2. Sajjad 상원의장은 지난 5월 최광수 대통령특사 당지 방문시 한·파 친선협회 주최 만찬 주빈으로 참석하고, 최근에는 상원내 파·한 의원 친선협회를 구성하는등 아국과의 관계증진에 매우 적극적인 인사임을 첨언합니다.

첨 부 : 동 서한 사본. 끝.

주 파 키 스 탄 대 사

선 결			결재		
접수일시	1991. 9. 30				
처리과	54082				

0053

Mr. Park

بسم الله الرحمن الرحيم

CHAIRMAN

SENATE OF PAKISTAN

ISLAMABAD

The 21 September, 1991.

H.E. Mr. Park Jyun Kyu,
Speaker,
National Assembly,
Republic of Korea,
Seoul,
Republic of Korea.

Excellency,

I am very glad to learn that the Republic of Korea has been admitted to the United Nations as a member State. On behalf of the Members of the Senate of Pakistan and on my own behalf, I extend to you, Excellency, our heartiest congratulations and sincere good wishes on admission of the Republic of Korea to the UN fold. We are sure that the U.N. membership will enable the Republic of Korea to develop the relations of friendship and fruitful cooperation with all member states of the U.N. more vigorously and join them in efforts to promote world peace.

Assuring you, Excellency, of my highest esteem,

Yours sincerely,

Wasim Sajjad

(WASIM SAJJAD)

→ Copy to: The Ambassador,
Embassy of Korea,
Islamabad.

0060

관리 번호	91 -1159

원 본

외 무 부

1

종 별 :

번 호 : IVW-0492 일 시 : 91 0927 1600

수 신 : 장 관(국연,아프일)

발 신 : 주 코트디브와르 대사

제 목 : UN 가입 축전

대:AM-0198

1. 주재국 HOUPHOUET-BOIGNY 대통령은 노태우 대통령께 아국의 UN 가입에 대한 9.26 자 별첨 축전을 타전하여 온바 요지는 아래와 같음

가. 금번 한국의 가입은 세계 평화와 안보의 유지 및 보다 나은 국제 사회의 도래를 향한 우호, 협력의 장으로서의 UN 의 보편성을 더욱확대하는것임.

나. 국제사회 제반부문에서 이미활발한 활동을 전개해오고있는 한국이 동 가입을 시점으로 UN 의 목적과 제원칙 구현을 위해 더욱 공헌할것으로 확신함.

다. 양국간의 기존 우호, 협력관계 심화를 위한 주재국 정부의 확고한 의지와 노력 강화를 재차 다짐함.

2. 축전에 대한 답전을 건의함.

첨부: 상기 축전

(대사 양태규-국장)

예고:91.12.31 일반

SON EXCELLENCE MONSIEUR ROH TAE WOO

PRESIDENT DE LA REPUBLIQUE DE COREE

SEOUL

NO. 75440

PRIORITE ABSOLUE

C'EST AVEC UN REEL PLAISIR QUE JE VOUS ADRESSE MES VIVES FELICITATIONS A L'OCCASION DE L'ADMISSION DE VOTRE PAYS A L'ORGANISATION DES NATIONS-UNIES.

CETTE ADMISSION RENFORCE DAVANTAGE LE CARACTERE UNIVERSEL DE

국기국 차관 1차보 중아국 분석관 청와대 안기부

PAGE 1 91.09.28 08:19

외신 2과 통제관 BS

0061

L'ORGANISATION DES NATIONS-UNIES CONCUE COMME UN CENTRE OU S'HARMONISENT LES EFFORTS DES NATIONS POUR LE MAINTIEN DE LA PAIX ET DE LA SECURITE INTERNATIONALES, ET LE DEVELOPPEMENT DE RELATIONS AMICALES ENTRE LES ETATS EN VUE DE L'AVENEMENT D'UN MONDE MEILLEUR.

JE SUIS CERTAIN QUE LA REPUBLIQUE DE COREE QUI A DONNE TOUTE LA MESURE DE SA VITALITE DANS DIVERSES INSTITUTIONS INTERNATIONALES SAURA APPORTER A L'ONU UNE CONTRIBUTION PRECIEUSE ET EFFICACE A LA MISE EN OEUVRE DES BUTS ET PRINCIPES DE LA CHARTE DE NOTRE ORGANISATION COMMUNE.

JE VOUDRAIS SAISIR CETTE OCCASION POUR REAFFIRMER LA NETTE DETERNINATION DU GOUVERNEMENT IVOIRIEN A POURSUIVRE ET RENFORCER DAVANTAGE LES RELATIONS DE COOPERATION CORDIALE ET MUTUELLEMENT AVANTAGEUSE QUE NOS DEUX PAYS ENTRETIENNENT.

TRES HAUTE CONSIDERATION.

FELIX HOUPHOUET-BOIGNY

PRESIDENT DE LA REPUBLIQUE DE COTE D'IVOIRE

LE 26/09/91

A A P S O

AFRO-ASIAN PEOPLES' SOLIDARITY ORGANIZATION

Consultative status: NAM, ECOSOC, UNESCO, UNCTAD, UNIDO

THE PERMANENT SECRETARIAT

89, Abdel Aziz Al Saoud St., Manial, Cairo, Egypt. Tel. 3622946, Tx 92627 AAPSO UN, Fax (202) 3637361, Cable AFROASIACO Cairo

TELE-FAX

Serial Number: 248
Date: 29.09.1991
drafted by: E.V.
sent by: G.I.A.
Fax-Number: 82 2 7395986
OR " " 7395990

Country: KOREA - SEOUL

TEXT:

To: His Excellency Roh Tae WU,
President of the Republic
of Korea,
S E O U L

On behalf of the Permanent Secretariat of AAPSO and on our own behalf, we convey our congratulations to Your Excellency, and the people of Korea on the happy occasion of the admission of the Republic of Korea to the United Nations.

Since its inception, AAPSO had been consistently advocating the cause of the peaceful settlement of the Korean question and we do hope that Koreas' membership in the U.N. will be a great step in achieving the dream of the korean re-unification.

With warm greetings.

Nouri Abdul Razzak
Secretary General
of AAPSO

Dr. Morad Ghaleb
President
of AAPSO

0063

47342

기 안 용 지

분류기호 문서번호	연일 2031 -	(전화:)	시 행 상 특별취급	
보존기간	영구·준영구. 10. 5. 3. 1	장 관		
수 신 처 보존기간				
시행일자	1991.9.30.			

보조기관	국 장	전결	협조기관		문서통제 1991.10.01
	심의관				
	과 장				
기안책임자		김성진			발송인 1991.10.01 외무부

경 유		발신명의	
수 신	대통령비서실장		
참 조	의전수석비서관		

제 목	대통령각하 앞 축전접수

연 : 연일 2031-46017(9.19)

연호, 우리의 유엔가입에 대하여 4개국 국가원수가 대통령각하 앞 축전을 보내 왔는 바, 동 축전사본을 별첨 송부합니다.

첨부 : 1. 호주 호크수상 및 중화민국 이등휘총통 축전 각1부.

칠레 아소까르 대통령, 투니지아 벤알리 대통령

(주한대사관 경유)

/계속/

0064

(2)

2. 코트디브와르 브와그니 대통령 축전 1부.

(주재 한국대사관 경유)

~~3. 칠레 아소까르 대통령 축전 1부(텔렉스).~~ 끝.

0065

AUSTRALIAN EMBASSY
SEOUL

NOTE NO. 108/91

The Embassy of Australia presents its compliments to the Ministry of Foreign Affairs of the Republic of Korea and has the honour to request the Ministry's assistance in conveying the following message from the Prime Minister of Australia, the Honourable R.J.L. Hawke, to the President of the Republic of Korea, His Excellency Roh Tae Woo.

Begins

"My dear President,

I want to extend my congratulations and those of all Australians on the admission of the Republic of Korea to the United Nations.

My Government has been a staunch advocate of the Republic of Korea's admission to the United Nations. Australia co-sponsored the General Assembly resolution on the admission of both the Republic of Korea and the Democratic People's Republic of Korea.

We assess that prospects for cooperation and an improved security environment can only be enhanced by the membership of the two Koreas in the United Nations.

I am therefore delighted with this successful result, which will allow your country to assume its rightful role and responsibility in international affairs.

Australia values highly the strong bilateral relationship we share, and our close and continuing consultation on important regional and international issues, particularly APEC. Our close cooperation will be further strengthened by your country's membership of and contribution to the United Nations.

With warmest good wishes

Yours sincerely,

BOB HAWKE"

Ends

0066

The Embassy of Australia avails itself of this opportunity to renew to the Ministry of Foreign Affairs of the Republic of Korea the assurances of its highest consideration.

AUSTRALIAN EMBASSY
AUSTRALIA
SEOUL

SEOUL
19 SEPTEMBER 1991

0067

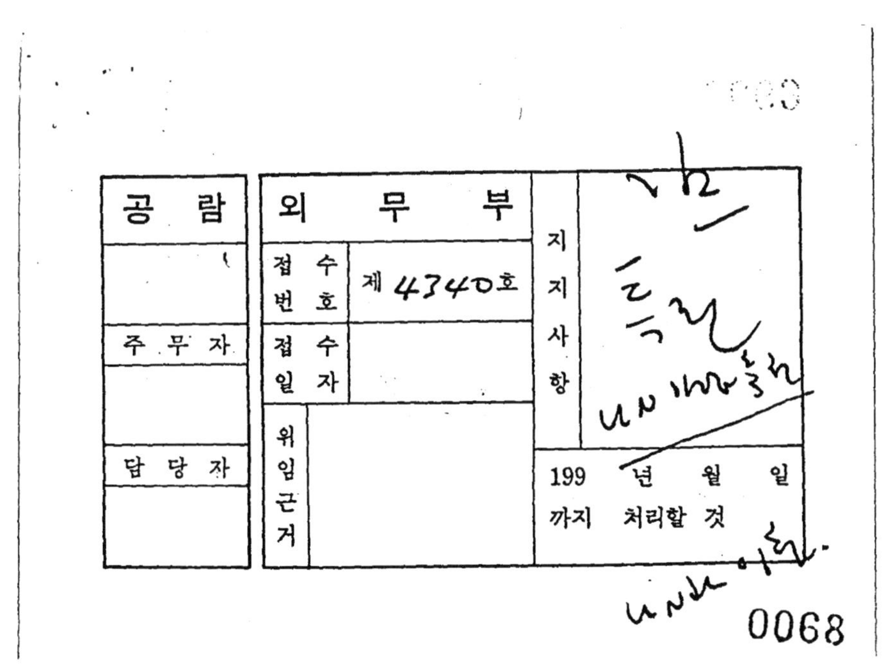

공 람	외 무 부		지시사항	
	접수번호	제 4340 호		
주무자	접수일자			
	위임근거			
담당자			199 년 월 일 까지 처리할 것	

0068

0069

배 부 처

기획실		아주국		국제기구조약국		영교국	
정책실		미주국		국제경제국		총무과	
의전실	—	구주국		통상국		감사관실	
특전실		중아국		문화협력국		여권과	

0063

EMBAJADA DE CHILE SEUL, COREA

No.39/91

The Embassy of Chile presents its compliments to the Ministry of Foreign Affairs and has the honour to attache herewith a Telex that the President of Chile H.E.Mr.Patricio Aylwin is sending to the President of the Republic of Korea, H.E.Mr.Roh Tae Woo.

The Embassy of Chile will thank the Ministry of Foreign Affairs to hand over the message enclosed to its high addressee.

The Embassy of Chile avails itself of this opportunity to renew to the Ministry of Foreign Affairs the assurances of its highest consideration.

Seoul, September 26, 1991.

0070

EMBAJADA DE CHILE SEUL, COREA

TELEX

SEPTEMBER 25.1991.

AL
EXCELENTISIMO SEÑOR
ROH TAE-WOO
PRESIDENTE DE LA REPUBLICA DE COREA
SEUL

RECIBA VUESTRA EXCELENCIA MIS MAS AFECTUOSAS FELICITACIONES CON MOTIVO DEL INGRESO DE LA REPUBLICA DE COREA COMO ESTADO MIEMBRO DE LA ORGANIZACION DE LAS NACIONES UNIDAS.

JUNTO CON FORMULAR VOTOS POR VUESTRA VENTURA PERSONAL Y POR EL ESTRECHAMIENTO DE LOS VINCULOS ENTRE NUESTROS PAISES, EXPRESOLE LAS SEGURIDADES DE MI MAS ALTA Y DISTINGUIDA CONSIDERACION.

PATRICIO AYLWIN AZOCAR
PRESIDENTE DE LA REPUBLICA DE CHILE

0071

번　역　문

1991.9.25. 산티아고

노 태 우
대한민국 대통령 각하

본인은 대한민국이 UN 회원국으로 정식 가입하게 된 것에 대해 각하께 진심으로 축하를 드립니다.

각하의 건안을 축원드리며 양국관계가 더욱 긴밀해지기를 기원하면서 각하께 본인 최대의 경의와 안부를 전합니다.

빠뜨리시오 앨윈 아소까르
칠레공화국 대통령

0072

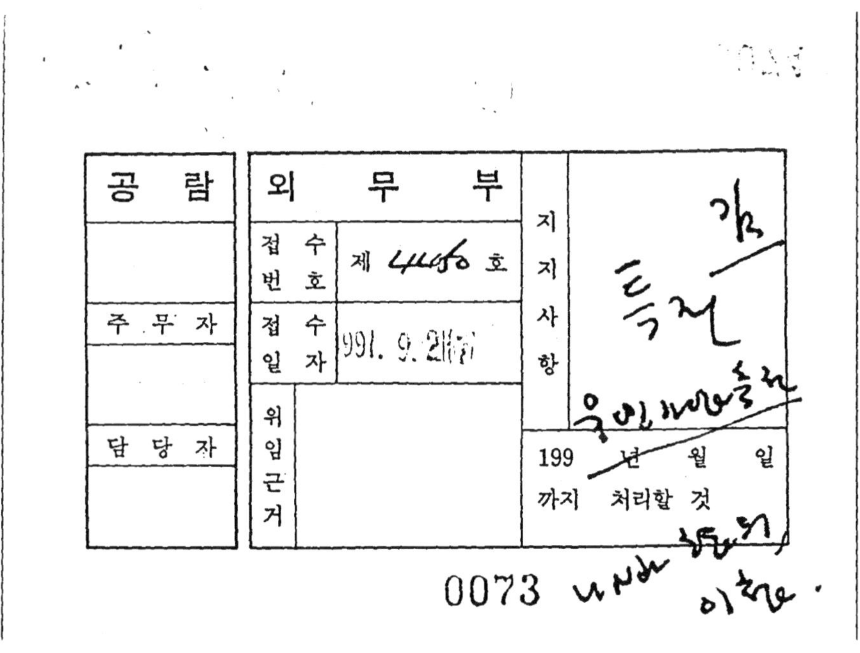

공 람	외 무 부		지시사항	특 검 / 유엔, 사무총장
	접수번호	제 44050 호		
주 무 자	접수일자	1991. 9. 21		
	위임근거		199 년 월 일 까지 처리할 것	
담 당 자				

0073

배 부 처

기획실		아주국		국제기구조약국		영교국	
정책실		미주국		국제경제국		총무과	
의전실	/	구주국		통상국		감사관실	
특전실		중아국		문화협력국		여권과	

0074

EMBASSY OF TUNISIA

SEOUL

No.526/91/Prot.

Séoul, le 24 septembre 1991

L'Ambassade de Tunisie présente ses compliments au Ministère des Affaires Etrangères et a l'honneur de le prier de bien vouloir transmettre le message de félicitations ci-joint, adressé par Son Excellence Zine El Abidine BEN ALI, Président de la République tunisienne à Son Excellence ROH Tae-Woo, Président de la République de Corée.

Tout en remerciant le Ministère des Affaires Etrangères de sa diligence, l'Ambassade de Tunisie saisit cette occasion pour lui renouveler les assurances de sa très haute considération.

Ministère des Affaires Etrangères
77-6, Sejong-ro, Chongro-ku,
Séoul

0075

Son Excellence Monsieur ROH Tae Woo
Président de la République de Corée

L'Adhésion de la République de Corée à l'Organisation des Nations Unies nous offre l'heureuse occasion d'exprimer à Votre Excellence nos très vives félicitations.

Votre participation active aux Nations Unies renforcera, nous en sommes convaincus, la paix dans le monde et favorisera la poursuite du dialogue inter-coréen pour réaliser dans la paix la réunification de la péninsule coréenne.

Zine El Abidine BEN ALI
Président de la République tunisienne

0076

편철

PRIME MINISTER
REPUBLIC OF KOREA

Seoul, September 30, 1991

Excellency,

I was very much pleased to receive your Excellency's congratulatory message kindly extended to me on the occasion of my country's admission to the United Nations at the current 46th Session of the United Nations General Assembly.

I would like to express, on behalf of the Government and people of the Republic of Korea, our deep appreciation to the Government and people of Thailand for the valuable support to our effort to join the United Nations.

I am certain that on this occasion new areas of cooperation will be opened in which Thailand and Korea would work together more closely for the benefits of our two countries and the world as a whole.

Please accept, Excellency, the renewed assurances of my highest consideration.

Won-Shik Chung

Won-Shik Chung

His Excellency Anand Panyarachun,
Prime Minister of the Kingdom of Thailand.

0077

No. 660/2534

Royal Thai Embassy
Seoul

24 September B.E. 2534 (1991)

Excellency,

I have the honour to convey to Your Excellency the message from His Excellency Mr. Anand Panyarachun, Prime Minister of Thailand, to His Excellency Mr. Chung Won-shik, Prime Minister of the Republic of Korea, which reads as follows :

BEGIN

Office of the Prime Minister
Government House, Bangkok,
THAILAND.

20 September B.E. 2534 (1991)

Excellency,

It is indeed a great pleasure for me to learn of the unanimous admission of the Republic of Korea to the United Nations at the current 46th Session of the United Nations General Assembly.

On this happy occasion, may I express, on behalf of the Government and people of Thailand, our sincere congratulations and best wishes to Your Excellency, and through Your Excellency, to the Government and people of the Republic of Korea.

In /...

His Excellency Mr. Lee Sang-ock
Minister of Foreign Affairs,
Ministry of Foreign Affairs,
Seoul.

0078

In this connection, I fervently hope that, as fellow-members of this distinguished world body, the Republic of Korea and Thailand will join hands and work closely together, both within and outside the framework of the United Nations, in bringing about peace, prosperity and harmony to our region and to the world as a whole.

Please accept, Excellency, the renewed assurances of my highest consideration.

(Anand Panyarachun)

Prime Minister of Thailand

END.

I shall be most grateful if the above message could be transmitted to its highest destination.

Please accept, Excellency, the renewed assurances of my highest consideration.

Chuchai Kasemsarn

(Chuchai Kasemsarn)

Ambassador

0073

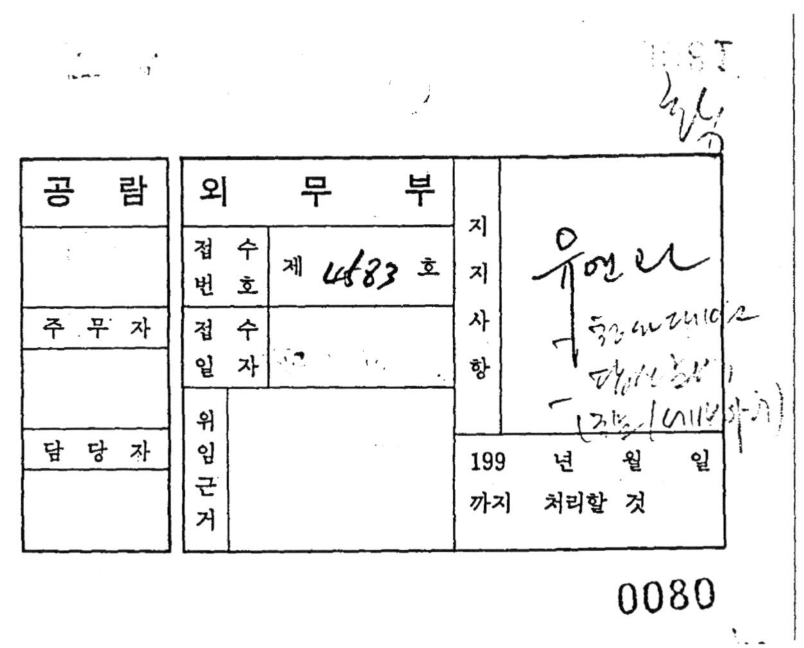

공 람	외 무 부		지 지 사 항	유엔 LL
	접 수 번 호	제 4583 호		
주 무 자	접 수 일 자			
	위 임 근 거			199 년 월 일 까지 처리할 것
담 당 자				

0080

0080

배 부 처

기 획 실		아 주 국		국제기구 조 약 국		영 교 국	
정 책 실		미 주 국		국 제 경 제 국		총 무 과	
의 전 실	―	구 주 국		통 상 국		감사관실	
특 전 실		중 아 국		문 화 협 력 국		여 권 과	

0081

EMBAJADA DEL PERU
SEÚL, COREA

M/26

The Embassy of Peru presents its compliments to the Ministry of Foreign Affairs and has the honor to request its kind cooperation to deliver the enclosed message which has been sent by Mr. Alberto Fujimori, President of the Republic of Peru to His Excellency Mr. Roh Tae Woo, President of the Republic of Korea on the occasion of the admission of the Republic of Korea to the United Nations Organization.

The Embassy of Peru avails itself of the opportunity to renew to the Ministry of Foreign Affairs the assurances of its highest consideration.

Seoul, 30 September 1991

TO
THE MINISTRY OF FOREIGN AFFAIRS
S E O U L

0082

EMBAJADA DEL PERU
SEÚL, COREA

EXCELENTISIMO SEÑOR
ROH TAE WOO
PRESIDENTE DE LA
REPUBLICA DE COREA
SEUL.-

TENGO A HONRA DIRIGIRME A VUESTRA EXCELENCIA PARA HACERLE LLEGAR MI FELICITACION Y LA DEL GOBIERNO Y PUEBLO PERUANOS POR LA RECIENTE ADMISION DE SU ILUSTRE PAIS A LA ORGANIZACION DE LAS NACIONES UNIDAS EL PASADO 17 DEL CORRIENTE MES.

ESTOY PLENAMENTE CONVENCIDO QUE LA REPUBLICA DE COREA ENCONTRARA EN EL SENO DE LAS NACIONES UNIDAS UN FORO ADECUADO QUE, SIN DUDA ACOGERA LOS VALIOSOS APORTES QUE SU ILUSTRADO GOBIERNO HAGA EN FAVOR DE LA DISTENSION Y PAZ MUNDIAL DENTRO DE LA ACTUAL TENDENCIA A LA DISTENSION DE LOS BLOQUES DE PODER, ASI COMO EN PRO DEL FORTALECIMIENTO DEL MULTILATERALISMO.

AL HACER VOTOS POR EL BIENESTAR Y PROSPERIDAD DE LA NOBLE NACION COREANA Y POR LA VENTURA PERSONAL DE VUESTRA EXCELENCIA, APROVECHO LA OPORTUNIDAD PARA REITERARLE LAS SEGURIDADES DE MI MAS ALTA Y DISTINGUIDA CONSIDERACION.

ALBERTO FUJIMORI F.
PRESIDENTE DE LA REPUBLICA DEL PERU

0083

EMBAJADA DEL PERU

EXCELENTISIMO SEÑOR
ROH TAE WOO
PRESIDENTE DE LA REPUBLICA
DE COREA
SEUL.-

0034

EMB=Y OF PAKISTAN
SEOUL

No.Pol.2/6/91. 1 October, 1991.

The Embassy of the Islamic Republic of Pakistan presents its compliments to Ministry of Foreign Affairs, Republic of Korea, and has the honour to reproduce the following message of felicitations from His Excellency Mr. Muhammad Siddique Khan Kanju, Minister of State for Foreign Affairs, Pakistan, for His Excellency Mr. Lee Sang-Ock, Minister for Foreign Affairs, the Republic of Korea:

Message Begins

Excellency,

Please accept my sincere felicitations on Republic of Korea's membership of the United Nations. The unanimous decision of the United Nations General Assembly reflects the confidence of the international community that the Republic of Korea would not only uphold, but also contribute effectively to the principles and purposes of United Nations.

It is a matter of great satisfaction that the Republic of Korea has got its rightful place in the community of nations and I am confident that it would cooperate with other countries in achieving the UN ideals of peace and security.

Please accept, Excellency, the assurances of my highest considerations.

Muhammad Siddique Khan Kanju,
Minister of State for Foreign Affairs,
Government of the Islamic Republic of Pakistan.

Message Ends

58-1 SHINMOON-RO, CHONGRO-KU, SEOUL TEL: 739-4422 FAX: 739-0428 CABLE: PAREP. TELEX: 29346

0085

The Embassy would be grateful if the message is placed before the Foreign Minister.

The Embassy of the Islamic Republic of Pakistan avails itself of this opportunity to renew to the esteemed Ministry of Foreign Affairs, Republic of Korea, the assurances of its highest consideration.

EMBASSY OF PAKISTAN SEOUL

Ministry of Foreign Affairs,
Republic of Korea,
SEOUL.

0086

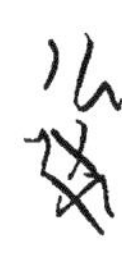

관리 번호	91 -1170

UN 1

외 무 부

종 별 :

번 호 : NDW-1594 일 시 : 91 1001 1800

수 신 : 장 관(아서, 연일)

발 신 : 주 인도 대사

제 목 : 아프간 외상의 유엔가입 축하 멧세지

1. 당지 주재 아프가니스탄 대사관은 금 10.1. 동대사관 서한으로 아래내용의 동국 ABDUL WAKIL 외무장관 멧세지를 이상옥장관께 송부하여 주도록 요청하여왔음.

ON THE OCCASION OF THE ACCEPTANCE OF THE REPUBLIC OF KOREA IN THE OFFICIAL MEMBERSHIP OF THE ORGANIZATION OF THE UNITED NATIONS, IT GIVES ME GREAT PLEASURE TO EXTEND MY SINCERE FELICITATIONS TO YOUR EXCELLENCY AND THROUGH YOU TO THE LEADERSHIP AND PEOPLE OF THE REPUBLIC OF KOREA.

I AM CONFIDENT THAT BY THE RE-ESTABLISHMENT OF RELATIONS BETWEEN OUR COUNTRIES, THE EXISTING RELATIONS BETWEEN OUR TWO COUNTRIES AND PEOPLE WILLFURTHER DEVELOP AND STRENGTHEN IN THE INTEREST OF OUR COUNTRIES AND PEOPLE AND FOR THE BENEFIT OF WORLD PEACE AND INTERNATIONAL UNDERSTANDING AND COOPERATION.

2. 상기 서한 및 멧세지 파편 송부하겠음.

(대사-국장)

예고:91.12.31 일반 고문에 의거 일반문서로 재분류됨

아주국 장관 차관 1차보 국기국 분석관 청와대 안기부

PAGE 1 91.10.02 01:08

외신 2과 통제관 CE

0087

◎ 다른 나라 외상들의

發言에 따라 회견도

함께 고려

— [illegible]

[illegible]

10/8

0088

중동아국

관리 번호	

	분류번호	보존기간

발 신 전 보

번 호 : 종별 :

수 신 : 주 나미비아, ~~일본~~ 대사. ~~총영사~~ (사본: 주일, 유엔대사)

발 신 : 장 관 (아프이)

제 목 : 남아공 외무장관앞 답전

대 : NMW-0756, JAW-5486

연 : WNM-0381

대호 남아공 외무장관 명의 축전에 대한 본직 명의 답전을 하기 타전하니 남아공측에 적의 전달하고 결과 보고 바람.

EXCELLENCY,

I WOULD LIKE TO EXTEND MY GRATITUDE TO YOUR EXCELLENCY FOR THE KIND MESSAGE OF CONGRATULATIONS ON THE OCCASION OF THE ADMISSION OF THE REPUBLIC OF KOREA TO THE UNITED NATIONS.

I ALSO WISH TO TAKE THIS OPPORTUNITY TO MENTION THAT THE GOVERNMENT OF THE REPUBLIC OF KOREA WELCOMES THE RECENT POSITIVE DEVELOPMENTS IN YOUR COUNTRY AND HOPES THAT NEGOTIATIONS ON A NEW CONSTITUTION WILL REACH A FRUITFUL CONCLUSION, THUS COMPLETELY DISMANTLING APARTHEID.

PLEASE ACCEPT, YOUR EXCELLENCY, THE ASSURANCES OF MY HIGHEST CONSIDERATION.

끝.

~~(중동아국장 이 해 순)~~
(장 관)

예고문 : 91.12.31 일반

보안 통제	

앙 고 재	91년 10월 2일	아프2과	기안자 성명		과 장	심의관	국 장	제1차관보	차 관	장 관

외신과통제

0089

공동아 3

Excellency,

I have the pleasure of acknowledging the receipt of your kind letter of Septmber 22, 1991, transmitted through your Embassy in India.

Expressing my deep gratitude to you for your felicitations on my country's admission to the United Nations, I would like to inform you that the Republic of Korea wishes to have friendly relations with all countries. Accordingly, the Government and the people of the Republic of Korea, sincerely hope that the political situations in and around your country will develop to create conditions favorable to early resumption of diplomatic relations between our countries.

I avail myself of this opportunity to extend to your Excellency the assurances of my highest consideration.

Sang Ock LEE
Minister of Foreign Affairs
Republic of Korea
Seoul

H.E. Abdul Wakil
Minister of Foreign Affairs
Republic of Afghanistan

0090

'소득은 정당하게, 소비는 알뜰하게'

주 인 도 대 사 관

인도(정) 20274- 718

1991. 10. 4.

수신 : 외무부장관

참조 : 아주국장

제목 : 아프가니스탄 외무장관 서한

연 : NDW-1594

연호 표지 보고드린 바 있는 Abdul Wakil 아프가니스탄 외무장관의 이상옥 장관님 앞 서한을 별첨과 같이 송부합니다.

첨부 : 동 서한 1부. 끝.

주 인 도 대 사

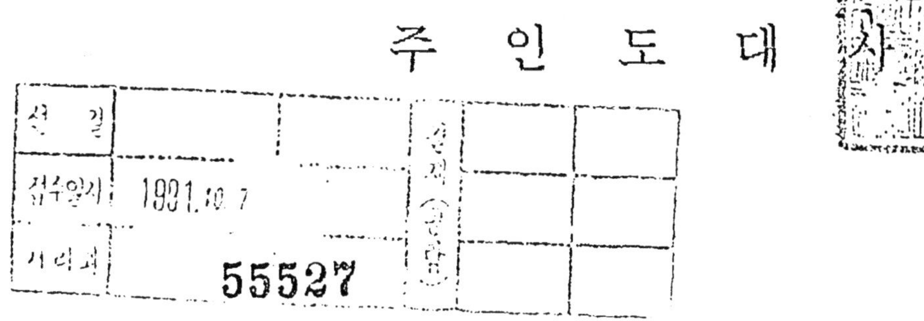

선 결			공 람		
접수일시	1991.10.7				
처리과	55527				

0091

10.1 수령.

EMBASSY OF
THE REPUBLIC OF AFGHANISTAN
NEW DELHI

PS/AE/ZN/70/91/464 24th September, 1991.

The Embassy of the Republic of Afghanistan in India presents its compliments to the Embassy of the Republic of Korea and has the honour to enclose a message for His Excellency Mr Lee Sang Ock, Minister of Foreign Affairs of the Republic of Korea from His Excellency Mr Abdul Wakil, Minister of Foreign Affairs of the Republic of Afghanistan.

The Embassy of the Republic of Afghanistan requests the esteemed Embassy of the Republic of Korea to kindly arrange to send the enclosed message to its highest destination.

The Embassy of the Republic of Afghanistan avails itself of this opportunity to renew to the Embassy of the Republic of Korea the assurances of its highest consideration.

Embassy of the Republic of Korea
9, Chandragupta Marg
Chanakyapuri
New Delhi - 110021.

0092

M E S S A G E

His Excellency
Mr Lee Sang Ock
Minister of Foreign Affairs
of the Republic of Korea
Seoul.

On the occasion of the acceptance of the Republic of Korea in the official membership of the organization of the United Nations, it gives me great pleasure to extend my sincere felicitations to your Excellency and through you to the leadership and people of the Republic of Korea.

I am confident that by the re-establishment of reltations between our countries, the existing relations between our two countries and people will further develop and strengthen in the interest of our countries and people and for the benefit of world peace and international understanding and cooperation.

I avail myself of this opportunity, to express my best wishes for Your Excellency's well being, as well as for the further progress and prosperity of the friendly people of the Republic of Korea.

With warm regards

Abdul Wakil
Minister of Foreign Affairs
of the Republic of Afghanistan
Kabul, September 22, 1991.

....

0093

√. 기ㅅ

주 트 리 니 다 드 토 바 고 대 사 관

주트리니다드(정) 800-175　　　　1991. 10. 4

수 신: 장 관

참 조: 미주국장, 국제기구국장

제 목: 유엔가입 축하서한

그레나다의 전 수상 겸 외무장관인 Ben Jones 국민당(The National Party: TNP) 당수는 아국의 유엔가입과 관련, 별첨의 장관님 앞 축하서한을 당관으로 송부, 전달 의뢰하여왔음을 보고합니다.

첨부: 상기 서한 1부. 끝.

주 트 리 니 다 드 토 바 고 대 사

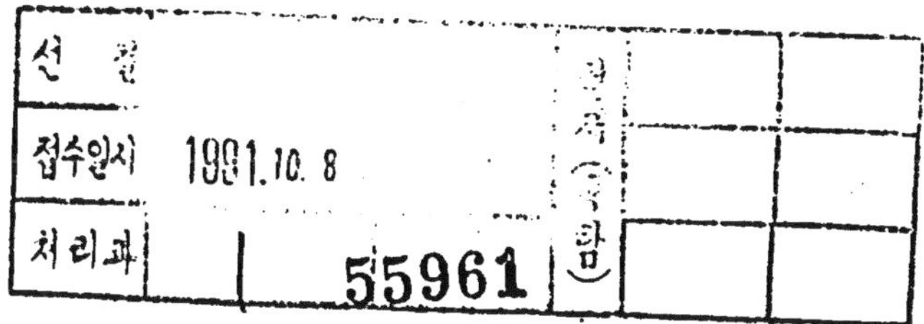

선 결		결재 (공람)		
접수일시	1991. 10. 8			
처리과	55961			

0094

Ben J. Jones, LLB.

BARRISTER-AT-LAW

Phone No. 7-335

Chambers,
Victoria,
Grenville,
St. Andrews',
Grenada W.I.

26th September, 1991

The Minister of Foreign Affairs,
The Republic or Korea,
Soeul,
South Korea.

Dear Mr. Minister,

I send sincere greetings to the Government and People of your country from the officers and members of The National Party (The Herbert Blaize Party) which I am now privileged to lead, and from the people of Grenada and I wish to congratulate your Government on its continued development of both the Economy and Democracy.

It was in early 1985 when I was Minister of External Relations, that our two Governments established Diplomatic Relationship and I note, with pride, the warmth and cordiality that charactized that relationship through our term of office. It is therefore my hope that the friendship and understanding established during that period will continue to grow to mutual benefit.

During the 1988 session of the United Nations General Assembly, Grenada proposed that the time had come for the peoples of the Korean Peninsula to be allowed representation at the United Nations and that if there were difficulties in determining which should be seated as between the two Koreas then both should be admitted on the basis that we could not properly continue to deny representation to the over sixty million people of the Peninsula. That proposal was repeated to the assembly in 1989.

I note, with great satisfaction, that the 1991 Session of the General Assembly which began a few days ago granted admission to both Koreas so that you have now rightfully taken your seat among the family of Nations. I want on behalf of my party and on my own behalf to offer my warmest congratulations, through you, to the Government and people of your couhtry and to express the hope that membership of the Organization will provide your country with greater opportunity and scope to continue contributing towards International Peace and understanding.

I am,
Yours respectfully,

Ben J. Jones
Political leader of T.N.P

0095

주 제 네 바 대 표 부

제네(정) 2031-851　　　　　　　　　　　　　　1991. 10. 4

수신 : 장관

참조 : 국제기구국장

제목 : 유엔가입 축하

Sadako Ogata 유엔 난민 고등판무관은 장관님앞 축전을 통하여 우리의 유엔가입을 축하해온바, 이를 별첨 송부합니다.

첨부 : 상기 축전 1부. 끝.

주 제 네 바 대 사

1991.10.8

55963

0096

NNNN

415519 KOGE CH
412962X UNO CH

415519 KOGE CH

415740V HCR CH

3748039 (UNHCR) GENEVA 02OCT91 1144Z

ST00-9110-0005 011. 010.RUR (NEW FILE)
HCR/MSC/7191
H.E.
MR. LEE SANG-OCK
MINISTER FOR FOREIGN AFFAIRS
C/O THE OFFICE OF THE PERMANENT OBSERVER OF THE REPUBLIC OF KOREA TO THE UNITED NATIONS OFFICE AT GENEVA 20 ROUTE DE PRE-BOIS CASE POSTALE 566 1215 GENEVA 15 PLEASE ACCEPT MY SINCERE CONGRATULATIONS ON YOUR COUNTRY'S RECENT ELECTION AS A MEMBER OF THE UNITED NATIONS. EACH NEW MEMBERSHIP OF THE UNITED NATIONS IS A MOST IMPORTANT EVENT AND DEMONSTRATES A STRENGTHENING OF INTERNATIONAL SOLIDARITY AND COOPERATION. I AM CONFIDENT THAT YOUR COUNTRY'S MEMBERSHIP OF THE UNITED NATIONS WILL PROVIDE A VALUABLE CONTRIBUTION TOWARDS THE ONGOING PROCESS OF INTERNATIONAL PEACE AND UNDERSTANDING, AND ULTIMATELY BENEFIT REFUGEES WORLD-WIDE. ASSURANCES HIGHEST CONSIDERATION SADAKO OGATA UNITED NATIONS HIGH COMMISSIONER FOR REFUGEES (UNHCR GENEVA)

COL 00 9110 0005 011 010 7191 20 566 1215 15

NNNN

415519 KOGE CH

0097

ZCZC SJC018 BSM971 TRI144
KRSJ CO TRAX 205
LEFKOSA AC.09 205/216 5 0900

19 5 [illegible]

HE MR ROH TAE WOO
PRESIDENT OF THE REPUBLIC OF KOREA
SEOUL
REPUBLIC OF KOREA

YOUR EXCELLENCY

I HAVE THE HONOUR TO CONVEY TO YOUR EXCELLENCY MY HEARTFELT CONGRATULATIONS ON THE OCCASION OF THE REPUBLIC OF KOREAS ACCESSION TO THE UNITED NATIONS ORGANISATION AS A NEW MEMBER OF THE INTER-NATIONAL FAMILY OF THE UNITED NATIONS AND MY BEST WISHES FOR THE WELL BEING OF THE PEOPLE OF THE REPUBLIC OF KOREA

IT IS MY STRONG BELIEF THAT YOUR COUNTRY WILL DO THE UTMOST TO CONTRIBUTE TO THE ENHANCEMENT OF THE VALUES AND IDEALS OF THE UN CHARTER

YOUR EXCELLENCY THE TURKISH CYPRIOT PEOPLE WHO HAVE A LONG TRADITION OF DEMOCRATIC PLURALISM AND THE UPHOLDING OF THE SANCTITY OF THE RULE OF LAW WITH ITS INHERENT RIGHT TO SELF DETERMINATION AS ENSHRINED IN THE UN CHARTER DECLARED INDEPENDENCE ON 15 NOVEMBER IN 1983 THE TURKISH REPUBLIC OF NORTH CYPRUS WILL BE CELEBRATING THE EIGHTH YEAR OF ITS ESTABLISHMENT ON 15 NOVEMBER 1991 ONCE MORE AFFIRMING ITS COMMITMENT TO CONTEMPORARY VALUES AND IDEALS AS SHARED BY THE INTERNATIONAL FAMILY OF THE UNITED NATIONS

PLEASE ACCEPT YOUR EXCELLENCY THE ASSURANCES OF MY HIGHEST CONSIDERATION

(RAUF R. DENKTAS)
PRESIDENT
TURKISH REPUBLIC OF
NORTHERN CYPRUS
LEFKOSA KIBRIS VIA
MERSIN10 TURKEY +

0098

외 무 부

종 별 :

번 호 : UNW-3251 일 시 : 91 1008 1945

수 신 : 장 관(연일,아프일)

발 신 : 주 유엔 대사

제 목 : 축하멧세지

당지 BENIN 대표부는 아국 유엔가입을 축하하는 동국 HOLO 외무장관의 장관앞 메세지를 보내온바, 이를 별첨송부함.(FAX)

첨부:동 축하메세지 1부: UNW(F)-616 끝

(대사 노창희-국장)

국기국 1차보 중아국 외정실 분석관 청와대 안기부

PAGE 1

91.10.09 09:40 WG

외신 1과 통제관

0093

UNW(Fi)-616 11○○ 19○○
(연_, 아프일) 총 1매

MESSAGE DE FELICITATIONS A S.E.M. SANG OCK LEE
MINISTRE DES AFFAIRES ETRANGERES
DE LA REPUBLIQUE DE COREE

MONSIEUR LE MINISTRE,

C'EST AVEC UN REEL PLAISIR QUE J'AI APPRIS LA NOUVELLE DE L'ADMISSION DE VOTRE PAYS A L'ORGANISATION DES NATIONS UNIES.

JE SAISIS CETTE HEUREUSE CIRCONSTANCE POUR VOUS PRESENTER MES PLUS CHALEUREUSES FELICITATIONS.

JE SUIS CONVAINCU QUE LA PRESENCE DE LA REPUBLIQUE DE COREE A L'ORGANISATION DES NATIONS UNIES LUI PERMETTRA D'APPORTER SA PRECIEUSE CONTRIBUTION AU SEIN DE CETTE ORGANISATION, A LA RECHERCHE DE SOLUTIONS AUX PROBLEMES DE NOTRE MONDE ET QU'ELLE SERA UNE ETAPE DECISIVE DANS LE PROCESSUS DE LA REUNIFICATION PACIFIQUE DE LA NATION COREENNE.

JE VOUDRAIS PAR AILLEURS VOUS ASSURER DE MON ENTIERE DISPONIBILITE A OEUVRER, DE CONCERT AVEC VOUS A L'INSTAURATION DE RELATIONS D'AMITIE ET DE COOPERATION FRUCTUEUSE ENTRE NOS DEUX ETATS.

EN VOUS REITERANT MES SINCERES FELICITATIONS, JE VOUS PRIE D'AGREER, MONSIEUR LE MINISTRE, L'EXPRESSION DE MA HAUTE CONSIDRATION.

SIGNE: THEODORE HOLO
MINISTRE DES AFFAIRES ETRANGERES
ET DE LA COOPERATION DU BENIN

UNW-7251
첨부

1 — 1

0100

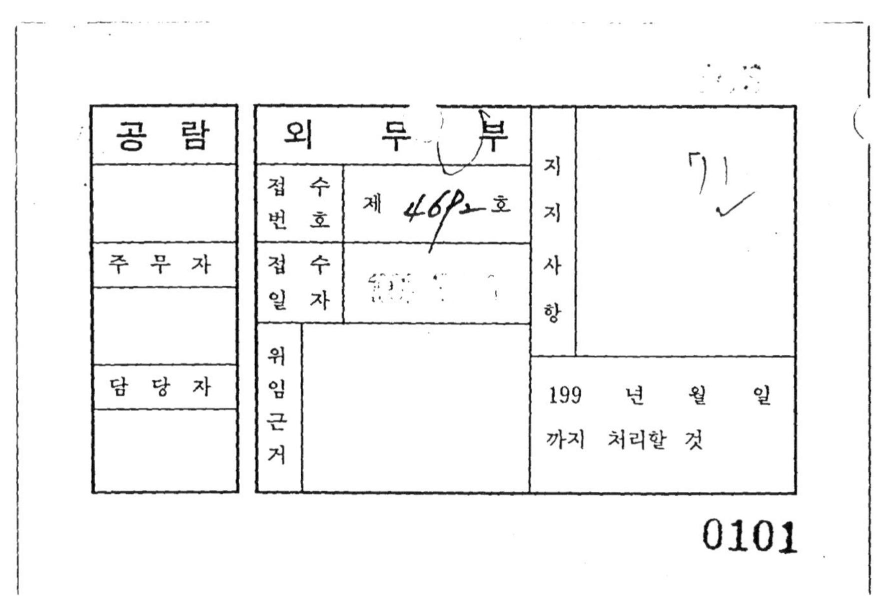

공 람	외 무 부		지 지 사 항	기
	접 수 번 호	제 4692 호		
주 무 자	접 수 일 자			
	위 임 근 거		199 년 월 일 까지 처리할 것	
담 당 자				

0101

배 부 처

장관실

기획실		아주국		국제기구국		문화협력국	
정책실		미주국		조약국		영교국	
의전실		구주국		국제경제국		총무과	
특전실		중아국		통상국		감사관실	

0102

EMBASSY OF INDIA
C.P.O. BOX 3466, SEOUL
TEL : 798-4257, 798-4268
TELEX: K24641 INDEMB
FAX : 796-9534

सत्यमेव जयते

भारतीय राजदूतावास
सिओल

No.SEO/123/1/88

October 8, 1991.

The Embassy of India presents its compliments to the Ministry of Foreign Affairs of the Government of the Republic of Korea and has the honour to forward herewith a letter from H.E. Mr. Eduardo Faleiro, Minister of State for External Affairs, Government of India to H.E. Mr. Lee Sang Ock, Minister of Foreign Affairs of the Republic of Korea, Seoul. It would be appreciated if the letter is transmitted to its high destination.

The Embassy of India avails itself of this opportunity to renew to the Ministry of Foreign Affairs of the Republic of Korea the assurances of its highest considertion.

Embassy of India, Seoul

Ministry of Foreign Affairs
Republic of Korea,
SEOUL.

0103

विदेश राज्य मंत्री
भारत
MINISTER OF STATE
FOR EXTERNAL AFFAIRS
INDIA

New Delhi

September 22, 1991.

Excellency,

Please accept my sincere felicitations on admission of the Republic of Korea as a Member of the United Nations Organisation.

India has consistently supported the aspirations of the Korean people to actively contribute towards the realisation of the purposes and principles of the United Nations through representation in this world body.

It is our sincere hope that entry of the Republic of Korea and the Democratic People's Republic of Korea into the United Nations will further promote the process of peaceful dialogue and reduction of tensions in the Korean peninsula.

With my good wishes for your personal well-being and happiness and the prosperity of the friendly people of the Republic of Korea.

(EDUARDO FALEIRO)

H.E. Mr. Lee Sang Ock,
Minister for Foreign Relations
of the Republic of Korea,
SEOUL.

0104

50239

기안용지

분류기호 문서번호	연일 2031 -	(전화 :)	시 행 상 특별취급	
보존기간	영구 · 준영구. 10. 5. 3. 1	장 관		
수 신 처 보존기간				
시행일자	1991. 10. 10.			

보조기관			협조기관		
	국 장	전 결			문서통제
	심의관				검열 1991. 10. 12 통제관
	과 장				
기안책임자		황준국			발송인

경 유		발신명의		
수 신	대통령비서실장			
참 조	의전수석비서관			
제 목	대통령각하 앞 축전접수			

연 : 연일 2031-47342 (9.30)

연호, 우리의 유엔가입에 대하여 페루대통령이 대통령각하 앞 축전을 보내 왔는 바 동 축전사본을 별첨 송부합니다.

첨 부 : 동 사본 1부. 끝.

0105

기안용지

분류기호 문서번호	연일 2031 -	(전화 :)	시행상 특별취급	
보존기간	영구·준영구. 10. 5. 3. 1	차 관	장 관	
수신처 보존기간				
시행일자	1991.10.10.			

보조기관			협조기관		문서통제
	국 장			제1차관보 아주국장 미주국장 구주국장 중동아국장	
	심의관				
	과 장				
기안책임자		김성진			발송인

경유 수신 참조	건 의	발신명의		
제 목	유엔가입 축전에 대한 장관님 명의 회신발송			

1. 9.17. 우리의 유엔가입 관련, '허드' 영국 외무장관등 12개국 외무장관을 포함하여 각국 인사 20명이 장관님 앞으로 축전을 보내 왔는 바, 이에 대한 장관님 명의 회신 (일본 및 멕시코 외무장관은 제외)을 별첨(안)과 같이 발송코자 하오니 재가하여 주시기 바랍니다.

2. 상기 회신중 서한(12건)은 주한 해당국 대사관을 통하여, 그리고 케이블 메세지(5건)는 해당국 주재 우리공관을

0106 /계속/

통하여 각각 전달할 예정임을 첨언합니다.

첨부 : 1. 장관님 앞 축전접수 현황 1부.

2. 회신(안) 17부. 끝.

0107

(첨부 1)

유엔가입 관련 장관님 앞 축전 접수현황

91.10.10. 현재

I. 각국 외무장관(12명)

순번	국 가	접수일자	전 달 경 위	형 식	비 고(지역국 협의필)
1	일 본 (나까야마외상)	9.17. 9.18.	주유엔 일본대사 주한 일본대사관	케이블 메세지 "	o 9.23. 조찬회담시 구두사의 표명, 답신 불필요 (아주국)
2	영 국 (허드외상)	9.17. 9.18.	주한 영국대사대리 주유엔 영국대사	" "	o 답 신(서한)
3	남 아 공 (보타외상)	9.17. 9.18. 9.25.	주유엔 남아공대사 주나미비아대사관 (경유) 주일 남아공총영사관	" " "	o 답신(케이블메세지)
4	멕 시 코 (솔라나외상)	9.18.	주멕시코대사관 (경유)	"	o 멕시코 방문관련 친서에 포함예정, 답신 불필요 (미주국)
5	호 주 (블레웨트 외상대리)	9.19. 9.26.	주한 호주대사대리 주한 호주대사관	" 친필서한	o 답 신(서한)
6	브루나이 (볼키아외상)	9.20.	주한 브루나이 대사관	케이블 메세지	o 답 신(서한)
7	루마니아 (나스타세외상)	9.24.	주한 루마니아 대사관	"	o 답 신(서한)
8	인 도 (팔레리오 외무 담당 국무상)	9.25.	주한 인도대사	"	o 답 신(서한)

0108

순번	국 가	접수일자	전 달 경 위	형 식	비 고(지역국 협의필)
9	칠 레 (시마외상)	9.25. 9.26.	일반 텔렉스 주한 칠레대사관	케이블 메세지 (스페 인어)	ㅇ 답 신(서한, 스페인어)
10	아 프 간 (와킬외상)	10.1.	주인도 아프간 대사관	케이블 메세지	ㅇ 답신(케이블메세지)
11	파키스탄 (칸주외상)	10.1.	주한 파키스탄 대사관	"	ㅇ 답 신(서한)
12	베 넹 (홀로외상)	10.8.	주유엔대사(경유)	"	ㅇ 답신(케이블메세지)

Ⅱ. 기타 인사(8명)

순번	국 가	접수일자	내용 및 전달	비고(지역국협의필)
1	Nye 하바드대 국제 관계센타 학장	9.17.	ㅇ 가입축하, 외무부와 하바드대 간 긴밀한관계 유지 희망 (주유엔대표부경유 FAX)	ㅇ ~~답 신(서한)~~ 不要
2	Etre 주한 헝가리대사	9.18.	ㅇ 가입축하 (친필서한, 국문)	ㅇ ~~답 신(서한, 국문)~~ 不要
3	Kasenda 주한 인니대사	9.18.	ㅇ 가입축하 (친필서한)	ㅇ ~~답 신(서한)~~ 不要
4	Urjinlhundev 주한 몽골대사	9.18.	ㅇ 가입축하 (친필서한, 몽골어 및 국문)	ㅇ 답 신(서한, 국문)
5	R. Allen 친한 미측인사	9.18.	ㅇ 가입축하 (친필서한, FAX)	ㅇ 10.11-15. 방한 예정, 답신 불필요 (미주국)

0103

순번	국 가	접수일자	내용 및 전달	
6	Cholkamy 주한 이집트 총영사	9.19.	o 가입축하 (일반 Telex)	o ~~답 신(서한)~~ 不要
7	Ogata UNHCR 고등판무관	9.20.	o 가입축하 (주제네바대표부 경유 일반 Telex)	o 답 신(케이블 메세지)
8	Jones 그레나다 국민당 당수 (전 수상겸 외상)	9.26.	주 TNT대사관(경유) (친필서한)	o 답신(케이블 메세지)

0110

(첨부 2)

회신 대상자 명단 (17명)

I. 각국 외무장관 (10명)

1. 영　　국　　Douglas Hurd 외무장관 (서한)
2. 호　　주　　Neal Blewett 외무장관대리 (서한)
3. 인　　도　　Eduardo Falerio 외무담당 국무상 (서한)
4. 루마니아　　Adrian Nastase 외무장관 (서한)
5. 브루나이　　Mohamed Bolkiah 외무장관 (서한)
6. 파키스탄　　Muhammad S.K. Kanju 외무장관 (서한)
7. 칠　　레　　Enrique S. Cimma 외무장관 (서한)
8. 남 아 공　　Roelof F. Botha 외무장관 (케이블 메세지)
9. 아 프 간　　Abdul Wakil 외무장관 (케이블 메세지)
10. 베　　냉　　Theodore Holo 외무장관 (케이블 메세지)

II. 기타인사 (7명)

1. Sandor Etre　　주한 헝가리 대사 (서한)
2. Rudolf Kasenda　　주한 인니 대사 (서한)
3. P. Urjinlhundev　　주한 몽골 대사 (서한)
4. Mohamed A. Cholkamy　　주한 이집트 총영사 (서한)
5. Sadako Ogata　　UNHCR 고등판무관 (케이블 메세지)
6. Ben J. Jones　　그레나다 국민당 당수 (케이블 메세지)
7. Joseph S. Nye Jr.　　하바드대 국제관계센터 학장 (서한)

0111

MINISTER OF FOREIGN AFFAIRS
SEOUL, KOREA

October 14, 1991

Excellency,

I was very much pleased to receive Your Excellency's congratulatory message transmitted to me through the Romanian Embassy in Seoul on the occasion of my country's admission to the United Nations.

Taking this opportunity, I should like to express our deep appreciation to the Government of Romania, in particular as a member of the Security Council, for the invaluable support to our efforts to attain United Nations membership.

I hope that our two countries will henceforth closely cooperate at the United Nations.

Looking forward to welcoming you soon in Seoul, I wish to extend my best wishes and warmest regards.

Yours sincerely,

LEE Sang-Ock

His Excellency
Mr. Adrian Nastase
Minister of Foreign Affairs
Romania

0112

MINISTER OF FOREIGN AFFAIRS
SEOUL, KOREA

October 14, 1991

Dear Mr. Secretary,

I wish to extend my sincere gratitude to you for sending me a kind message of congratulations on the occasion of my country's admission to the United Nations through the British Embassy in Seoul.

I would like to express our deep appreciation to the Government and people of the United Kingdom for the invaluable support to our efforts to attain United Nations membership.

It is my firm belief that the friendly and cooperative relations happily existing between our two countries will be further strengthened through close cooperation at the United Nations.

Taking this opportunity, I am also happy to invite you to visit Korea at your convenience in the near future. I am confident that the visit will contribute to enhancing the ties of friendship between our two countries.

With my best wishes,

Yours sincerely,

LEE Sang-Ock

The Right Honourable
Douglas Hurd
Secretary of State for Foreign and
Commonwealth Affairs
United Kingdom

0113

MINISTER OF FOREIGN AFFAIRS
SEOUL, KOREA

October 14, 1991

Dear Dr. Blewett,

I was very much pleased to receive your congratulatory letter of September 23, 1991 on the occasion of my country's admission to the United Nations.

Taking this opportunity, I should like to express our deep appreciation to the Government of Australia for the invaluable support to our efforts to attain United Nations membership.

As you indicated, I also believe that our U.N. membership will help improve inter-Korean relations and create favourable atmosphere for national reconciliation.

It is my firm belief that the friendly and cooperative relations happily existing between our two countries will be further strengthened through close cooperation at the United Nations.

I would like to extend to you my best wishes and warmest regards.

Yours sincerely,

Lee Sang-Ock

His Excellency
Dr. Neal Blewett
Minister for Trade and Overseas Development
Australia

0114

MINISTER OF FOREIGN AFFAIRS
SEOUL, KOREA

October 14, 1991

Your Royal Highness,

I was very much pleased to receive a congratulatory message of Your Royal Highness transmitted to me through the Embassy of Brunei Darussalam in Seoul on the occasion of my country's admission to the United Nations.

Taking this opportunity, I would like to express our deep appreciation to the Government of Brunei Darussalam for the valuable support to our efforts to attain United Nations membership.

I hope that our two countries will henceforth closely cooperate at the United Nations.

Please accept, Your Royal Highness, the assurances of my highest consideration.

LEE Sang-Ock

His Royal Highness
Prince Mohamed Bolkiah
Minister of Foreign Affairs
Brunei Darussalam

0115

MINISTER OF FOREIGN AFFAIRS
SEOUL. KOREA

October 14, 1991

Excellency,

I was very much pleased to receive Your Excellency's congratulatory message transmitted to me by the Indian Ambassador in Seoul, H.E. Mr. L.T. Pudaite, on the occasion of my country's admission to the United Nations.

Taking this opportunity, I should like to express our deep gratitude to the Government of India for the invaluable support to our efforts to attain United Nations membership. In particular, we highly appreciate your country's role in presenting a draft resolution on the admission of both Koreas to the Unted Nations at the current session of the General Assembly.

I am confident that our two countries will henceforth closely cooperate at the Untied Nations.

Please accept, Excellency, the renewed assurances of my highest consideration.

LEE Sang-Ock

His Excellency
Mr. Eduardo Falerio
Minister of State for External Affairs
India

0116

MINISTER OF FOREIGN AFFAIRS
SEOUL, KOREA

October 14, 1991

Excellency,

I was very much pleased to receive Your Excellency's congratulatory message transmitted to me through your Embassy in Seoul on the occasion of my country's admission to the United Nations.

Taking this opportunity, I should like to express our deep appreciation to the Government of the Islamic Republic of Pakistan for the valuable support to our efforts to attain United Nations membership.

I am confident that our two countries will henceforth closely cooperate at the United Nations.

Please accept, Excellency, the assurances of my highest consideration.

LEE Sang-Ock

His Excellency
Mr. Muhammad Siddique Khan Kanju
Minister of State for Foreign Affairs
Islamic Republic of Pakistan

0117

MINISTER OF FOREIGN AFFAIRS
SEOUL, KOREA

Seúl, 11 de Octubre de 1991

Excelentísimo Señor Ministro:

Fue, para mí, una gran alegría recibir el gentil mensaje de felicitación, fechado 25 de septiembre pasado, que Vuestra Excelencia tuviera a bien enviarme por conducto de la Embajada de Chile en Seúl con ocasión de la admisión de la República de Corea en las Naciones Unidas.

Debo, igualmente, manifestarle mi hondo agradecimiento por el valioso apoyo que nos fuera brindado por el ilustrado Gobierno de Chile en favor de nuestros esfuerzos para ser miembro de las Naciones Unidas. Esperamos que Corea y Chile sigan estrechando más la cooperación en las Naciones Unidas y en otros organismos internacionales.

Quiero aprovechar esta grata oportunidad para expresar mi sincera congratulación por los notables logros que Chile viene alcanzando tanto en la consolidación del sistema democrático como en el crecimiento económico bajo la distinguida conducción del Excelentísimo señor Presidente Aylwin.

Acepte, Excelencia, mis mejores votos por la ventura personal de Vuestra Excelencia con las seguridades de mi más alta consideración.

LEE Sang-Ock

Al Excelentísimo Señor
Enrique Silva Cimma
Ministro de Relaciones Exteriores
de la República de Chile

0118

(번역문)

1991년 10월 11일

각 하,

금번 대한민국의 유엔가입에 즈음하여 각하께서 주한 칠레 대사관을 통하여 본인에게 보내주신 9월 25일자 축전을 기쁘게 받아보았습니다.

본인은 칠레공화국정부가 그동안 우리의 유엔가입 노력에 대해 적극적으로 지지해 준데 대하여 심심한 사의를 표하는 바입니다.

금후 한·칠레 양국이 유엔등 국제무대에서 보다 긴밀히 협조할 수 있게 되기를 기원하오며, 아울러 최근 귀국이 앨윈 대통령의 영도하에 착실한 민주발전과 안정적인 경제성장을 구가하고 있는데 대하여 진심으로 축하를 드립니다.

본인 최대의 경의와 안부를 전합니다.

이 상 옥

엔리께 실바 시마
칠레공화국 외무장관

0119

MINISTER OF FOREIGN AFFAIRS
SEOUL, KOREA

October 14, 1991

Dear Mr. Nye,

I was very pleased to receive your congratulatory letter of September 16, 1991 on the occasion of my country's admission to the United Nations.

As you mentioned in your letter, my Ministry has long maintained close ties of cooperation with Harvard University, especially through the steady participation of our diplomats in the Fellows Program at the Center for International Affairs. I am sure that our close relationship will be further strengthened in the future with your kind cooperation and assistance.

With my best wishes and warmest personal regards, I remain,

Yours sincerely,

LEE Sang-Ock

Mr. Joseph S. Nye, Jr.
Director of the Center for
International Affairs
Harvard University

0120

(남아공외상 : 케이블메세지)

His Excellency
Mr. Roelof F. Botha
Minister of Foreign Affairs
Republic of South Africa

Excellency, October 11, 1991

I would like to extend my gratitude to Your Excellency for the kind message of congratulations on the occasion of the admission of the Republic of Korea to the United Nations.

I also wish to take this opportunity to mention that the Government of the Republic of Korea welcomes the recent positive developments in your country and hopes that negotiations on a new constitution will reach a fruitful conclusion, thus completely dismantling apartheid.

Please accept, Excellency, the assurances of my highest consideration.

LEE Sang-Ock
Minister of Foreign Affairs
Republic of Korea

0121

(아프간외상 : 케이블메세지)

His Excellency
Mr. Abdul Wakil
Minister of Foreign Affairs
Republic of Afghanistan

Excellency, October 11, 1991

I have the pleasure of acknowledging receipt of Your Excellency's kind message of September 22, 1991 transmitted to me through your Embassy in India.

Expressing my deep gratitude to you for your congratulatory message on my country's admission to the United Nations, I would like to inform you that the Republic of Korea wishes to have friendly relations with all countries. Accordingly, the Government and the people of the Republic of Korea sincerely hope that the political situations in and around your country will develop to create conditions favorable to an early resumption of diplomatic relations between our two countries.

I avail myself of this opportunity to extend to Your Excellency the assurances of my highest consideration.

LEE Sang-Ock
Minister of Foreign Affairs
Republic of Korea

0122

(베냉외상 : 케이블메세지)

His Excellency
Mr. Theodore Holo
Minister of Foreign Affairs and Cooperation
Benin

Excellency,

October 11, 1991

I was very much pleased to receive Your Excellency's congratulatory message transmitted through your Permanent Mission to the U.N. in New York on the occasion of my country's admission to the United Nations.

I sincerely hope that our two countries will henceforth closely cooperate at the United Nations. In particular, I believe that your official visit to Korea schedueled in December this year will be a milestone in further strengthening the close relations between our two countries.

Please accept, Excellency, the assurances of my highest consideration.

LEE Sang-Ock
Minister of Foreign Affairs
Republic of Korea

0123

(UNHCR 고등판무관 : 케이블메시지)

Mrs. Sadako Ogata
High Commissioner
Office of the UNHCR
Geneva

Dear Mrs. Ogata, October 11, 1991

I was very pleased to receive your kind telex of October 2, 1991 transmitted to me through the Korean Permanent Mission to the U.N. at Geneva.

Expressing my deep appreciation to you for your congratulatory message on our entry into the United Nations, I would like to inform you that the Republic of Korea will make every effort to contribute to the works of the United Nations in a manner commensurate with its standing in the international community.

I would like to extend to you my best wishes and warmest regards.

LEE Sang-Ock
Minister of Foreign Affairs
Republic of Korea

0124

(그레나다 국민당 당수 : 케이블메시지)

Mr. Ben J. Jones
Political Leader of The National Party (T.N.P.)
Grenada

Dear Mr. Jones, October 11, 1991

I would like to express my deep appreciation to you for your congratulatory letter conveyed to me through our Embassy in Trinidad and Tobago on the occasion of my country's admission to the United Nations.

I am confident that the close relations between Grenada and the Republic of Korea will be further strengthened in the future.

I wish you good health and every success in discharging your important responsibilities.

LEE Sang-Ock
Minister of Foreign Affairs
Republic of Korea

0125

50240

기 안 용 지

분류기호 문서번호	연일 2031 -	(전화:)	시 행 상 특별취급	
보존기간	영구·준영구. 10. 5. 3. 1	장 관		
수 신 처 보존기간				
시행일자	1991. 10. 11.			

보조기관			협조기관		문서통제
	국 장	전 결			검열 1991. 10. 12 통제관
	심의관				
	과 장				
기안책임자		황준국			발 송 인

경 유		발신명의	
수 신	대통령비서실장		
참 조	의전수석비서관		
제 목	대통령각하 앞 축전 답신		

연 : 연일 2031-46017(9.19), 47342(9.30), 50239(10.12)

연호 송부한 대통령각하 앞 유엔가입 축전(6개국) 및 코트디봐르의 축전(전문 IVW-0492)에 대하여 대통령 명의 답신을 별첨과 같이 건의합니다.

첨 부 : 1. 일본수상 앞 답신안 (국.영문)

2. 호주수상 앞 답신안 (국.영문)

/ 계속 /

0126

(2)

3. 중화민국총통 앞 답신안 (국.영문)

4. 칠레대통령 앞 답신안 (국.영문)

5. 페루대통령 앞 답신안 (국.영문)

6. 튀니지대통령 앞 답신안 (국.영문)

7. 코트디브와르대통령 앞 답신안(국.영문).

끝.

0127

유엔가입 축전에 대한 대통령 답신 (국.영문 안)

1. 일본 수상
2. 호주 수상
3. 중화민국 총통
4. 칠레 대통령
5. 페루 대통령
6. 튀니지 대통령
7. 코트디봐르 대통령

앙 91년 고 10월 재 10일	담 당	과 장	국 장
	(서명)	(서명)	

0128

1991년 10월 11일

총리대신 각하,

금번 우리의 유엔가입에 즈음하여 축전을 보내 주신데 대해 감사 드립니다.

본인은 그동안 우리가 유엔가입을 위해 외교적 노력을 경주함에 있어서 일본정부가 보여준 확고한 지원과 협조에 심심한 사의를 표하는 바 입니다.

우리는 남북한의 유엔가입이 이 지역의 긴장완화에 기여하고 또한 한반도의 평화통일을 촉진시킬 것으로 희망하고 있으며, 각하께서도 우리와 같은 희망을 표명해 주신 것을 기쁘게 생각합니다.

본인은 우리 두나라가 유엔을 위시한 국제무대에서 상호협력의 영역을 확대하면서 인류공동의 번영을 위해 함께 노력해 나가기를 희망하며, 이를 통하여 양국간의 우호협력 관계도 더욱 강화될 수 있을 것으로 믿습니다.

각하의 건승하심과 귀국의 무궁한 번영을 기원합니다.

노 태 우

일본국
카이후 토시키 내각총리대신 각하

0129

11 October 1991

Dear Prime Minister,

I thank you very much for your thoughtful message on the occasion of my country's admission to the United Nations.

Your Government's full support for our diplomatic campaign for United Nations membership has been highly appreciated.

It is reassuring to see that Your Excellency is sharing my hope that both Koreas' entry into the United Nations will reduce tensions in the region and provide a new momentum to our efforts to accelerate the process of the peaceful reunification of the Korean peninsula.

I also hope that Japan and the Republic of Korea will make concerted efforts towards the common interests of humankind by expanding the scope of cooperation in the multilateral forums including the United Nations. This will surely lead to ever closer bilateral relations between our two countries.

Please accept my best wishes for your good health and the everlasting prosperity of your great nation.

Yours sincerely,

/s/ Roh Tae Woo

H.E. Toshiki Kaifu
Prime Minister
Japan

0130

1991년 10월 11일

수상각하,

금번 우리의 유엔가입에 즈음하여 축전을 보내주신데 대해 감사드립니다.

본인은 그동안 우리가 유엔가입을 위해 외교적 노력을 경주함에 있어서 호주정부가 보여준 확고한 지원과 협조에 심심한 사의를 표하는 바입니다.

각하의 축전에서도 언급하셨듯이, 우리의 유엔가입은 북한과 함께 이루어졌다는 점에서 더욱 그 의의가 크다고 하겠습니다. 우리는 이 같은 사태발전이 한반도의 평화통일이라는 우리의 궁극적인 목표에 기여할 것으로 희망하고 있습니다.

또한 우리의 유엔가입으로 호주와 대한민국과의 긴밀한 협력관계도 더욱 강화될 수 있을 것이라는 각하의 기대에 전적으로 동감입니다.

각하의 건승하심과 귀국의 무궁한 번영을 기원합니다.

노 태 우

호주
로버트 호크 수상 각하

0131

11 October 1991

Dear Prime Minister,

I thank you very much for your kind words on the occasion of my country's admission to the United Nations.

I wish to take this opportunity to express my heartfelt gratitude for the unwavering support and cooperation that your Government has given to our diplomatic campaign for United Nations membership.

As your message said, the entry of the Republic of Korea into the United Nations was all the more significant because the Democratic People's Republic of Korea was also admitted at the same time. It is my earnest hope that a momentum can now be maintained which will lead in the fullness of time towards our ultimate goal of the peaceful reunification of the Korean peninsula.

I also fully agree to your view that my country's membership of the United Nations will greatly help to further strengthen the close and cooperative relationship between Australia and the Republic of Korea.

Please accept my best wishes for your good health and the everlasting prosperity of your great country.

Yours sincerely,

/s/ Roh Tae Woo

The Honourable R.J.L. Hawke
Prime Minister of Australia

0132

1991년 10월 11일

총통각하,

금번 우리의 유엔가입에 즈음하여 축전을 보내주신데 대해 감사드립니다.

우리는 남북한의 유엔가입이 이 지역의 긴장완화에 기여하기를 희망하고 있습니다.

각하의 건승하심과 귀국의 무궁한 번영을 기원합니다.

노 태 우

중화민국
이등휘 총통각하

0133

11 October 1991

Dear Mr. President,

I thank you very much for your thoughtful message on the occasion of my country's admission to the United Nations.

It is my sincere hope that both Koreas' entry into the United Nations will contribute to reducing tensions in the region.

Please accept my best wishes for your good health and the everlasting prosperity of your great country.

Yours sincerely,

/s/ Roh Tae Woo

His Excellency
Lee Teng-hui
President of the Republic of China

0134

1991년 10월 11일

대통령 각하,

금번 우리의 유엔가입에 즈음하여 축전을 보내 주신데 대해 감사드립니다.

본인은 그동안 우리가 유엔가입을 위해 외교적 노력을 경주함에 있어서 칠레 정부가 보여준 확고한 지원과 협조에 심심한 사의를 표하는 바 입니다.

우리는 유엔에서 상호협력을 확대해 나감으로써 양자간 우호관계도 더욱 강화될 수 있을 것으로 믿습니다.

각하의 건승하심과 귀국의 무궁한 번영을 기원합니다.

노 태 우

칠 레

빠뜨리시오 엘윈 아소깔 대통령 각하

0135

11 October 1991

Dear Mr. President,

I thank you very much for your thoughtful message on the occasion of my country's admission to the United Nations.

I wish to take this opportunity to express my heartfelt gratitude for the firm support that your Government has given to our diplomatic campaign for United Nations membership.

It is my sincere hope that the expanded contacts and cooperation in the United Nations will lead to ever closer bilateral relations between our two countries.

Please accept my best wishes for your good health and the everlasting prosperity of your nation.

Yours sincerely,

/s/ Roh Tae Woo

His Excellency
Patricio Aylwin Azocar
President of the Republic of Chile

0136

1991년 10월 11일

대통령 각하,

금번 우리의 유엔가입에 즈음하여 축전을 보내 주신데 대해 감사 드립니다.

본인은 그동안 우리가 유엔가입을 위해 외교적 노력을 경주함에 있어서 페루 정부가 보여준 확고한 지원과 협조에 심심한 사의를 표하는 바 입니다.

우리는 유엔에서 상호협력을 확대해 나감으로써 양자간 우호 관계도 더욱 강화될 수 있을 것으로 믿습니다.

각하의 건승하심과 귀국의 무궁한 번영을 기원합니다.

노 태 우

페 루

알베르토 후지모리 대통령 각하

0137

11 October 1991

Dear Mr. President,

I thank you very much for your thoughtful message on the occasion of my country's admission to the United Nations.

I wish to take this opportunity to express my heartfelt gratitude for the firm support that your Government has given to our diplomatic campaign for United Nations membership.

It is my sincere hope that the expanded contacts and cooperation in the United Nations will lead to ever closer bilateral relations between our two countries.

Please accept my best wishes for your good health and the everlasting prosperity of your nation.

Yours sincerely,

/s/ Roh Tae Woo

His Excellency
Alberto Fujimori
President of the Republic of Peru

0138

1991년 10월 11일

대통령 각하,

금번 우리의 유엔가입에 즈음하여 축전을 보내 주신데 대해 감사 드립니다.

본인은 그동안 우리가 유엔가입을 위해 외교적 노력을 경주함에 있어서 튀니지 정부가 보여준 확고한 지원과 협조에 심심한 사의를 표하는 바 입니다.

우리는 유엔에서 상호협력을 확대해 나감으로써 양자간 우호 관계도 더욱 강화될 수 있을 것으로 믿습니다.

각하의 건승하심과 귀국의 무궁한 번영을 기원합니다.

노 태 우

튀니지

진엘 아비딘 벤 알리 대통령 각하

0139

11 October 1991

Dear Mr. President,

I thank you very much for your thoughtful message on the occasion of my country's admission to the United Nations.

I wish to take this opportunity to express my heartfelt gratitude for the firm support that your Government has given to our diplomatic campaign for United Nations membership.

It is my sincere hope that the expanded contacts and cooperation in the United Nations will lead to ever closer bilateral relations between our two countries.

Please accept my best wishes for your good health and the everlasting prosperity of your nation.

Yours sincerely,

/s/ Roh Tae Woo

His Excellency
Zine El Abidine BEN ALI
Republic of Tunisia

0140

1991년 10월 11일

대통령 각하,

금번 우리의 유엔가입에 즈음하여 축전을 보내 주신데 대해 감사 드립니다.

본인은 그동안 우리가 유엔가입을 위해 외교적 노력을 경주함에 있어서 코트디봐르 정부가 보여준 확고한 지원과 협조에 심심한 사의를 표하는 바 입니다.

우리는 유엔에서 상호협력을 확대해 나감으로써 양자간 우호 관계도 더욱 강화될 수 있을 것으로 믿습니다.

각하의 건승하심과 귀국의 무궁한 번영을 기원합니다.

노 태 우

코트디봐르

페릭스 우프에 브와니 대통령 각하

0141

11 October 1991

Dear Mr. President,

I thank you very much for your thoughtful message on the occasion of my country's admission to the United Nations.

I wish to take this opportunity to express my heartfelt gratitude for the firm support that your Government has given to our diplomatic campaign for United Nations membership.

It is my sincere hope that the expanded contacts and cooperation in the United Nations will lead to ever closer bilateral relations between our two countries.

Please accept my best wishes for your good health and the everlasting prosperity of your nation.

Yours sincerely,

/s/ Roh Tae Woo

His Excellency
Felix Houphouet-Boigny
President of the Republic of Cote d'Ivoire

0142

외 무 부 장 관

서울, 1991년 10월 11일

친애하는 우르쥔루훈데브 대사 귀하,

금번 대한민국의 유엔가입에 즈음하여 귀하께서 보내주신 9월 18일자 축하서한을 기쁘게 받아 보았습니다.

이 기회를 빌어 그동안 우리정부의 유엔가입 노력에 있어서 몽골 정부가 깊은 관심을 갖고 지지해 준데 대해 심심한 사의를 표하는 바입니다.

본인은 곧 있을 몽골 대통령의 역사적 방한을 계기로 한.몽골 양국이 제반분야에서 실질협력관계를 더욱 발전시키고, 유엔에서도 긴밀한 협조관계를 계속 강화해 나갈 수 있기를 기대합니다.

대사의 건승을 기원합니다.

이 상 옥

페렌레인 우르쥔루훈데브 대사
주한 몽골대사관

0143

不要

외 무 부 장 관

서울, 1991년 10월 11일

친애하는 애뜨래 대사 귀하,

금번 대한민국의 유엔가입에 즈음하여 귀하께서 보내주신 9월 18일자 축하서한을 기쁘게 받아 보았습니다.

이 기회를 빌어 그동안 우리정부의 유엔가입 노력에 있어서 헝가리정부가 보내준 아낌없는 지지와 성원, 그리고 귀하가 보여준 각별한 관심에 대하여 깊은 사의를 표하는 바입니다.

본인은 앞으로 한·헝가리 양국이 제반분야에서 실질협력 관계를 착실히 발전시키면서, 유엔에서도 긴밀한 협력관계를 유지해 나가게 되기를 기대합니다.

대사의 건승을 기원합니다.

이 상 옥

샨도르 애뜨래 대사
주한 헝가리대사관

0144

THE MINISTER OF FOREIGN AFFAIRS
SEOUL, KOREA

October 14, 1991

Dear Mr. Ambassador,

I was very much pleased to receive your congratulatory letter of September 18, 1991 on the occasion of my country's admission to the United Nations.

Taking this occasion, I would like to express our deep appreciation to the member countries of ASEAN for their invaluable support to our efforts to attain United Nations membership.

I am confident that our relations with the member countries of ASEAN will be further enhanced through close cooperation at the United Nations.

I would also like to take this opportunity to highly compliment Your Excellency on your able chairmanship of the ASEAN Committee in Seoul for the past six months, during which we elevated the ROK-ASEAN relations to a Full Dialogue Partnership.

With my best wishes and warmest personal regards, I remain,

Yours sincerely,

LEE Sang-Ock

His Excellency
Mr. Rudolf Kasenda
Ambassador of the Republic of Indonesia
Seoul

0145

MINISTER OF FOREIGN AFFAIRS
SEOUL, KOREA

October 14, 1991

Dear Mr. Cholkamy,

I was very pleased to receive your congratulatory telegram of September 19, 1991 on the occasion of my country's admission to the United Nations.

Taking this opportunity, I hope that our two countries will henceforth closely cooperate at the United Nations. I also hope that the bilateral relations will be further strengthened during your term of office in Seoul.

With my best wishes,

Yours sincerely,

LEE Sang-Ock

Mr. Mohamed Amin Cholkamy
Consul General of Egypt
Seoul

0146

주 제 네 바 대 표 부

제네(정) 730- 874 1991. 10. 11.

수신 : 장 관

참조 : 국제기구국장

제목 : 아국 유엔가입 축하 서한

당지 도미니카 공화국 Hugo Lodrini대사는 아국의 유엔가입 축하 서한을 장관앞으로 보내왔는바, 동 서한을 별첨 송부합니다.

첨부 : 상기 서한 1부. 끝.

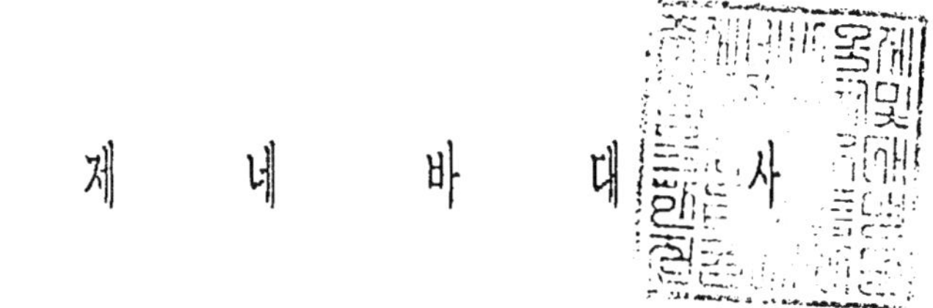

주 제 네 바 대 사

57518 0147

기 안 용 지

분류기호 문서번호	연일 2031 - 37886 (전화:)	시 행 상 특별취급	
보존기간	영구 · 준영구. 10. 5. 3. 1	장 관	
수 신 처 보존기간			
시행일자	1991. 10. 14.		

보조기관	국 장	전 결	협조기관		문서통제 검열 1991. 10. 15 통제관
	심의관				
	과 장				
기안책임자		김성진			발 송 인

경 유 / 수 신 / 참 조	주유엔대사	발신명의	

제 목	하바드대 국제문제센타 학장 앞 장관명의 답신 송부

우리의 유엔가입과 관련, 본직에게 축하서한(9.16자)을 보내온 하바드대학 Joseph S. Nye 국제문제센타 학장에 대한 본직명의 답신을 별첨 송부하니 동인에게 적의 전달하고 결과 보고바랍니다.

첨 부 : 표제답신 및 사본 각 1부. 끝.

0148

91-1309

기 안 용 지

분류기호 문서번호	연일 2031-2465	(전화:)	시 행 상 특별취급	
보존기간	영구 · 준영구. 10. 5. 3. 1	장	관	
수 신 처 보존기간				
시행일자	1991. 10. 14.			

보조기관	국 장	전 결	협조기관		문서통제
	심의관				검열 1991. 10. 15 통제관
	과 장				
기안책임자		김성진			발 송 인

경 유 수 신 참 조	수신처 참조	발신명의		
제 목	주재국 외무장관에 대한 장관명의 답신 송부			

9.17. 우리의 유엔가입 관련 귀주재국 외무장관이 보내온 축전 및 이에대해 10.14. 주한대사관을 통하여 주재국측에 전달한 본직명의 답신을 별첨 송부하니 참고바랍니다.

첨 부 : 상기 축전 및 답신 사본 각 1부. 끝.

수신처 : 주영, 호주, 인도, 루마니아, 브루나이, 파키스탄, 및 칠레대사

0149

OGI 91-873

The Ministry of Foreign Affairs presents its compliments to the British Embassy and has the honour to acknowledge receipt of the congratulatory message from The Right Honourable Douglas Hurd, Secretary of State for Foreign and Commonwealth Affairs of the United Kingdom, to H.E. LEE Sang-Ock, Minister of Foreign Affairs, on the occasion of the admission of the Republic of Korea to the United Nations.

The Ministry has further the honour to enclose herewith a reply letter of H.E. LEE Sang-Ock addressed to The Right Honourable Douglas Hurd. It would be appreciated if the letter is conveyed to its high destination.

The Ministry avails itself of this opportunity to renew to the British Embassy the assurances of its highest consideration.

Enclosure : as stated

Seoul, October 14, 1991

검열 1991. 10. 16 통제관

심의관:

양고재 91년 10월 10일	담당	과장	국장
	김성리		

0150

MINISTRY OF FOREIGN AFFAIRS
REPUBLIC OF KOREA

OGI 91-893

The Ministry of Foreign Affairs presents its compliments to the British Embassy and has the honour to acknowledge receipt of the congratulatory message from The Right Honourable Douglas Hurd, Secretary of State for Foreign and Commonwealth Affairs of the United Kingdom, to H.E. LEE Sang-Ock, Minister of Foreign Affairs, on the occasion of the admission of the Republic of Korea to the United Nations.

The Ministry has further the honour to enclose herewith a reply letter of H.E. LEE Sang-Ock addressed to The Right Honourable Douglas Hurd. It would be appreciated if the letter is conveyed to its high destination.

The Ministry avails itself of this opportunity to renew to the British Embassy the assurances of its highest consideration.

Enclosure : as stated

Seoul, October 14, 1991

0151

OCI 91-868

The Ministry of Foreign Affairs presents its compliments to the Embassy of Australia and has the honour to acknowledge receipt of the congratulatory letter from H.E. Neal Blewett, Minister for Trade and Overseas Development of Australia, to H.E. LEE Sang-Ock, Minister of Foreign Affairs, on the occasion of the admission of the Republic of Korea to the United Nations.

The Ministry has further the honour to enclose herewith a reply letter of H.E. LEE Sang-Ock addressed to H.E. Neal Blewett. It would be appreciated if the letter is conveyed to its high destination.

The Ministry avails itself of this opportunity to renew to the Embassy of Australia the assurances of its highest consideration.

Enclosure : as stated

Seoul, October 14, 1991

검열 1991. 10. 16 통제관

신디안 :

앙 고 재	91년 10월 14일	담 당	과 장	국 장
		김상인		

0152

MINISTRY OF FOREIGN AFFAIRS
REPUBLIC OF KOREA

OGI 91-869

The Ministry of Foreign Affairs presents its compliments to the Embassy of Australia and has the honour to acknowledge receipt of the congratulatory letter from H.E. Neal Blewett, Minister for Trade and Overseas Development of Australia, to H.E. LEE Sang-Ock, Minister of Foreign Affairs, on the occasion of the admission of the Republic of Korea to the United Nations.

The Ministry has further the honour to enclose herewith a reply letter of H.E. LEE Sang Ock addressed to H.E. Neal Blewett. It would be appreciated if the letter is conveyed to its high destination.

The Ministry avails itself of this opportunity to renew to the Embassy of Australia the assurances of its highest consideration.

Enclosure : as stated

Seoul, October 14, 1991

0153

OGI 91-874

The Ministry of Foreign Affairs presents its compliments to the Embassy of India and has the honour to acknowledge receipt of the congratulatory message from H.E. Eduardo Falerio, Minister of State for External Affairs of India, to H.E. LEE Sang-Ock, Minister of Foreign Affairs, on the occasion of the admission of the Republic of Korea to the United Nations.

The Ministry has further the honour to enclose herewith a reply letter of H.E. LEE Sang-Ock addressed to H.E. Eduardo Falerio. It would be appreciated if the letter is conveyed to its high destination.

The Ministry avails itself of this opportunity to renew to the Embassy of India the assurances of its highest consideration.

Enclosure : as stated

Seoul, October 14, 1991

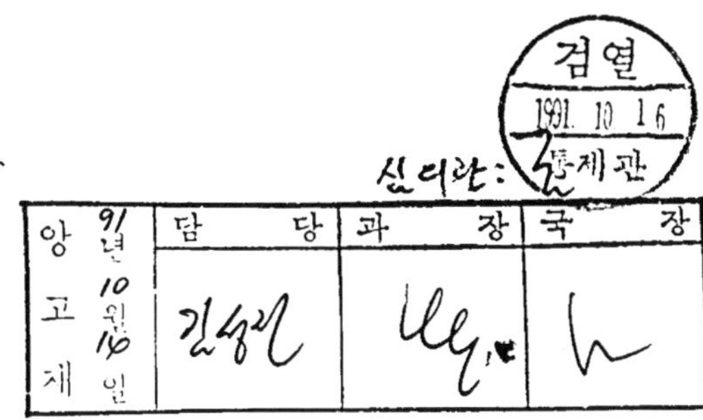

0154

MINISTRY OF FOREIGN AFFAIRS
REPUBLIC OF KOREA

OGI 91-84V

The Ministry of Foreign Affairs presents its compliments to the Embassy of India and has the honour to acknowledge receipt of the congratulatory message from H.E. Eduardo Falerio, Minister of State for External Affairs of India, to H.E. LEE Sang-Ock, Minister of Foreign Affairs, on the occasion of the admission of the Republic of Korea to the United Nations.

The Ministry has further the honour to enclose herewith a reply letter of H.E. LEE Sang Ock addressed to H.E. Eduardo Falerio. It would be appreciated if the letter is conveyed to its high destination.

The Ministry avails itself of this opportunity to renew to the Embassy of India the assurances of its highest consideration.

Enclosure : as stated

Seoul, October 14, 1991

0155

OGI 91-845

The Ministry of Foreign Affairs presents its compliments to the Embassy of Romania and has the honour to acknowledge receipt of the latter's Note No. 565 dated September 24, 1991 which enclosed the congratulatory message from H.E. Adrian Nastase, Minister of Foreign Affairs of Romania, to H.E. LEE Sang-Ock, Minister of Foreign Affairs, on the occasion of the admission of the Republic of Korea to the United Nations.

The Ministry has further the honour to enclose herewith a reply letter of H.E. LEE Sang-Ock addressed to H.E. Adrian Nastase. It would be appreciated if the letter is conveyed to its high destination.

The Ministry avails itself of this opportunity to renew to the Embassy of Romania the assurances of its highest consideration.

Enclosure : as stated

Seoul, October 14, 1991

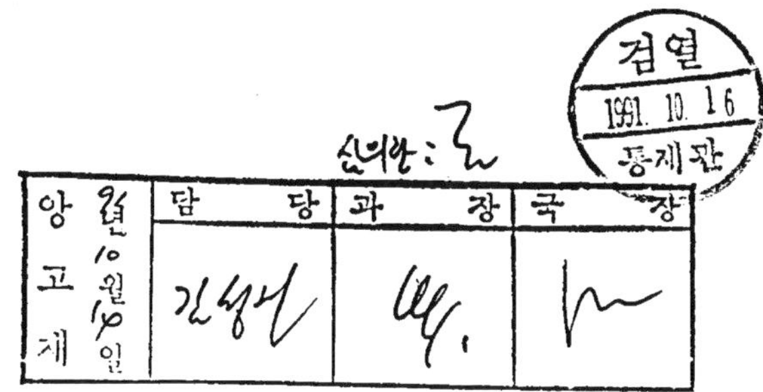

0156

MINISTRY OF FOREIGN AFFAIRS
REPUBLIC OF KOREA

OCI 91-845

The Ministry of Foreign Affairs presents its compliments to the Embassy of Romania and has the honour to acknowledge receipt of the latter's Note No. 565 dated September 24, 1991 which enclosed the congratulatory message from H.E. Adrian Nastase, Minister of Foreign Affairs of Romania, to H.E. LEE Sang-Ock, Minister of Foreign Affairs, on the occasion of the admission of the Republic of Korea to the United Nations.

The Ministry has further the honour to enclose herewith a reply letter of H.E. LEE Sang-Ock addressed to H.E. Adrian Nastase. It would be appreciated if the letter is conveyed to its high destination.

The Ministry avails itself of this opportunity to renew to the Embassy of Romania the assurances of its highest consideration.

Enclosure : as stated

Seoul, October 14, 1991

0157

OGI 91-870

The Ministry of Foreign Affairs presents its compliments to the Embassy of Brunei Darussalam and has the honour to acknowledge receipt of the latter's Note No. 276 dated September 20, 1991 which enclosed the congratulatory message from His Royal Highness Prince Mohamed Bolkiah, Minister of Foreign Affairs of Brunei Darussalam, to H.E. LEE Sang-Ock, Minister of Foreign Affairs, on the occasion of the admission of the Republic of Korea to the United Nations.

The Ministry has further the honour to enclose herewith a reply letter of H.E. LEE Sang-Ock addressed to His Royal Highness Prince Mohamed Bolkiah. It would be appreciated if the letter is conveyed to its high destination.

The Ministry avails itself of this opportunity to renew to the Embassy of Brunei Darussalam the assurances of its highest consideration.

Enclosure : as stated

Seoul, October 14, 1991

검열 1991. 10. 16 통제관

신여부: [illegible]

앙 고 재	91년 10월 10일	담 당	과 장	국 장
		[signature]	[signature]	[signature]

0158

MINISTRY OF FOREIGN AFFAIRS
REPUBLIC OF KOREA

OGI 91-840

The Ministry of Foreign Affairs presents its compliments to the Embassy of Brunei Darussalam and has the honour to acknowledge receipt of the latter's Note No. 276 dated September 20, 1991 which enclosed the congratulatory message from His Royal Highness Prince Mohamed Bolkiah, Minister of Foreign Affairs of Brunei Darussalam, to H.E. LEE Sang-Ock, Minister of Foreign Affairs, on the occasion of the admission of the Republic of Korea to the United Nations.

The Ministry has further the honour to enclose herewith a reply letter of H.E. LEE Sang Ock addressed to His Royal Highness Prince Mohamed Bolkiah. It would be appreciated if the letter is conveyed to its high destination.

The Ministry avails itself of this opportunity to renew to the Embassy of Brunei Darussalam the assurances of its highest consideration.

Enclosure : as stated

Seoul, October 14, 1991

0159

OGI 91-871

The Ministry of Foreign Affairs presents its compliments to the Embassy of the Islamic Republic of Pakistan and has the honour to acknowledge receipt of the latter's Note No. 2/6/91 dated October 1, 1991 which enclosed the congratulatory message from H.E. Muhammad Siddique Khan Kanju, Minister of State for Foreign Affairs of Pakistan, to H.E. LEE Sang-Ock, Minister of Foreign Affairs, on the occasion of the admission of the Republic of Korea to the United Nations.

The Ministry has further the honour to enclose herewith a reply letter of H.E. LEE Sang-Ock addressed to H.E. Muhammad Siddique Khan Kanju. It would be appreciated if the letter is conveyed to its high destination.

The Ministry avails itself of this opportunity to renew to the Embassy of the Islamic Republic of Pakistan the assurances of its highest consideration.

Enclosure : as stated

Seoul, October 14, 1991

검열 1991. 10. 15 통제관

신의관:

앙 고 재	91년 10월 14일	담 당	과 장	국 장
		김성진		

0160

MINISTRY OF FOREIGN AFFAIRS
REPUBLIC OF KOREA

OGI 91- 871

The Ministry of Foreign Affairs presents its compliments to the Embassy of the Islamic Republic of Pakistan and has the honour to acknowledge receipt of the latter's Note No. 2/6/91 dated October 1, 1991 which enclosed the congratulatory message from H.E. Muhammad Siddique Khan Kanju, Minister of State for Foreign Affairs of Pakistan, to H.E. LEE Sang-Ock, Minister of Foreign Affairs, on the occasion of the admission of the Republic of Korea to the United Nations.

The Ministry has further the honour to enclose herewith a reply letter of H.E. LEE Sang-Ock addressed to H.E. Muhammad Siddique Khan Kanju. It would be appreciated if the letter is conveyed to its high destination.

The Ministry avails itself of this opportunity to renew to the Embassy of the Islamic Republic of Pakistan the assurances of its highest consideration.

Enclosure : as stated

Seoul, October 14, 1991

0161

OGI 91-872

The Ministry of Foreign Affairs presents its compliments to the Embassy of Chile and has the honour to acknowledge receipt of the latter's Note No. 38/91 dated September 26, 1991, which enclosed the congratulatory message from H.E. Enrique Silva Cimma, Minister of Foreign Affairs of Chile, to H.E. LEE Sang-Ock, Minister of Foreign Affairs, on the occasion of the admission of the Republic of Korea to the United Nations.

The Ministry has further the honour to enclose herewith a reply letter of H.E. LEE Sang-Ock addressed to H.E. Enrique Silva Cimma. It would be appreciated if the letter is conveyed to its high destination.

The Ministry avails itself of this opportunity to renew to the Embassy of Chile the assurances of its highest consideration.

Enclosure : as stated

Seoul, October 14, 1991

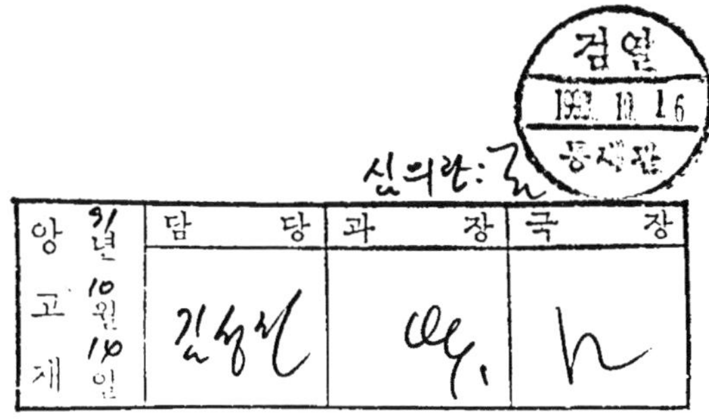

0162

MINISTRY OF FOREIGN AFFAIRS
REPUBLIC OF KOREA

OGI 91- 872

The Ministry of Foreign Affairs presents its compliments to the Embassy of Chile and has the honour to acknowledge receipt of the latter's Note No. 38/91 dated September 26, 1991, which enclosed the congratulatory message from H.E. Enrique Silva Cimma, Minister of Foreign Affairs of Chile, to H.E. LEE Sang-Ock, Minister of Foreign Affairs, on the occasion of the admission of the Republic of Korea to the United Nations.

The Ministry has further the honour to enclose herewith a reply letter of H.E. LEE Sang-Ock addressed to H.E. Enrique Silva Cimma. It would be appreciated if the letter is conveyed to its high destination.

The Ministry avails itself of this opportunity to renew to the Embassy of Chile the assurances of its highest consideration.

Enclosure : as stated

Seoul, October 14, 1991

0163

관리 번호	91-5277

분류번호	보존기간

발 신 전 보

번 호 : WGV-1395 911015 1543 BE 종별 :

수 신 : 주 제네바 대사. 총영사

발 신 : 장 관 (연일)

제 목 : UNHCR 고등판무관 앞 답전

대 : 재네(정) 2031-859

대호 Ogata UNHCR 고등판무관 명의 축전에 대한 본직명의 답전을 하기 타전하니 동인에게 적의 전달하고 결과 보고바람.

Mrs. Sadako Ogata
High Commissioner
Office of the UNHCR
Geneva

October 14, 1991

Dear Mrs. Ogata,

I was very pleased to receive your kind telex of October 2, 1991 transmitted to me through the Korean Permanent Mission to the U.N. at Geneva.

Expressing my deep appreciation to you for your congratulatory message on our entry into the United Nations, I would like to inform you that the Republic of Korea will make every effort to contribute to the works of the United Nations in a manner commensurate with its standing in the international community.

I would like to extend to you my best wishes and warmest regards.

LEE Sang-Ock
Minister of Foreign Affairs
Republic of Korea. 끝.

예 고 : 19 91.12.31. 일반문에 의거 일반문서로 재분류됨

(장 관)

보안 통제	

앙 고 재	91년 10월 14일	유엔1과	기안자 성명		과 장	심의관	국 장		차 관	장 관
			김성리				전결			

외신과통제

0164

관리 번호	91-5176

	분류번호	보존기간

발 신 전 보

번 호 : WTT-0127 911015 1544 BE 종별 :

수 신 : 주 트리니다드토바고 대사. 총영사

발 신 : 장 관 (연일, 미중)

제 목 : 그레나다 국민당당수 앞 답전

대 : 주트리니다드(정) 800-175

대호 Jones 그레나다 국민당 당수 명의 축하서한에 대한 본직 명의 답전을 하기 타전하기 동인에게 적의 전달하고 결과 보고바람.

Mr. Ben J. Jones
Political Leader of The National Party (T.N.P.)
Grenada

October 14, 1991

Dear Mr. Jones,

I would like to express my deep appreciation to you for your congratulatory letter conveyed to me through our Embassy in Trinidad and Tobago on the occasion of my country's admission to the United Nations.

I am confident that the close relations between Grenada and the Republic of Korea will be further strengthened in the future.

I wish you good health and every success in discharging your important responsibilities.

LEE Sang-Ock
Minister of Foreign Affairs
Republic of Korea. 끝.

예 고 19 1991.12.31. 일반에 의거 일반문서 (장 관)

보 안 통 제	

앙 고 재	91년 10월 14일	유엔 1 과	기안자 성 명		과 장	심의관	국 장		차 관	장 관
			김성진				전결			

외신과통제

0165

관리 번호	91-5179

	분류번호	보존기간

발 신 전 보

번 호 : WNM-0429 911015 1714 ED 종별 :

수 신 : 주 나미비아 대사. 총영사 (사본 : 주일, 유엔대사) WJA -4652 WUN -3562

발 신 : 장 관 (연일, 아프이)

제 목 : 남아공 외무장관 앞 답전

대 : NMW-0756

연 : WNM-0381

대호 남아공 외무장관 명의 축전에 대한 본직명의 답전을 하기 타전하니 남아공측에 적의 전달하고 결과 보고바람.

His Excellency
Mr. Roelof F. Botha
Minister of Foreign Affairs
Republic of South Africa

October 14, 1991

Excellency,

I would like to extend my gratitude to Your Excellency for the kind message of congratulations on the occasion of the admission of the Republic of Korea to the United Nations.

I also wish to take this opportunity to mention that the Government of the Republic of Korea welcomes the recent positive developments in your country and hopes that negotiations on a new constitution will reach a fruitful conclusion, thus completely dismantling apartheid.

Please accept, Excellency, the assurances of my highest consideration.

LEE Sang-Ock
Minister of Foreign Affairs
Republic of Korea 끝

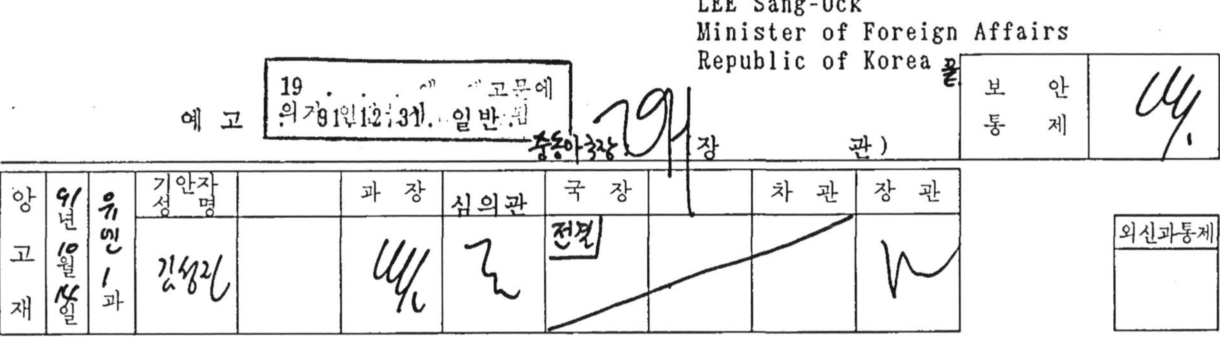

예 고 19 . . . 에 고문에 의거 91.12.31. 일반 (중동아국장 장 관)

보안 통제	

앙 고 재	91년 10월 14일	유엔 1 과	기안자 성 명		과 장	심의관	국 장		차 관	장 관
			김성길				전결			

외신과통제

0166

(남아공외상 : 케이블메세지)

His Excellency
Mr. Roelof F. Botha
Minister of Foreign Affairs
Republic of South Africa

Excellency, October 11, 1991

I would like to extend my gratitude to Your Excellency for the kind message of congratulations on the occasion of the admission of the Republic of Korea to the United Nations.

I also wish to take this opportunity to mention that the Government of the Republic of Korea welcomes the recent positive developments in your country and hopes that negotiations on a new constitution will reach a fruitful conclusion, thus completely dismantling apartheid.

Please accept, Excellency, the assurances of my highest consideration.

LEE Sang-Ock
Minister of Foreign Affairs
Republic of Korea

0167

관리 번호	91-5218

	분류번호	보존기간

발 신 전 보

번 호 : WUN-3563 911015 1715 ED 종별 :

수 신 : 주 유엔 대사. 총영사 (사본 : 주코트디브와르대사) WIV -0327

발 신 : 장 관 (연일, 아프일)

제 목 : 베냉 외무장관 앞 답전

대 : UNW-0381

대호 베냉 외무장관 명의 축전에 대한 본직명의 답전을 하기 타전하니 베냉측에 적의 전달하고 결과 보고바람.

His Excellency
Mr. Theodore Holo
Minister of Foreign Affairs and Cooperation
Benin

October 14, 1991

Excellency,

I was very much pleased to receive Your Excellency's congratulatory message transmitted through your Permanent Mission to the U.N. in New York on the occasion of my country's admission to the United Nations.

I sincerely hope that our two countries will henceforth closely cooperate at the United Nations. In particular, I believe that your official visit to Korea schedueled in December this year will be a milestone in further strengthening the close relations between our two countries.

Please accept, Excellency, the assurances of my highest consideration.

LEE Sang-Ock
Minister of Foreign Affairs
Republic of Korea. 끝

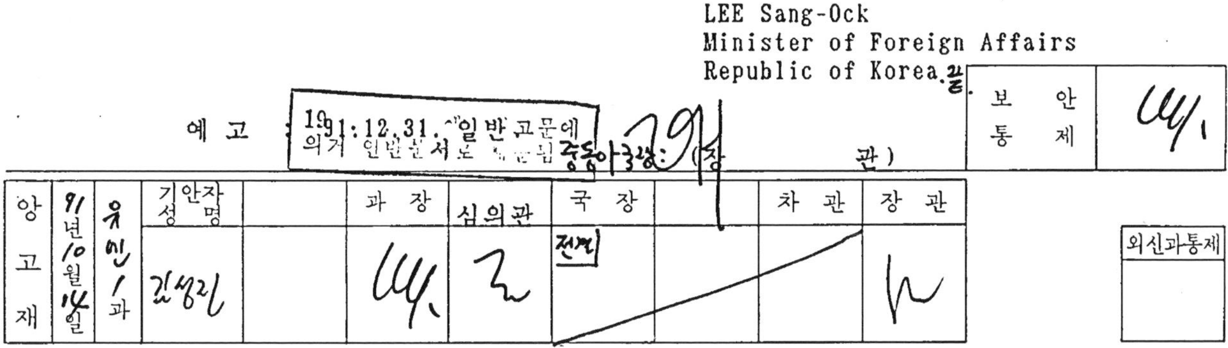

예 고 : 1991.12.31. 일반고문에 의거 인반문서로 재분류됨 (장 관)

보 안 통 제	

앙 고 재	91년 10월 14일	유엔 1과	기안자 성 명		과 장	심의관	국 장		차 관	장 관
			김성리				전결			

외신과통제

0168

(베넹외상 : 케이블메세지)

His Excellency
Mr. Theodore Holo
Minister of Foreign Affairs and Cooperation
Benin

Excellency, October 11, 1991

I was very much pleased to receive Your Excellency's congratulatory message transmitted through your Permanent Mission to the U.N. in New York on the occasion of my country's admission to the United Nations.

I sincerely hope that our two countries will henceforth closely cooperate at the United Nations. In particular, I believe that your official visit to Korea schedueled in December this year will be a milestone in further strengthening the close relations between our two countries.

Please accept, Excellency, the assurances of my highest consideration.

LEE Sang-Ock
Minister of Foreign Affairs
Republic of Korea

0169

관리 번호	91-5180

	분류번호	보존기간

발 신 전 보

번 호 : WND-0890 911015 1716 ED 종별 :

수 신 : 주 인도 대사. 총영사

발 신 : 장 관 (연일, 중동일)

제 목 : 아프가니스탄 외무장관 앞 답전

대 : NDW-1594, 인도(정) 20274-712

대호 아프가니스탄 외무장관 명의 축전에 대한 본직명의 답전을 하기 타전하니 아프가니스탄측에 적의 전달하고 결과 보고바람.

His Excellency
Mr. Abdul Wakil
Minister of Foreign Affairs
Republic of Afghanistan

October 14, 1991

Excellency,

I have the pleasure of acknowledging receipt of Your Excellency's kind message of September 22, 1991 transmitted to me through your Embassy in India.

Expressing my deep gratitude to you for your congratulatory message on my country's admission to the United Nations, I would like to inform you that the Republic of Korea wishes to have friendly relations with all countries. Accordingly, the Government and the people of the Republic of Korea sincerely hope that the political situations in and around your country will develop to create conditions favorable to an early resumption of diplomatic relations between our two countries.

I avail myself of this opportunity to extend to Your Excellency the assurances of my highest consideration.

LEE Sang-Ock
Minister of Foreign Affairs
Republic of Korea 끝

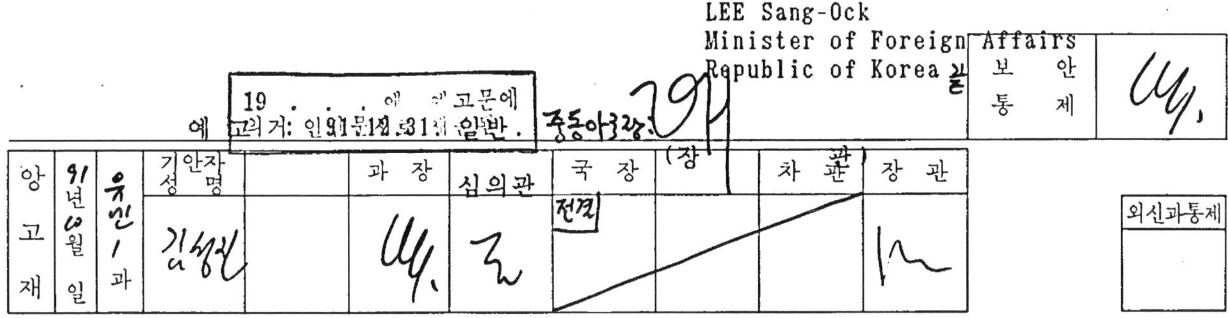
예 고 : 19 . . . 에 일반 고문에 의거: 인91.12.31. 일반.

앙 고 재	91 년 10 월 일	유엔 1 과	기안자 성 명		과 장	심의관	국 장	(장)	차 관	장 관
			김성진				전결			

보 안 통 제	

외신과통제

0170

(아프간외상 : 케이블메세지)

His Excellency
Mr. Abdul Wakil
Minister of Foreign Affairs
Republic of Afghanistan

Excellency, October 11, 1991

I have the pleasure of acknowledging receipt of Your Excellency's kind message of September 22, 1991 transmitted to me through your Embassy in India.

Expressing my deep gratitude to you for your congratulatory message on my country's admission to the United Nations, I would like to inform you that the Republic of Korea wishes to have friendly relations with all countries. Accordingly, the Government and the people of the Republic of Korea sincerely hope that the political situations in and around your country will develop to create conditions favorable to an early resumption of diplomatic relations between our two countries.

I avail myself of this opportunity to extend to Your Excellency the assurances of my highest consideration.

LEE Sang-Ock
Minister of Foreign Affairs
Republic of Korea

0171

AUSTRALIAN EMBASSY SEOUL

REF :

16 October 1991

Mr Hae Moon JUNG
Director
Southeast Asia Division
Ministry of Foreign Affairs
SEOUL

Dear Mr Jung,

I am enclosing, for transmission to His Excellency the Minister of Foreign Affairs, the original of a letter of congratulations from the Australian Acting Minister for Foreign Affairs and Trade, the Honourable Neal Blewett, on Korea's entry to the United Nations. The text of the letter was previously passed to His Excellency under cover of the Embassy's letter of 19 September 1991.

Yours sincerely,

(Andrew Mullin)
Counsellor

0172

TELEPHONE 720-6491, Y-6759, TELEX.23663, K.P.O. BOX 562 SEOUL

Minister for Trade and Overseas Development and Acting Minister for Foreign Affairs and Trade

Parliament House
CANBERRA ACT 2600

18 SEP 1991

His Excellency Lee Sang-Ock
Minister of Foreign Affairs
Republic of Korea

Dear Mr Lee

I am writing to congratulate you on the admission of your country to the United Nations. Australia has been a staunch advocate of the ROK's admission to the UN and co-sponsored the General Assembly resolution on the admission of the ROK and the DPRK. I am therefore delighted with this result, which will allow your country to assume its rightful role and responsibility in international affairs.

You will recall that when I wrote to you in April, I indicated that Australia would support either separate or simultaneous admission to the UN by the ROK and the DPRK in line with our support for the principle of universal UN membership. Australia is therefore also pleased to welcome the DPRK to the United Nations.

I believe the simultaneous entry of both Koreas into the UN will assist the process of Korean reconciliation as well as contributing to an improved security environment in the Asia Pacific region.

I am confident our close bilateral relationship and cooperation on international and regional issues can only be strengthened by your country's admission to the UN.

I wish you and your nation every success.

Yours sincerely

NEAL BLEWETT

0173

원 본

외 무 부

종 별 :

번 호 : TTW-0177　　　　　　일 시 : 91 1016 1430

수 신 : 장관(연일,미중)

발 신 : 주 트리니 다드대사

제 목 : 그레나다 국민당당수 앞 답전

대:WTT-0127

연: 주트리니다드(정)800-175

대호 그레나다 BEN JONES 국민당당수의 아국 유엔가입 축하서한에 대한장관님명의 답전을 금 10.16(수) 본직명의 서한 첨부 전달(우송)하였음을보고함.

(대사 박부열-장관)

예고:91.12.31 일반

에고문에 의거 일반문서로 재분류됨

국기국　장관　미주국

PAGE 1　　　　91.10.17 10:49

외신 2과 통제관 BD

0174

관리번호 91-5342

원 본

외 무 부

종 별 :

번 호 : GVW-2050 일 시 : 91 1017 1500

수 신 : 장관(연일)

발 신 : 주 제네바 대사

제 목 : UNHCR 고등 판무관앞 답전

대: WGV-1395

대호 답전 무위 전달하였음.

(대사 박수길-국장)

예고: 91.12.31. 일반문에 의거 일반문서로 재분류됨

국기국

PAGE 1

91.10.19 07:54

외신 2과 통제관 BD

0175

주 트 리 니 다 드 토 바 고 대 사 관

주 트리니다드(정) 800-177 1991. 10. 18

수 신: 장 관

참 조: 미주국장, 국제기구국장

제 목: 유엔가입 축하 공한

도미니카 연방 정부는 별첨과 같이 아국의 유엔가입에 대해 축하를 표시하는 공한을 당관으로 송부하여왔음을 보고합니다.

첨부: 상기 공한 1부. 끝.

선 결			결 재 (공람)		
접수일시	1991.10.22				
처리과	59530				

0176

TELEGRAMS, EXTERNAL DOMINICA
TELEX: 8613 *EXTERNAL DO*
TELEFAX: 809 44 85200
TELEPHONE: 809 44 82401 (*Ext.* 276)

Ref. No.: EX 211/01-1026

MINISTRY OF EXTERNAL AFFAIRS
AND OECS UNITY,
GOVERNMENT HEADQUARTERS,
ROSEAU
COMMONWEALTH OF DOMINICA,
WEST INDIES.

The Ministry of External Affairs and OECS Unity of the Commonwealth of Dominica presents its compliments to the Embassy of the Republic of Korea and has the honour to refer to the motion for the admission of the Republic of Korea to the membership of the United Nations Organization.

The Ministry has the special honour of extending warm congratulations from the People and Government of the Commonwealth of Dominica to the People and Government of the Republic of Korea on their attainment of such unparalleled recognition of their sovereignty as a nation of the world and acceptance into the United Nations Organization.

The Ministry looks forward to the further deepening of the friendly relations between our countries and the active co-operation between our nations within the United Nations Organization.

The Ministry of External Affairs and OECS Unity avails itself of the opportunity to renew to the Embassy of the Republic of Korea, the assurances of its highest consideration.

Embassy of the Republic of Korea
61 Dundonald Street
Port-of-Spain
P.O. Box 118
TRINIDAD & TOBAGO

1st October, 1991

0177

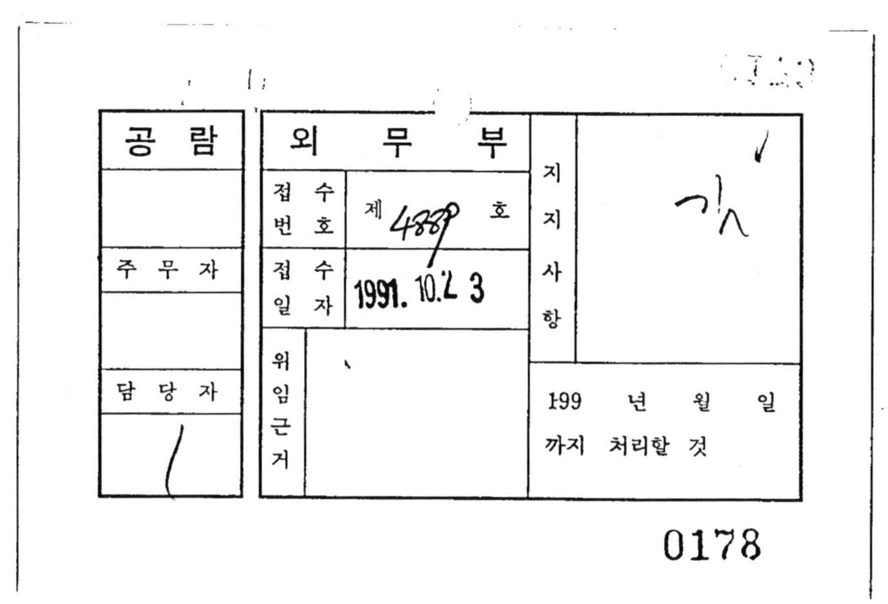

공 람	외 무 부		지시사항	
	접수번호	제 4889 호		
주 무 자	접수일자	1991. 10. 23		
	위임근거		199 년 월 일 까지 처리할 것	
담 당 자				

0178

배 부 처

기 획 실		아 주 국		국제기구국	✓	문 화 협 력 국	
정 책 실		미 주 국		조 약 국		영 교 국	
의 전 실		구 주 국		국 제 경 제 국		총 무 과	
특 전 실	/	중 아 국		통 상 국		감사관실	

0179

Note No: 112

Her Britannic Majesty's Embassy presents its compliments to the Ministry of Foreign Affairs of the Republic of Korea and has the honour to acknowledge receipt of the Ministry's Note No OGI91-873 covering a letter from His Excellency the Minister of Foreign Affairs to the Secretary of State for Foreign and Commonwealth Affairs which has been forwarded to the Foreign and Commonwealth Office in London.

Her Britannic Majesty's Embassy avails itself of this opportunity to renew to the Ministry of Foreign Affairs the assurances of its highest consideration.

British Embassy
Seoul

21 October 1991

0180

원 본

암호수신

외 무 부

종 별 : 지 급

번 호 : UNW-3474 일 시 : 91 1023 1820

수 신 : 장관 (연일,아프일)

발 신 : 주 유엔 대사

제 목 : 베넹 외무장관앞 답전

대: WUN-3563

대호 당관 공한으로 베넹측에 전달함. 끝

(대사 노창희-국장)

국기국 중아국

PAGE 1

91.10.24 07:59

외신 2과 통제관 BD

0181

52480

기 안 용 지

분류기호 문서번호	연일 2031 -	(전화:)	시 행 상 특별취급	
보존기간	영구 · 준영구. 10. 5. 3. 1	장 관		
수 신 처 보존기간				
시행일자	1991. 10. 25.			

보조기관	국 장	전 결	협조기관		문서통제
	심의관				1991. 1 . . 통제관
	과 장				
기안책임자		황준국			발 송 인

경 유		발신명의		
수 신	대통령비서실장			
참 조	의전수석비서관			
제 목	대통령각하 앞 유엔가입 축전			

연 : 연일 2031-50240

루안다 대통령으로부터의 대통령각하앞 유엔가입 축전을 별첨 송부하오며, 이에 대한 답신안(국.영문)을 별첨과 같이 건의합니다.

첨 부 : 1. 루안다 축전

2. 루안다 축전에 대한 답신안(국.영문). 끝.

0182

주 일 대 사 관

일본(정)700-8207 1991. 10.14.

수신 장관

참조 중동아프리카국장, 국제기구조약국장

제목 루안다 대통령 멧세지 송부

당지 루안다대사관은 루안다 대통령의 아국대통령 앞 별첩 축하멧세지를 전달해 줄 것을 요청해 왔는바, 이를 송부하니 적의 조치하여 주시기 바랍니다.

첨부 : 1. UN가입 축하멧세지 1부 : 국제연합1과로 이송

2. 국경일 축하멧세지 1부

3. 루안다대사관 공한 사본 1부. 끝.

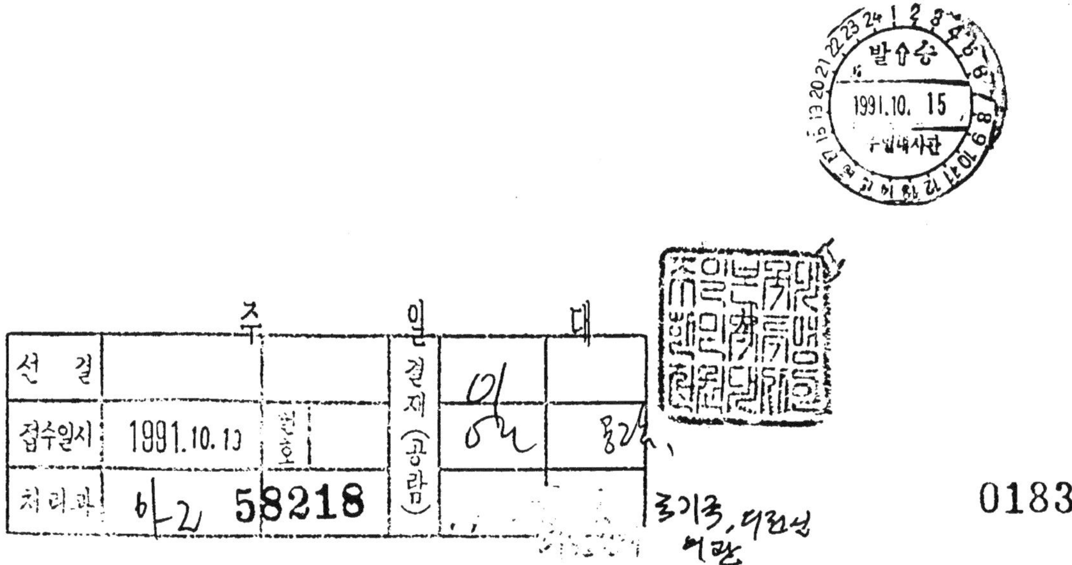

선 결			결재(공람)		
접수일시	1991.10.15	번호			
처리과		58218			

0183

AMBASSADE DE LA
REPUBLIQUE RWANDAISE

TOKYO

No 255/91/16.11.20/H29

The Embassy of the Rwandan Republic in Tokyo presents its compliments to the Embassy of the Republic of Korea and has the honour to inform the latter that it received by telex two messages from His Excellency the President of the Republic of Rwanda to His Excellency the President of the Republic of Korea.

The two congratulation messages are relating to the admission of the Republic of Korea as a member of the United Nations Organization and to the celebration of the Anniversary of the foundation of the Republic of Korea.

The Embassy of the Rwandan Republic would be very grateful if the Embassy of the Republic of Korea should help in conveying as quickly as possible the two messages to their high destinee.

The Embassy of the Rwandan Republic av'
itself of this opportunity to renew to the Embassy of Republic of Korea the assurances of its highest con'

Tokyo, 4th october, 1991

REPUBLIQUE RWANDAISE
AMBASSADE A TOKYO

Embassy of the Republic
of KOREA

TOKYO

0184

TELEGRAMME OFFICIEL

DESTINATAIRE : SON EXCELLENCE MONSIEUR ROH TAE WOO
PRESIDENT DE LA REPUBLIQUE DE COREE
SEOUL

TEXTE : MONSIEUR LE PRESIDENT COMMA A L'OCCASION DE L'ADMISSION DE VOTRE PAYS A L'ORGANISATION DES NATIONS UNIES COMMA J'AI L'HONNEUR DE VOUS ADRESSER MES PLUS VIVES ET CHALEUREUSES FELICITATIONS STOP JE SAISIS CETTE HEUREUSE OPPORTUNITE POUR EXPRIMER LA CONVICTION QUE VOTRE PAYS NE MENAGERA AUCUN EFFORT POUR FAVORISER LE RENFORCEMENT DES RELATIONS D'AMITIE QUI UNISSENT LE PEUPLE COREEN ET LE PEUPLE RWANDAIS COMMA AFIN DE LES CONCRETISER PAR UNE SOLIDARITE PLUS AGISSANTE DANS LA PROMOTION DU DEVELOPPEMENT SOCIO-ECONOMIQUE ET CULTUREL STOP JE SUIS HEUREUX DE VOUS RENOUVELER MON ENTIERE DISPONIBILITE A CONTRIBUER AVEC VOUS AU RENFORCEMENT DE CES RELATIONS AU PROFIT DE NOS DEUX PEUPLES TANT SUR LE PLAN BILATERAL QUE DANS LE CADRE DE L'ORGANISATION DES NATIONS UNIES DONT NOS DEUX PAYS SONT MEMBRES STOP TRES HAUTE CONSIDERATION FULLSTOP.

KIGALI LE 2 OCTOBRE 1991

HABYARIMANA JUVENAL
GENERAL-MAJOR
PRESIDENT DE LA REPUBLIQUE RWANDAISE

REPUBLIQUE RWANDAISE • PRESIDENT DE LA REPUBLIQUE •

0185

1991년 10월 25일

대통령 각하,

금번 우리의 유엔가입에 즈음하여 축전을 보내 주신데 대해 감사 드립니다.

또한 본인은 그동안 우리의 유엔가입 노력에 대하여 보여준 루안다 정부의 협조에 심심한 사의를 표하는 바 입니다.

우리는 유엔에서 상호협력을 확대해 나감으로써 양자간 우호 관계도 더욱 강화될 수 있을 것으로 믿습니다.

각하의 건승하심과 귀국의 무궁한 번영을 기원합니다.

노 태 우

루안다

하비아리마나 쥬브날 대통령 각하

0186

25 October 1991

Dear Mr. President,

I thank you very much for your thoughtful message on the occasion of my country's admission to the United Nations.

I wish to take this opportunity to express my heartfelt gratitude for your Government's cooperation in our efforts towards attaining United Nations membership.

It is my sincere hope that the expanded contacts and cooperation at the United Nations will help to further strengthen our bilateral relations.

Please accept my best wishes for your good health and the everlasting prosperity of your nation.

Yours sincerely,

/s/ Roh Tae Woo

His Excellency
Habyarimana Juvenal
President of the Republic of Rwanda

0187

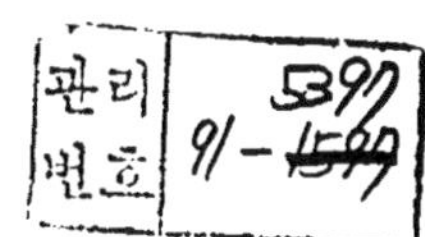

長 官 報 告 事 項

報 告 畢

1991. 10. 26.
아프리카2課

題 目 : 유엔 加入祝賀 마다가스칼 大統領 메세지

「라치라카」(Ratsiraka) 마다가스칼 大統領은 유엔 加入을 祝賀하는 우리 大統領앞 메시지를 駐日大使館 經由하여 送付하여 온 바, 關聯事項을 아래와 같이 報告 드립니다.

1. 메시지 內容
   - o 大韓民國의 유엔 加入은 南北會談에 새로운 章을 열고 韓半島 統一을 促進시킬 것으로 確信
   - o 韓.마다가스칼間 友好協力關係가 빠른 時日內 發展 되기를 希望
2. 關聯 措置 內容
   - o 금번 메시지 發送이 우리나라와의 關係改善을 意圖하는 것인지의 與否 및 同 메시지 發送의 背景 등에 관해 把握, 報告토록 駐日大使에게 指示(10.26)
   - o 駐日 大使로 부터 報告 받는대로 우리 大統領 名義 答信 建議 豫定
     - 兩國間 關係 正常化 촉구 및 가까운 時日內 兩國 兼任 大使 交換토록 提議
3. 參考事項
   - o 마다가스칼은 62.6 兩國 修交 이래 我國單獨 修交國이었으나 72년 政治的 混亂에 따른 軍政實施 및 左傾化로 인해 親北韓으로 急旋回.
   - o 72.7 我國大使의 아그레망 申請에 응답을 回避한 이래 UN 등 國際 舞臺에서 北韓 立場을 代辯해 오고 있음.
4. 言論對策 : 該當 없음

예고문 : 92.6.30 일반

0188

발 신 전 보

	분류번호	보존기간

번 호 : WTT-0137 911031 1800 FN 종별 :

암호송신

수 신 : 주 트리니다드토바고대사. 총영사

발 신 : 장 관 (연일)

제 목 : 유엔가입 축하 공한

대 : 주트리니다드(정) 800-177

대호 아래 요지로 귀관명의 회신 공한 발송바람.

- 우리의 유엔가입 노력에 대한 그간 도미니카 연방의 지원에 감사
- 유엔에서의 협력강화가 양국관계 발전에도 크게 기여할 것으로 믿음. 끝.

(국제기구국장 문동석)

보안 통제	

앙 고 재	91년 10월 31일	과	기안자 성명		과 장	심의관	국 장		차 관	장 관

외신과통제

0189

주 우 간 다 대 사 관

1991. 10. 31

우대(정) 700 - 181

수 신 : 외무부장관

참 조 : 국제기구국장

제 목 : 유엔가입축하공한

주재국 외무부는 제2부수상 겸 외무장관 Paul K. Ssemogerere 의 이상옥 외무장관앞 아국의 유엔가입축하공한을 10.23 송부하여 왔는바 사본 1부를 별첨과 같이 보고합니다.

첨 부 : 공한 1부. 끝

주 우 간 다 대

W62732

0190

TELEGRAMS: "EXTERIOR, KAMPALA."
TELEPHONE: 257525-258251.
TELEX: 61007, KAMPALA.

IN ANY CORRESPONDENCE ON THIS SUBJECT PLEASE QUOTE NO. XC. 1182

THE REPUBLIC OF UGANDA

MINISTRY OF FOREIGN AFFAIRS,
P.O. BOX 7048,
KAMPALA, UGANDA.

The Ministry of Foreign Affairs of the Republic of Uganda presents its compliments to the Embassy of the Republic of Korea in Kampala and has the honour to forward hereunder a message of Congratulations from the 2nd Deputy Prime Minister and Minister of Foreign Affairs to His Excellency Mr. Lee Sang-Ock, Minister of Foreign Affairs of the Republic of Korea.

Your Excellency,

On the occasion of the admission of the Republic of Korea to the United Nations, I congratulate you most sincerely and wish you happiest days as full members of this august family of nations.

As you very well know, the Government of the National Resistance Movement enjoys excellent relations with the Governments in Seoul and Pyongyang and it is our policy that we encourage inter-Korean relations both on the Korean peninsula and abroad. In this regard, the simultanesous joining of the United Nations by South and North Korea becomes most welcome and fitting.

I take this opportunity to reaffirm the desire of the Government of Uganda to strengthen further the ties of friendship and cooperation which so happily exist between our two countries.

Accept, Your Excellency, the assurances of my highest consideration and esteem

Paul K. Ssemogerere
2ND DEPUTY PRIME MINISTER/
MINISTER OF FOREIGN AFFAIRS

His Excellency
Lee Sang-Ock
MINISTER FOREIGN AFFAIRS
OF THE REPUBLIC OF KOREA,
SEOUL

27 September, 1991.

......./2

0191

The Ministry of Foreign Affairs of the Republic of Uganda avails itself of this opportunity to renew to the Embassy of the Republic of Korea the assurances of its highest consideration. J.N.

KAMPALA: 23rd October, 1991

The Embassy of the Republic
of Korea,
Kampala.

0192

	분류번호	보존기간

발 신 전 보

번 호 : WJA-4972 911101 1820 BE 종별 : 암호송신

WZR -0434

수 신 : 주 일본 대사. 총영사 (사본 : 주자이르대사)

발 신 : 장 관 (연일)

제 목 : 축전답신

대 : 일본(정) 700-8207 (91.10.14)

대호, 루안다 대통령의 아국 유엔가입 축전에 대한 우리대통령의 답전을 하기 타전하니 귀지 루안다대사관측에 공한으로 전달바람. 끝.

첨부 : 대통령 답전. 끝

(국제기구국장 문동석)

보안 통제	

앙 고 재	91년 11월 1일	연 1 과	기안자 성명		과 장	심의관	국 장		차 관	장 관
							전결			

외신과통제

0193

le 28 octobre 1991

Monsieur le Président,

J'ai été très sensible au message de félicitations que vous avez bien voulu m'adresser à l'occasion de l'admission de la République de Corée à l'Organisation des Nations Unies et vous en remercie vivement.

Je voudrais exprimer ma profonde gratitude pour le concours et l'appuie de votre gouvernement à l'égard de nos efforts pour entrer à l'ONU.

J'espère que nos deux pays continuent d'élargir la coopération mutuelle dans l'arène internationale dont l'ONU, de telle sorte que les liens d'amitié bilatéraux se renforceront davantage.

En vous renouvelant les voeux que je forme pour votre santé personnelle et pour la prospérité éternelle de votre pays, je vous prie d'agréer, Monsieur le Président, l'assurance de ma très haute considération.

Roh Tae Woo

S.E. le Général-Major
Habyarimana Juvénal
Président de la
République Rwandaise

0194

1991년 10월 28일

대통령 각하,

금번 한국의 유엔가입에 즈음하여 축전을 보내 주신데 대해 감사드립니다.

본인은 한국의 유엔가입 노력에 대해 그간 귀 정부가 보여준 협조에 심심한 사의를 표하는 바 입니다.

본인은 우리 양국이 유엔을 비롯한 국제무대에서 상호 협력을 확대해 나가기를 희망하며, 이를 통해 양국간의 우호관계도 더욱 강화되기를 바라마지 않습니다.

각하의 건승하심과 귀국의 무궁한 번영을 기원합니다.

노 태 우

루안다
하비아리마나 쥬브날 대통령 각하

0195

	분류번호	보존기간

발 신 전 보

번 호 : WCS-0382 911101 1835 BE 종별 : 암호송신

수 신 : 주 칠레 대사. 총영사

발 신 : 장 관 (연일)

제 목 : 축전 답신

주한 칠레대사관이 송부해온 칠레대통령의 아국 유엔가입 축전(9.25자)에 대한 우리대통령의 답전을 하기 타전하니 귀주재국측에 공한으로 전달바람.

첨 부 : 대통령 답전. 끝.

(국제기구국장 문동석)

보안통제	

미주국장:

앙고재	91년 11월 1일	연1과	기안자 성명		과 장	심의관	국 장		차 관	장 관
			송영완				전결			

외신과통제

0196

Seul, 28 de octubre de 1991

Excelencia;

Tengo el honor de dirigirsme a Vuestra Excelencia para manifestarle mi agradecimiento por el gentil mensaje de felicitacion que Vuestra Excelencia me enviara con ocasion de la admision de la Republica de Corea en las Naciones Unidas.

De igual manera, apreciamos mucho el firme apoyo y la colaboracion brindados por el ilustrado Gobierno de Chile en nuestros esfuerzos para ser miembro del dicho organismo mundial.

Es el deseo de mi Govierno seguir estrechando mas la cooperacion con Chile en las Naciones Unidas y en otros foros internacionales para, asi, fortalecer aun mas las relaciones de amistad entre los dos paises.

Reciba, Excelencia, mis mejores votos por Vuestra ventura personal y la continua prosperidad de Chile.

/ Fdo. /

Roh Tae Woo

Al Excelentisimo Senor
Patricio Aylwin Azocar
Presidente Constitucional de la Republica de Chile

0197

1991년 10월 28일

각 하,

금번 한국의 유엔가입에 즈음하여 축전을 보내 주신데 대해 감사드립니다.

본인은 한국의 유엔가입 노력에 대해 그간 귀 정부가 보여준 확고한 지원과 협조에 심심한 사의를 표하는 바 입니다.

본인은 우리 양국이 유엔을 비롯한 국제무대에서 상호 협력을 확대해 나가기를 희망하며, 이를 통해 양국간의 우호관계도 더욱 강화되기를 바라마지 않습니다.

각하의 건승하심과 귀국의 무궁한 번영을 기원합니다.

노 태 우

칠레

빠뜨리시오 앨윈 아소갈 대통령 각하

0198

	분류번호	보존기간

발 신 전 보

번 호 : WTN-0274 911101 1836 BE 종별 : 암호송신

수 신 : 주 튀니지 대사. 총영사

발 신 : 장 관 (연일)

제 목 : 축전 답신

대 : TNW-0361

대호, Ben Ali 대통령의 축전에 대한 우리 대통령의 답전을 하기 타전하니 주재국측에 공한으로 전달바람.

첨부 : 대통령 답전. 끝

(국제기구국장 문동석)

중동아국장 :

				보안통제	

앙고재	91년 11월 1일	UN 1과	기안자 성명		과장	심의관	국장	차관	장관
			송영완				전결		

외신과통제

0199

le 28 octobre 1991

Monsieur le Président,

J'ai été très sensible au message de félicitations que vous avez bien voulu m'adresser à l'occasion de l'admission de la République de Corée à l'Organisation des Nations Unies et vous en remercie vivement.

Je voudrais exprimer ma profonde gratitude pour le concours et l'appuie de votre gouvernement à l'égard de nos efforts pour entrer à l'ONU.

J'espère que nos deux pays continuent d'élargir la coopération mutuelle dans l'arène internationale dont l'ONU, de telle sorte que les liens d'amitié bilatéraux se renforceront davantage.

En vous renouvelant les voeux que je forme pour votre santé personnelle et pour la prospérité éternelle de votre pays, je vous prie d'agréer, Monsieur le Président, l'assurance de ma très haute considération.

Roh Tae Woo

Son Excellence
Monsieur Zine el Abidine Ben Ali
Président de la République Tunisienne

0200

1991년 10월 28일

각 하,

금번 한국의 유엔가입에 즈음하여 축전을 보내 주신데 대해 감사드립니다.

본인은 한국의 유엔가입 노력에 대해 그간 귀 정부가 보여준 확고한 지원과 협조에 심심한 사의를 표하는 바 입니다.

본인은 우리 양국이 유엔을 비롯한 국제무대에서 상호 협력을 확대해 나가기를 희망하며, 이를 통해 양국간의 우호관계도 더욱 강화되기를 바라마지 않습니다.

각하의 건승하심과 귀국의 무궁한 번영을 기원합니다.

노 태 우

튀니지

진엘 아비딘 벤알리 대통령 각하.

0201

분류번호	보존기간

발 신 전 보

번 호 : WPU-0421 911104 1517 BE 종별 : 암호송신

수 신 : 주 페루 대사. 총영사

발 신 : 장 관 (연일)

제 목 : 축전 답신

주한 페루대사관이 송부해온 페루대통령의 아국 유엔가입 축전(9.30자)에 대한 우리대통령의 답전을 하기 타전하니 귀주재국 측에 공한으로 전달바람.

첨부 : 대통령 답전. 끝.

(국제기구국장 문동석)

미주국장 : 전결

보안 통제	

앙 고 재	91년 11월 4일	유엔 1과	기안자 성명		과 장	심의관	국 장		차 관	장 관
							전결			

외신과통제

0202

Seul, 28 de octubre de 1991

Excelencia;

Tengo el honor de dirigirme a Vuestra Excelencia para manifestarle mi agradecimiento por el gentil mensaje de felicitacion que Vuestra Excelencia me enviara con ocasion de la admision de la Republica de Corea en las Naciones Unidas.

De igual manera, apreciamos mucho el firme apoyo y la colaboracion brindados por el ilustrado Gobierno del Peru en nuestros esfuerzos para ser miembro del dicho organismo mundial.

Es el deseo de mi Gobierno seguir estrechando la cooperacion con Peru en las Naciones Unidas y en otros foros internacionales y asi, fortalecer aun mas las relaciones de amistad entre los dos paises.

Reciba, Excelencia, mis mejores votos por Vuestra ventura personal y la continua prosperidad del Peru.

/ Fdo. /

Roh Tae Woo

Al Excelentisimo Senor
Alberto Fujimori Fujimori
Presidente de la Republica del Peru

0203

1991년 10월 28일

각 하,

금번 한국의 유엔가입에 즈음하여 축전을 보내 주신데 대해 감사드립니다.

본인은 한국의 유엔가입 노력에 대해 그간 귀 정부가 보여준 확고한 지원과 협조에 심심한 사의를 표하는 바 입니다.

본인은 우리 양국이 유엔을 비롯한 국제무대에서 상호 협력을 확대해 나가기를 희망하며, 이를 통해 양국간의 우호관계도 더욱 강화되기를 바라마지 않습니다.

각하의 건승하심과 귀국의 무궁한 번영을 기원합니다.

노 태 우

페루

알베르토 후지모리 대통령 각하

- 유엔가입축전에 대한 답전입니다.

- 번역, 타자해 주시고 번역본 clean copy 1부 함께 부탁드립니다

0204

관리 번호	91-5431

1 항

외 무 부

종 별 :

번 호 : NMW-0888　　　　일 시 : 91 1105 1420

수 신 : 장 관(아프이,국연)

발 신 : 주 나미비아 대사

제 목 : 앙골라외무성,아국의 유엔가입축하

당지 앙골라대사관은 당관앞 11.4. 자 공한을 통하여 앙골라외무성이 유엔가입을 축하한다고 통보해왔음을 보고함. 끝.

(대사 송학원-국장)

예고:91.12.31. 일반 고문에 의거 일반문서로 재분류됨

중아국 1차보 정와대 장관 차관 보좌관 국기국

PAGE 1　　　　91.11.06 03:30

외신 2과 통제관 FI

0205

/✓ 기스(회)

원 본

외 무 부

암호수신

종 별 :

번 호 : CSW-0859 일 시 : 91 1106 2050

수 신 : 장관(연일,미남)

발 신 : 주 칠레 대사

제 목 : 축전 답신 전달

대:WCS-0382

대호 답전, 11.4. 주재국측에 공한으로 무위 전달 하였음. 끝

(대사 문창화-국장)

국기국 미주국

PAGE 1

91.11.07 09:20

외신 2과 통제관 CA

0206

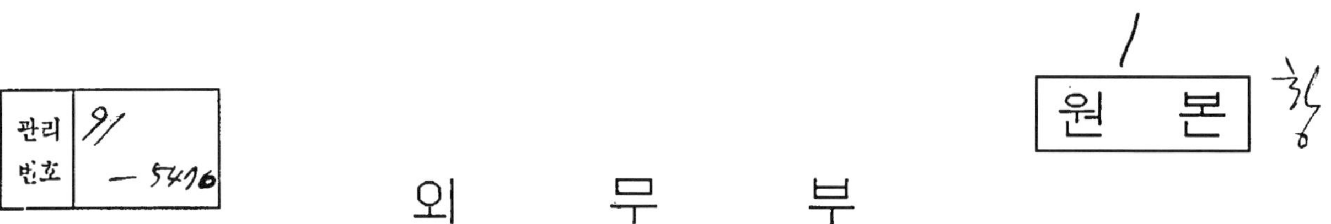
관리번호 91-5476

원 본

외 무 부

종 별 :

번 호 : IVW-0566 일 시 : 91 1111 1800

수 신 : 장관(국연,아프일)

발 신 : 주 코트디브와르 대사

제 목 : 베넹외상 장관님 앞서한.

연:IVW-0300

HOLO 베넹외상은 9.26 자 (금 11.11 당관도착) 아국의 유엔가입을 축하하는내용의 장관님앞 서한을 발송하여왔는바 동 서한 파편 송부함.

(대사 양태규-국장)

예고:1991.12.31.일반 고문에 의거 일반문서로 재분류

국기국 장관 차관 중아국

PAGE 1 91.11.12 08:00

외신 2과 통제관 BD

0207

L 6 SEP. 1991

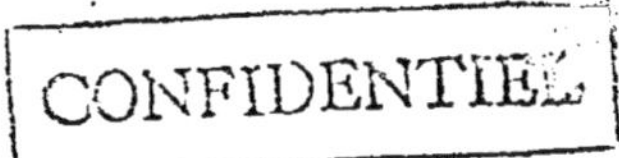

Le Ministre
des Affaires Etrangères
et de la Coopération

CONFIDENTIEL

Monsieur le Ministre,

C'est avec un réel plaisir que j'ai appris la nouvelle de l'admission de votre pays à l'Organisation des Nations Unies.

Je saisis cette heureuse circonstance pour vous présenter mes plus chaleureuses félicitations.

Je suis convaincu que la présence de la République de Corée à l'Organisation des Nations Unies lui permettra d'apporter sa précieuse contribution au sein de cette organisation, à la recherche de solutions aux problèmes de notre monde et qu'elle sera une étape décisive dans le processus de la réunification pacifique de la Nation coréenne.

Je voudrais par ailleurs vous assurer de mon entière disponibilité à oeuvrer, de concert avec vous, à l'instauration de relations d'amitié et de coopération fructueuse entre nos deux Etats.

En vous réitérant mes sincères félicitations, je vous prie d'agréer, Monsieur le Ministre, l'expression de ma haute considération.

MONSIEUR LEE SANK-OK
MINISTRE DES AFFAIRES ETRANGERES
DE LA REPUBLIQUE DE COREE

SEOUL

Théodore HOLO

0208

Monsieur le Ministre,

C'est avec un réel plaisir que j'ai appris la nouvelle de l'admission de votre pays à l'Organisation des Nations Unies.

Je saisis cette heureuse circonstance pour vous présenter mes plus chaleureuses félicitations.

Je suis convaincu que la présence de la République de Corée à l'Organisation des Nations Unies lui permettra d'apporter sa précieuse contribution au sein de cette organisation, à la recherche de solutions aux problèmes de notre monde et qu'elle sera une étape décisive dans le processus de la réunification pacifique de la Nation coréenne.

Je voudrais par ailleurs vous assurer de mon entière disponibilité à oeuvrer de concert avec vous, à l'instauration de relations d'amitié et de coopération fructueuse entre nos deux Etats.

En vous réitérant mes sincères félicitations, je vous prie d'agréer, Monsieur le Ministre, l'expression de ma haute considération.

MONSIEUR LEE SANK-OK
MINISTRE DES AFFAIRES ETRANGERES
DE LA REPUBLIQUE DE COREE

SEOUL

Théodore HOLO

0209

CONFIDENTIEL

MONSIEUR LEE SANK-OK
MINISTRE DES AFFAIRES ETRANGERES
DE LA REPUBLIQUE DE COREE

SEOUL

0210

관리 번호	91 -1545

주 코트디브와르 대사관

01 B.P 3950 01 ABIDJAN COTE D'IVORE / (225) 32-2290 . 22-5014

문서번호 코트디(정)720-323

시행일자 91.11.15

선결			지시		
접수	일자 시간		결재 공람		
	번호	5-251			
처리과		기 → 유엔과			
담당자					

수신 외무부 장관

참조 국제기구국장, 중동.아프리카국장

제목 베넹 외상 장관님앞 서한

연 : IVW-0566

1. 연호 HOLO 베넹 외상의 외무장관께 대한 아국의 UN 가입축하내용의 서한을 첨부와 같이 보고합니다.

2. 동 외상은 상기 서한을 통해 아국의 UN 가입이 현금의 재반 국제적인 문제점 해결에 기여 할것으로 믿으며, 한반도 통일과정에 있어 결정적인 도약의 계기가 될것으로 확신한다고 밝히고 있음을 첨언합니다.

첨 부 : 상기서한. 끝.

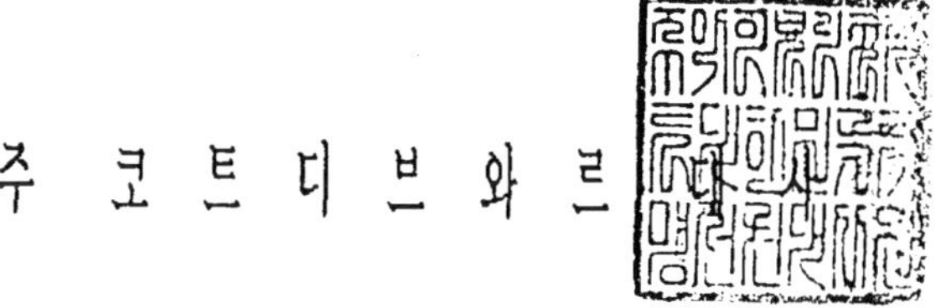

주 코트디브와르

0211

Le Ministre
des Affaires Etrangères
et de la Coopération

Monsieur le Ministre,

C'est avec un réel plaisir que j'ai appris la nouvelle de l'admission de votre pays à l'Organisation des Nations Unies.

Je saisis cette heureuse circonstance pour vous présenter mes plus chaleureuses félicitations.

Je suis convaincu que la présence de la République de Corée à l'Organisation des Nations Unies lui permettra d'apporter sa précieuse contribution au sein de cette organisation, à la recherche de solutions aux problèmes de notre monde et qu'elle sera une étape décisive dans le processus de la réunification pacifique de la Nation coréenne.

Je voudrais par ailleurs vous assurer de mon entière disponibilité à oeuvrer, de concert avec vous, à l'instauration de relations d'amitié et de coopération fructueuse entre nos deux Etats.

En vous réitérant mes sincères félicitations, je vous prie d'agréer, Monsieur le Ministre, l'expression de ma haute considération.

MONSIEUR LEE SANK-OK
MINISTRE DES AFFAIRES ETRANGERES
DE LA REPUBLIQUE DE COREE

SEOUL

Théodore HOLO

0212

주 카 메 룬 대 사 관

1991 년 11 월 25 일

카메룬 : 20334-169

수신 : 장관

참조 : 중동아프리카국장

제목 : 유엔가입축전

주재국 외무부는 아국의 유엔가입을 축하하는 "Jacques Roger Booh Booh" 외무부장관 명의 "이상옥" 장관앞 축전을 별첨과 같이 보내왔음을 보고합니다. 끝

첨부 : 동 축전 1부.

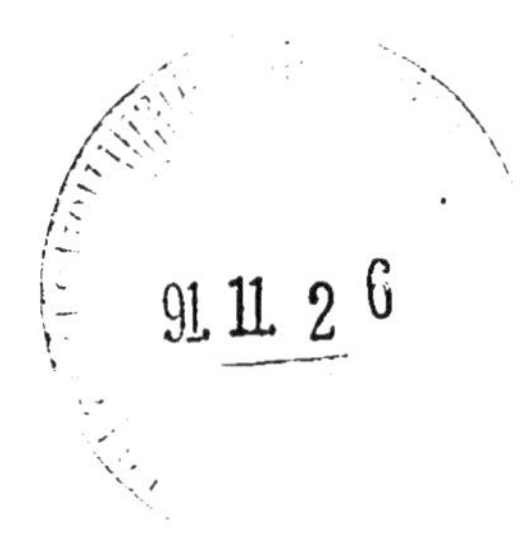

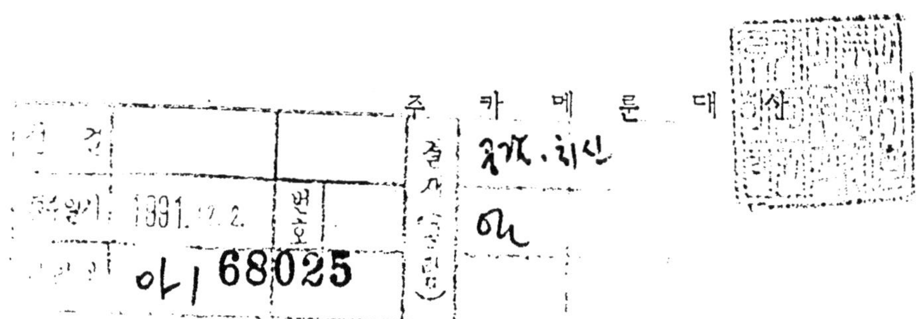

주 카 메 룬 대 사

0213

République du Cameroun — Republic of Cameroon

Ministère des Relations Extérieures — Ministry of External Relations

N° 07872 /DIPL/D1/SDAS/EO.-

Le Ministère des Relations Extérieures de la République du Cameroun présente ses compliments à l'Ambassade de la République de Corée à Yaoundé et a l'honneur de lui transmettre le message de félicitations de S.E.M. Jacques Roger BOOH BOOH, Ministre des Relations Extérieures du Cameroun à son homologue Sud-Coréen S.E.M. LEE SANG-OCK suite à la brillante admission de son pays à l'Organisation des Nations-Unies.

Citation :

<<Excellence, c'est avec un réel plaisir, au moment où votre pays célèbre son admission à l'ONU, que je vous réitére mes vives et chaleureuses félicitations.

L'admission de la République de Corée à l'Organisation des Nations-Unies est une marque de la volonté persistante de votre pays de contribuer au sein de notre grande organisation internationale, à la promotion des idéaux de paix qui en constituent le fondement.

Je suis persuadé que votre pays saura y apporter sa contribution constructive à l'édification d'un monde nouveau plus solidaire et plus juste.

Veuillez agréer Monsieur le Ministre, les assurances de ma très haute considération.

AMBASSADE DE LA REPUBLIQUE
DE COREE
YAOUNDE

.../...

0214

Jacques Roger BOOH BOOH
Ministre des Relations Extérieures
de la République du Cameroun>>.

Le Ministère des Relations Extérieures de la République du Cameroun remercie d'avance l'Ambassade de la République de Corée pour son aimable entremise et saisit cette occasion pour lui renouveler les assurances de sa haute considération.

YAOUNDE, le 11 NOV 1991

	분류번호	보존기간

발 신 전 보

번 호 : WJA-4942 911031 1719 FN 종별 :

수 신 : 주 일 대사. 총영사

발 신 : 장 관 (아일)

제 목 : 축전송부

우리의 유엔가입에 즈음한 카이후 일본수상의 노태우대통령앞 축전 송부와 관련, 노대통령의 카이후 일본수상앞 별첨 답전을 귀관에서 일본어 번역문을 작성 첨부하여 적의 전달바람(청와대측 요망이니 송부한 답전 및 번역문 복사본을 파편 송부바람).

첨부 : 답전 1부. 끝.

(아주국장 김석우)

보 안 통 제	

앙 고 재	91년 11월 31일	동북아1과	기안자 성명		과 장	심의관	국 장		차 관	장 관
			하태원							

외신과통제

0216

1991년 10월 28일

총리대신 각하,

금번 한국의 유엔가입에 즈음하여 축전을 보내 주신데 대해 감사드리며, 한국의 유엔가입 노력에 대해 그간 일본정부가 보여준 확고한 지원과 협조에 심심한 사의를 표하는 바 입니다.

본인은 남북한의 유엔가입이 이 지역의 긴장완화에 기여하고 또한 한반도의 평화통일을 촉진시킬 것으로 희망하고 있으며, 각하께서도 이와 같은 희망을 표명해 주신 것을 기쁘게 생각합니다.

본인은 우리 두나라가 유엔을 위시한 국제무대에서 상호협력의 영역을 확대하면서 인류공동의 번영을 위해 함께 노력해 나가기를 희망하며, 이를 통하여 양국간의 우호협력 관계도 더욱 강화될 수 있을 것으로 믿습니다.

각하의 건승하심과 귀국의 무궁한 번영을 기원합니다.

노 태 우

일본국
카이후 토시키 내각총리대신 각하

0217

정리보존문서목록

기록물종류	일반공문서철	등록번호	2020090097	등록일자	2020-09-21
분류번호	731.12	국가코드		보존기간	영구
명 칭	남북한 유엔가입, 1991.9.17. 전41권				
생 산 과	국제연합1과	생산년도	1990~1991	담당그룹	
권 차 명	V.34 유엔가입에 따른 제반 조치사항				
내용목차	1. 제반조치사항 점검 - 유엔가입신청 및 처리절차(국내조치 포함), 대통령 및 장관님 유엔방문 행사, 대유엔 활동 강화 방안 등 2. 신임장 제정 3. 예산.인력 추가확보 4. 주유엔대표부 현판제작 5. 유엔사무국 게양 태극기 제작 - 태극기 제작 오류 지적 민원 및 시정내용 포함(1991-93)				

0001

1. 제반 조치사항 검토

0002

관리	91
번호	-38

기 안 용 지

분류기호 문서번호	국연 2031-75	(전화 :)	시 행 상 특별취급	
보존기간	영구·준영구. 10. 5. 3. 1.	장 관		
수 신 처 보존기간				
시행일자	1991. 1. 9.			

보조기관	국 장	전 결	협조기관		문 서 통 제
	과 장				검열 1991. 1. 09
기안책임자	송영완				발 송 인

경 유 수 신 참 조	주유엔대사	발신명의		1991. 1. 09
제 목	유엔가입 추진관련 조치사항			

1. 유엔가입에 앞서 헌법규정에 따라 국내절차 (국무회의 심의 및 국회비준 동의)를 거쳐야 하는 바, 이에 대한 검토서 및 유엔가입에 따른 아국의 재정적 추가 부담액에 대한 검토서를 별첨 송부하오니 업무에 참고하시기 바랍니다.

2. 상기 국내절차와 관련, 아국이 유엔가입을 추진할 경우에는 안보리의 가입권고 결의 채택후에 국내절차를 취하는 방안 (별첨 검토서상의 제 2안)을 고려중임을 참고하시기 바랍니다.

/ 계속 /

0003

1505-25(2-1) 일(1)갑
85. 9. 9. 승인

190㎜×268㎜ 인쇄용지 2급 60g/㎡
가 40-41 1986. 2. 13.

3. 금년중 유엔가입 실현방침에 따라, 유엔가입후 아국이 취해야 할 국내적, 국제적 조치사항 및 고려 요망사항에 대한 귀견을 가급적 91.2월중순까지 종합 보고바랍니다.

첨 부 : 1. 유엔가입관련 국내 절차문제

2. 유엔가입에 따른 아국의 재정적 부담. 끝.

예 고 : 1991.12.31. 일반

검 토 필 (1991. 6. 30.)

0004

1505-25(2-2) 일(1)을
85. 9. 9. 승인
"내가아낀 종이 한장 늘어나는 나라살림"
190㎜×268㎜ 인쇄용지 2급 60g/㎡
가 40-41 1990. 5. 28

	분류번호	보존기간

발 신 전 보

번 호 : WUN-0441 910305 1609 DP 종별 : 지급 / 암호

수 신 : 주 유엔 대사. 총영사 (윤병세 참사관)

발 신 : 장 관 (국연과 이규형 배)

제 목 : 업 연

업무에 참고코자 하니 하기 사항을 3.5. 09:00시 유엔과 전화로 알려 주기 바람.

1. 동독의 유엔가입 수락연설 일자 및 연설자 성명, 최초 기조연설일자 및 연설자 성명

2. 리히텐슈타인의 최초 기조연설일자 및 연설자 성명. 끝.

보 안 통 제	

앙 고 재	91년 3월 5일	과	기안자 성 명		과 장		국 장		차 관	장 관

외신과통제
72

0005

가입후 2차

연 / 통 / 관리 / 반네 / 결재 / 원본 / 서류

원 본

외 무 부

암 호 수 신

종 별 : 지 급

번 호 : UNW-0506 일 시 : 91 0305 1200

수 신 : 장관(유엔과 이규형과장)

발 신 : 주 유엔 윤병세

제 목 : 업연

대:WUN-0441

1. 대호 아래와같음.

(가입일자, 가입수락 연설수락및 연설자, 최초 기조연설일자 및 연설자 순)

가. 동독:73.9.18 , 9.19 (WINZER 외상), 10.1.(WINZER 외상)

나. 서독: 73.9.18, 9.19(SCHEEL 외상), 9.26 (BRANDT 수상)

다. 리히텐스타인:90.9.18, 9.18 (BRUNHARDT 수상겸 외상), 10.4.(BRUNHARDT 수상겸 외상)

2. 동.서독 가입수락 연설문 및 기조연설문 전문은 UNGA OFFICIAL RECORDS (28 차 SESSION) 의 V01.I (PLENARY MEETINGS) 2119 차 본회의 (P 11,12) , 2128 차 본회의 (P 1-5) , 2134 차 본회의 (P 1-6) 기록참고바람. 끝.

국기국

PAGE 1 91.03.06 05:37

외신 2과 통제관 CA

0006

5

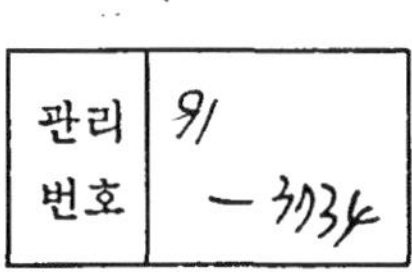

원 본

외 무 부

종 별 : 지 급

번 호 : UNW-1440 일 시 : 91 0601 0100

수 신 : 장관(문동석 국제기구조약국장)

발 신 : 주 유엔 대사

제 목 : 유엔가입문제

대:WUN-1567, 주국련 2031-25

연: 주국련 20312-263, UNW-1439

금년유엔가입 실현관련, 행정및 의전사항 이외에 당관및 본부에서 장단기적으로 검토내지 조치가 필요하다고 생각되는 분야를 아래보고하니 대호관련 우선 참고바라며, 추후 사안별 검토가 끝나는대로 별도 보고예정임.

1. 가입신청 및 의무수락서 준비(당관안 기송부)

2. 가입수락 연설문및 기조연설문

3.46 차 총회 적극 참가 대책강구(최초 참가 총회인점 감안)

0. 늦어도 7 월중 본부내 특별대책반 및 관계부처 협의체제 설치

0. 총회및 위원회 의제별 참가대책 협의

-약 150 개 의제

0. 예상 결의안별 입장확정(특히 표결대비)

-남북한간 대립예상 분야포함 (특히 제 1 위원회)

0. 위원회별 아국대표 발언문

-일반토의(제 1, 제 2 위원회)및 의제별 발언(전 위원회)

0. 대표단 구성

-관계부처 대표 포함문제

4. 경축행사

-국기게양식(가입승인 결의직후),-축하 리셉션

-경축공연등

5.ICJ 강제관할권 조항 수락문제

6. 남북한의 유엔내 좌석배치 (SEATING)문제

국기국

PAGE 1 91.06.01 14:33

외신 2과 통제관 CH

0007

-기존 국명표기 유지시 남북한간 격리착석

-동서독식 방안 검토 필요여부

7. 유엔주요활동 참가방안

0. 평화유지군 및 선거감시단

-걸프, 캄푸차

0. 아주그룹의장

0. 의장단 진출분야

-총회(및 위원회), 경사리, 각종 산하기구

0.RAPPORTEUR 활동 가능분야

8. 유엔기구 참여가능분야

0. 유엔사무국 진출요원 양성

0.ICJ 판사진출

0. 주요위원회 위원 출마

-ILC 등

0. 남북한 대사급 상설 협의회 설치문제

0. 통일지향적 특수협력방안

10. 유엔관련기구 및 회의 서울유치문제

11. 안보리 비상임 이사국 진출.끝

(대사 신기복)

예고:91.12.31. 일반고문에 의거 일반문서로 재분류됨

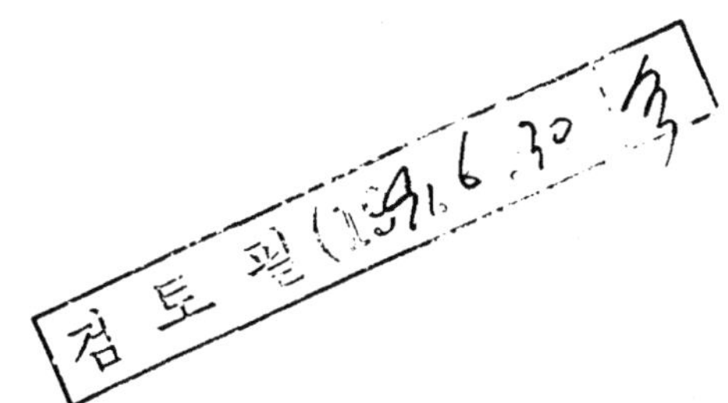

PAGE 2

0008

관리 번호	91 -576

연 1/ 송

외 무 부

가입이후 활용 File

종 별 : 지 급

번 호 : GVW-1037 일 시 : 91 0604 2350

수 신 : 장 관(국기,국연)

발 신 : 주 제네바 대사

제 목 : ILO 가입준비

대: WGV-0716

1. 대호 관련 당관 문봉주참사관이 금 5.4(화) ILO 사무국 MAUPAIN 법률고문과 면담, 파악한 사항을 아래 보고함(김종일서기관, ILO 파견 조주현 노동부과장 동석)

가. ILO 조약 비준

- 신규 회원국이 기존의 조약(COVENTION)을 비준해야 한다는 ILO 헌장(CONSTITUTION) 상의 명문 규정이 없으므로, 기존의 조약에 대한 비준여부는 회원국의 자발적, 정책적 결정사항임.(91.1. 현재 171 개 조약채택)

- 조약관련 신규 회원국의 의무는 ILO 가입이후 총회에서 새로이 채택되는 조약을 조약채태(450)후 1 년이내(부득이한 경우 18 개월 이내)에 국내 입법기관에 입법 또는 기타조치를 취하도록 부의하는것이 주된 의무임.(상세는 헌장 제 19조 참조)

나. 주요 조약의 우선적 비준의무

- 상기에 따라 신규 회원국이 결사의 자유에 관한 조약(제 87 호) 및 단결권 조약(제 98 호)등 주요 조약을 우선적으로 비준해야 한다는 의무도 없음.

- 다만, 조약 제 87 호 결사의자유(FREEDOM OF ASSOCIATION) 관련 신규 가입국이 동 조약을 비준하지 않터라도 국내 노동단체 등에서 단결권에 관한 COMPLAINTS 를 ILO 사무국에 제출할 경우, ILO 이사회 및 이사회 산하 "결사의 자유위원회"가 동 COMPLAINTS 를 검토, 해당 정부에 필요한 권고를 할수있음.

- 상기 이사회의 권고는 SANCTION 의 성격은 아니며, 이사회는 필요시 반복하여 해당정부에 대한 권고를 할수있으며, 이는 일종의 압력으로 작용될 수 있음.

다. 조약 비준시 유예기간 설정 및 유보가능 여부

- 조약비준 여부가 회원국의 정책적 결정에 따르는 것인 만큼, 유예기간 문제는 제기될수 없음.

국기국 장관 차관 1차보 2차보 국기국 분석관 청와대 안기부

PAGE 1

91.06.05 08:03

외신 2과 통제관 BS

0003

- 조약 유보관련, 조약 내용에 유보에 관한 조항이 있을 경우 자동적으로 유보가 가능하나, 일개 회원국이 특정조약 내용의 일부를 유보하는것은 불가능함.

라. 조약 미비준시 비준 촉구 압력 여부

- 회원국이 특정 조약을 비준하지 않았다고 해서 집행이사회등 ILO 내부기관에서 특정국에 대해 공식적으로 비준을 촉구하는 경우는 없음.

- 다만, 총회에서 특정조약 비준을 촉구하는 결의를 채택할 수 있으나 동 결의 내용도 개별국가를 대상으로 하는 것이 아니고 모든 회원국을 대상으로 하는 것임.

마. 아국가입시 분담금

- ILO 회원국에 대한 분담금은 집행이사회내의 할당 위원회가 유엔 분담금 배분율을 기초로하여 산정, 총회의 승인을 얻어 확정됨.(MAUPAIN 법률고문은 현상황에서 아국의 분담률에 대해 정확하게 언급할수는 없다고 양해를 구함)

- 참고: 92-93 년도 ILO 예산안은 379,479 천불 이며, WHO 에 대한 92 년도아국의 분담율은 0.21 퍼센트(727,905 불)임.

바. 기타 예상되는 문제점

- 아국이 유엔에 가입하고 ILO 에 가입하지 않더라도, 결사의 자유에 관한 문제는 1950 년 UN ECOSOC 과 ILO 간 체결된 협정에 따라 ECOSOC 이 ILO 에 의뢰하여 사실조사를 할수 있게 되므로 이경우는 ILO 회원국이 아니더라도 유엔회원국인 이상 ILO 의 조사를 받게됨.(단, ILO 가 사실 조사단을 파견할 경우에는 조사대상국 정부의 사전동의가 있어야 함).

2. 유엔가입과 병행, 유엔군축회의 및 유엔인권위 가입문제에 관하여 아래사항을 본부 참고로 보고함.

가. 유엔 군축회의(CD) 가입문제

- 유엔가입국이 아니더라도 CD 회원국이 될수있으며 또한 유엔가입국의 경우라도 현 CD 회원국(39 개국)의 합의가 없는한 반드시 CD 회원국이 되는것은 아니나, 한반도 군축문제의 중요성을 감안, 아국의 유엔가입후 남북한이 CD 에 공동으로 가입신청 하는 문제를 검토할 필요가 있을것으로 봄

- 현재 CD 에서는 독일 통일로 공석이된 1 개국과 신규 4 개 회원국 증가문제가 검토되고 있는바, 특히 신규 4 개 회원국 증가문제는 10 여년간 CD 에서 논의되고 있으나 회원국간 합의가 이루어 지지 않고 있는 상태임

- CD 회원국 가입을 신청한 국가는 현재까지 17 개국(신청순: 놀웨이, 핀랜드,

PAGE 2

0010

오지리, 터키, 세네갈, 방글라데시, 스페인, 베트남, 아일랜드, 튜니시아, 에쿠아돌, 카메룬, 그리스, 짐바브웨, 뉴질랜드, 칠레 및 스위스)임

나. 유엔인권위 참가

- 유엔 활동중 인권문제에 대한 관심 및 중요성이 증대되고 있음을 고려, 관련기구인 유엔인권위 및 유엔인권 소위에 위원 또는 위원국으로 선출되는 방안을 검토하는 것이 바람직함.(현재는 UN 회원국이 아니기 때문에 입후보자격이 없음)

- 인권위는 3 년 임기의 53 개국 위원국으로 구성되며, 매년 경사리에서 선출됨

- 인권소위는 인권위에서 선출되는 4 년임기 26 명의 위원으로 구성되며, 동 위원은 개인자격으로 활동함. 끝

(대사 박수길-장관)

예고:91.12.31. 까지

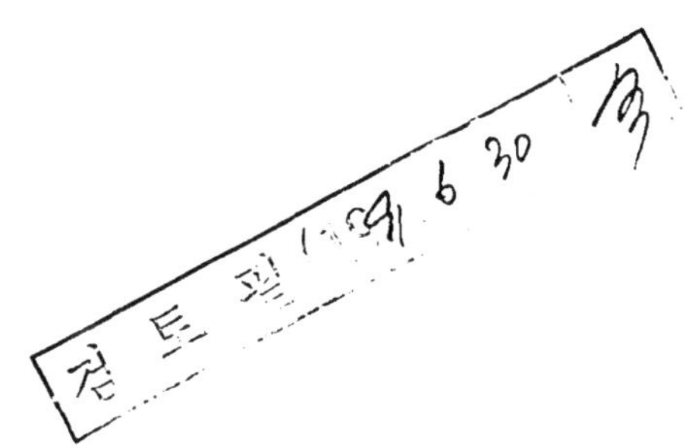

PAGE 3

0011

유엔가입에 따른 제반조치사항 점검

1991. 6. 19.

국 제 기 구 조 약 국

0012

목　　차

0013

I. 유엔가입 신청서 제출 및 처리관련 조치사항

국내조치

1. 국회동의

o 유엔가입을 위한 유엔헌장 수락 동의(7월초순)

- 당정회의 필요여부 협의(정무 1장관실 협조)
- 국회보고서 작성
- 질의.답변자료 작성

※ 국회전문위원에 대한 설명회 기개최(6.18)

- 설명자료 및 질의.답변자료 작성

2. 기타 검토사항

가. 국제사법재판소(ICJ)규정 선택조항 수락문제

o 선택조항 수락여부, 시기 및 유보내용은 각국의 재량사항

- ICJ 규정당사국 162개국중 총 49개국만 선택조항 수락
- 최근 유엔가입국은 통상 가입후 1-2년내에 선택조항 수락 경향

o 선택조항 수락문제는 유엔가입후 충분한 시간적 여유를 갖고 검토함이 바람직

나. 국제노동기구(ILO) 가입문제

o 유엔가입후 ILO 가입과 관련한 제반사항을 관련부처와 협의후 조치

- ILO의 제협약 가입관련 문제는 신중 검토

o ILO 헌장수락시 국무회의 및 국회동의 필요

1

0014

다. 유엔가입에 따른 회원국 분담금 예산 확보

o 아국의 분담금율은 92-94 기간중 유엔예산의 0.24%로 될 전망

o 따라서 92년의 경우 약 420만불의 추가분담금이 소요될 전망

- 유엔회원국 분담금 : 약 250만불
- 평화유지활동 분담금 : 약 70만불
- ILO 분담금(가입시) : 약 50만불
- 기타 기여금 : 약 50만불

o 상기와는 별도로 자발적 기여금도 우리의 국제적 위상에 맞게 증액되어야 할것인 바, UNDP, UNICEF등 주요기구에 대한 기여금이 약 300만불 추가소요될 전망

유엔가입 신청

1. 신청일시 결정

8.1(木)
8.2(金)

o 8월초(8.9이전) 가입신청서 제출

* 안보리 의장국 : 쿠바(7월), 에쿠아돌(8월)

2. 미국 및 CG와의 협의(7월중)

o 가입신청서 제출시기

o 안보리에서의 가입신청서 처리대책

- 남북한의 일괄 가입권고(단일결의안 또는 별개결의안) 채택문제

o 총회에서의 결의 채택

- 공동제안국 확보문제
- 전회원국의 박수로 결의 채택

3. 재외공관에 기본입장 통보(7월)

기안.

o 국회동의절차 완료후 금후 추진계획 통보

4. 가입신청서 및 유엔헌장 수락서 작성(7월중순)

o 신청서 및 수락서 작성(국회동의절차 완료후)

  * 장관 ASEAN 방문(7.20-8.2) 유의

o 대통령의 수락서 서명행사(7.15-7.19)

  - 행사계획 협의(청와대 의전, 외교안보)
  - 대통령 말씀자료 작성
  - 대외보도자료 준비

5. 가입신청서 제출(8월초)

o 정부대변인 명의 성명발표

  - 유엔에 가입하여 국제사회의 책임있는 일원으로서 주어진 책임과 기여를 다하고자 함.
  - 우리의 유엔가입은 통일시까지의 잠정조치임을 재천명
  - 남북한의 유엔가입은 한반도 긴장완화와 평화정착에 기여, 궁극적인 평화통일 촉진 기대

o 보도자료 작성, 배포

6. 주유엔대사 일시귀국

o 정무협의차 8월중(안보리 절차 완료후)

3

0016

남북한 유엔대사 회담

1. 회담대비 기본입장

- o 회담개최를 계속 추진하되, 북한이 끝내 불응시 별도 대처
- o 회의의제, 금후 추진방향 결정(6.17)
- o 필요시 사전교육(관계부처 전문가 파견) 검토
- o 보도자료 배포(회담일자 확정시)

2. 구체적인 논의사항

- o 가입신청서 처리방안
  - 가입신청서는 각기 편리한 시기에 별도제출
  - 안보리 및 총회의 남북한 유엔가입에 관한 결의(단일 또는 별개 결의안) 채택
- o 기 타(필요시)
  - 회의장내 남북한 seating 및 국명 영문표기 문제
  - 북한측의 총회개막일 및 기조연설 시행자 탐문

3. 회담개최결과 홍보

- o 회담 상세내용 국내외 언론 홍보 : 보도자료 배포
- o 재외공관 전파

4. 기 타

- o 회담 불개최시 미.중간 협의채널 활용
  - 금후 남북한 신청서 처리방안 협의

신청서 처리방향

1. 안보리 심의

- ㅇ 미국 및 CG와의 협의를 토대로 안보리 심의 시나리오 작성
  - 기본적으로 일괄가입권고 방식(단일 또는 별개결의) 채택 추진
  - 컨센서스(또는 전원찬성 표결) 처리 유도

- ㅇ 안보리에서의 표결시에 대비한 대책도 검토
  - 남북한 유엔가입에 관한 단일결의에 대한 일괄표결시에는 별문제 없으나, 결의항목을 개별적으로 표결할 경우도 상정 (단, 가능성 희박)
- ㅇ 안보리 관련 본부 관계관 파견 검토
  - 전원찬성 표결 또는 콘센서스 처리시 실무급 파견 검토
  - 안보리의 표결시 고위간부 파견 검토
- ㅇ 안보리 권고 결의 채택후 홍보 (8月)
  - 외무부대변인 성명, 보도자료 작성, 배포

2. 총회대책

가. 총회 결의추진 관련사항

- ㅇ 남북한 가입 권고결의안(단일 또는 별개) 추진
  - 공동제안국 검토(일단 남북한 동시수교국을 고려)
- ㅇ 남북한의 가입에 관한 별도 결의안 제출시 대책수립
  - 표결시 대비, 전재외공관의 득표교섭 시행

0018

나. 대표단 구성

- o 외무장관을 수석대표로 하되 국회등 부외인사 포함여부 검토
  - 대표 5명, 교체대표 5명(총회의사규칙의 제25조에 의거)
  - Advisor등 (인원 제한없음)
- o 청와대 및 당정협의

다. 국명표기 조기결정

- o 남북한 관계개선 의지 부각차원에서 "KOREA, Republic of"로 표기하여 북측의 "KOREA, D.P.R." 유도
- o 또는 남북한 각기 원래국명인 Republic of Korea, Democratic People's Republic of Korea로 표기

라. 가입결의 채택후 남북한대표 초청(안내) 관련 세부사항

- o 좌석배치 사전조정
- o 총회 좌석 안내시 참석자(6명 : 전열 3명, 후열 3명) 선정

마. 총회에서의 가입승인후 연설

- o 연설문 작성(외무부)
  - 금후 기조연설문 내용과 함께 청와대 보고

바. 가입결의 채택직후 Ceremony

- o 국기게양식
  - 국기제작 필요여부 확인
- o 가입축하 리셉션은 불개최
- o 유엔대표부 현판식 개최 검토
  - 새현판 제작 필요여부 확인
- o 사무총장에게 주유엔 상임대표 통보 및 신임장 제정문제 확인

사. 홍보활동

o 총회의 결의채택과정, 가입승인후 연설, 국기게양식등 국내전송

- TV 생중계 예상

- 전송 예상

o 가입승인에 따른 대통령(또는 정부대변인) 담화발표

- 보도자료 배포

아. 가입경축행사 개최(관계부처 협조)

o 청와대 주최 가입축하 리셉션 개최 또는 해외공연 경축예술단의 서울공연(9.18.저녁 잠실 올림픽 스타디움 또는 세종문화회관)

o 기념우표 발행

o 단, 10.24. 유엔의 날 기념행사와의 관련성도 검토

가입신청 및 처리관련 청와대 보고사항

1. 가입신청서 제출일시 ✓

o 미국등 우방국과 협의 이후

2. 가입신청서 제출관련 ✓

o 수락서 서명 행사

3. 가입신청서 처리방향 ✓

o 안보리 및 총회

* 단, 개략적인 사항은 6.3. 기보고

4. 대표단 구성문제(윤곽)

o 총회가입 승인시 대표단

o 대통령 유엔방문시 수행원

5. 연설관계

o 기조연설 개요

o 총회의 가입승인후 연설 개요

6. 가입승인 행사 개요

o 국명표기, 좌석안내, 수락연설, 국기게양식등

o 국내 가입 축하행사

Ⅱ. 장관 유엔방문 관련사항

방문 기본계획 수립

o 전체 방문일정안 작성

- 9.15(일) 출국, 9.19(목) 귀국
- 9.20(금) 청와대 귀국보고, 9.21(토) 지구촌행사 수행

o 대표단 구성

- 수석대표 : 장관
- 국회등 각계인사 포함여부 검토
- 아국대표단 신임장 사무국에 제출

o 방문계획 청와대 보고(8월말/9월초)

- 안보리 처리결과 포함
- 지구촌 행사계획 포함

* 지구촌행사 이후 별도 유엔방문(9.28-10.2) 검토

- 제2차 아태지역 외상 만찬 참석
- EC 의장국단과의 회담
- 주요국 외상들과의 개별면담

o 장관 경유지(앵커리지) 공관 통보

o 부인 별도일정 검토

9

0022

방문중 주요행사

1. 가입승인후 연설

o 관련자료 수집

- 외연원, 세종연구소등에 기전달

o 연설문 작성(7월말까지 1차안, 8.15까지 완료목표)

- 영문작업(8.15-31)

o 국내보도문제

- TV 위성중계

- 전송사진 예상

2. 유엔 사무총장 및 총회의장 예방

o 신임 가입국가 대표의 선례 참조

3. 총회가입 결의채택 직후 행사

o 총회장내 아국의석 착석

- 가입결의 채택후 안내, 착석절차 확인

- 대표단 좌석(6명) 착석자 선정

- 국내 TV 위성중계, 국내사진 전송(연통)

o 국기게양식 개최

- 국기제작 필요성 여부 확인

- 국기게양식 절차 확인

※ 북한측 행사참석여부 검토 필요

- 현지교민대표 참석여부 및 규모, 범위 결정
  . 현지교민 데모 가능성 대비
- 국내 TV 위성중계, 국내사진 전송(연통)

o 가입기념품 증정식 검토
- 기념품은 유엔측과 협의 선정
- 기념품 증정식 개최시기 검토
  . 지구촌 행사도 관련하여 검토
- 기념품 선정(관계부처 협의)

o 국내 기념행사 검토
- 기념우표 발행(9.18)

4. 핵심우방국 대사 초청 오(만)찬 개최

o 대상 : 미, 영, 불, 일, 카나다, 벨기에 대사

o 오(만)찬사 준비

5. 기타 주요활동 검토사항

가. 남북한 외무장관 회담개최문제

o 남북한 유엔대사간 협의 및 남북관계 전반을 보면서 신중검토

o 적절한 시기에 관계부처와 사전협의

나. 주요 언론회견

o 미국 주요언론 회견, 유엔 특파원(UNCA)과의 간담회

o 아국 특파원과의 간담회, 교포언론 간담회

다. 지구촌 행사 점검

o 세부일정 검토

o 주요행사 준비상태 확인

o 교민단체장 노고 치하

홍보관계

o 수행기자 결정

- 공보관실 협조

o 국내TV 위성중계 및 연합통신의 사진 전송 점검

- TV 위성중계 대상 행사

. 총회 결의채택, 총회 회의장내 아국의석 착석

. 가입에 제한 연설

. 국기게양식

※ 사무국측과의 사전협조

- 연합통신 사진 전송 점검

. TV 위성중계 대상 행사

. 유엔 사무총장, 유엔총회 의장 면담

. 기념품 증정식(시행시)

o 보도자료 배포

- 방문계획(출국전)

- 각 주요행사 종료 직후

- 유엔방문성과(귀국 직후)

o 출국 및 입국시 기자회견 여부 및 준비

- 유엔방문 의의(출국시) 및 성과(귀국시) 홍보

12

0025

대표단, 숙소, 경호

o 대표단 결정

- 본부직원 및 부외 주요인사 포함여부 결정

o 숙 소

- UN Plaza 호텔 예약(기조치)

. 2 BR Suite : 1실

. Single 8실, Twin 10실, 1 BR Suite 1실(대표부 연락실)

- 방배치(유엔대표부) + Single 10 (7.3)

o 경 호

- 미측 경호요청(주미대사관 및 주유엔대표부)

자료준비

o 가입에 제한 연설문

o 방문자료

- 방문일정

- 공통자료

- 유엔사무총장 및 총회의장 면담자료

- 핵심우방국대사 초청 오(만)찬사

- 주요언론 회견자료

- 출입국시 기자회견자료

o 귀국보고서

- 9.20. 청와대보고

행정 및 예산

o 항공편 예약

  - 대표단 확정 직후

o 예산집행계획 작성

o 선물결정

  - 선물대상자 선정

  - 선물구입 및 방문전 유엔대표부 송부(파편)

Ⅲ. 지구촌 행사

기본계획 수립

1. 第46차 유엔총회 기조연설 참석 기본보고(6.3. 기조치)

o 멕시코 방문포함

2. 기조연설일자 교섭

o 9.24(화) 오전 두번째 연설로 잠정예약(6.6. 기조치)

- 11:15-11:45중 연설 예상

※ 국내TV 위성중계시간 : 9.25(수) 00:15-00:45

3. 방문일정 결정(의전실 조치사항)

o 멕시코 방문의사 전달(기조치)

o 경유지 확정

o 영부인 별도일정 작성

4. 방문관계 청와대 보고

o 보고시기

- 1차 : 8월중순(유엔가입신청 안보리 처리 이후)
- 2차 : 9.14경(장관 뉴욕출국전)
- 3차 : 9.20.(유엔가입이후 지구촌 출국전)

o 보고내용

- 행사 세부일정
- 기조연설문 주안점
- 수행원 구성

※ 주미대사등 미국내 공관장 참석문제 검토

- 가입 경축행사 개요

방문중 주요행사

1. 기조연설

o 연설문 작성

- 연설문 작성 관련 자료수집
- 연설문 기본 골격(포함사항) 결정(7.15)

. 유엔대표부, 외연원, 세종연구소등 협조

- 연설 초안작성(7.15-7.31), 청와대 송부

o 연설 시행방법

- 국문 또는 영문연설 여부 확정

. 국문연설시 통역 선정

o 국내TV 위성중계

- KBS/MBC에서 추진예정

2. 각국 수뇌와의 회담 개최추진

o 대상국(기조연설 일시)

- 미국(9.23. 오전), 일본(9.23. 오후), 소련(9.24. 오전), 말련(9.24. 오후), 브라질(9.23. 오전), 호주(9.23. 오후)

o 수뇌회담 대상국 정상의 유엔총회 참석여부 및 일정확인

o 정상회담 개최교섭

- 부내 협의

- 청와대(외교안보, 의전)와의 사전 협의

3. 유엔 사무총장 면담

o 면담일시 및 장소 확정

4. 가입 경축행사

o 기념품 기증식 개최 추진(관례조사중)

- 기념품 선정 및 송부

- 기념품 전시장소등 교섭

- 국내TV 위성중계등 검토

o 리셉션 개최(9.24)

- 장소선정, 예약(The Plaza)

- 초청대상자 확정, 초청장 발송

o 경축 민속예술단 공연(9.25. 뉴욕 카네기홀)

5. 유엔 사무총장/총회의장 및 주요국 정상 주최 행사참석

o 참석대상행사 선정

- 미국 대통령주최 행사(9.23)

o 세부사항 확인

17

0030

6. 기타활동 검토

- o 주요언론사 회장등 접견
- o Dinkins 뉴욕시장 접견

자료준비

- o 기조연설문
  - \- 국.영문 연설문 인쇄
    - . 소요부수 확인 및 유엔대표부 송부
- o 방문일정(의전실)
- o 정상회담 자료
- o 주요인사 접견자료(필요시)
- o 출국 및 귀국성명

홍보대책

- o 지구촌행사 발표
  - \- 1차 발표(안보리 권고결의 채택 직후)
    - . 보도자료(개략일정, 방문의의) 준비
  - \- 2차 발표(총회 가입결의 채택 직후)
    - . 보도자료(기조연설 일시, 확정일정, 방문의의) 준비
- o 기조연설
  - \- 국내TV 위성중계
- o 각종 보도자료 작성
  - \- 기조연설, 정상회담, 주요인사 접견, 교민행사, 뉴욕출발시
- o 유엔과 우리나라와의 관계에 관한 다큐멘타리 TV 방영 및 좌담(9.24)

교민행사

- o 입.출국시 환영.환송행사
- o 교민 격려행사(9.22. 추석)

의전, 경호, 숙소

- o 의전, 경호사항
- o 숙 소
  - The Plaza Hotel 숙소예약 현황(6.11. 기조치)
    - . Presidential Suite : 1실
    - . Suite(13), Single(15), Twin(60)
  - St. Moritz Hotel : Twin(50실)
  - 기타 : W.A. 및 Intercontinental Hotel에 예약관련 협조요청중

주유엔대표부 지원

- o 인원 지원
  - 직원파견여부 검토
  - 타자수 파견, 임시직(운전원등) 고용여부 검토
- o 예산 지원
  - 예비비 신청(의전실, 기획관리실 조치)

19

0032

Ⅳ. 대유엔활동 강화방안

금년도 대유엔활동 종합계획

2. 총회 및 각 위원회별 참가대책 수립

가. 제45차 총회결과 검토

  o 제45차 총회 토의결과 책자발간(6.20.)

    - 주요의제에 관한 각국입장 정리

- 주요의제 토의내용 분석
- 주요결의수록

나. 제46차 총회 특별대책반 설치 검토(8월/9월)

o 관계부처 및 각실.국 참여

다. 의제별 아국입장 정립

o 총회 주석가의제 분석(7월/8월)

o 총회 각 의제별 주요쟁점사안 및 동사안에 대한 주요국 및 그룹별 입장 분석(8월/9월)

- 아주지역국가 및 동구권국가 대표부등과 의견교환 추진

o 상기 분석에 기초한 아국입장 정립(9월말)

라. 각 위원회 활동

o 일반토의 연설문 작성(8월/9월)

- 제 1, 2, 3, 5 위원회

o 각 위원회의 주요의제 토의시 능동적 참여 모색

- 주요결의안 작성 참여

. 비공식 협의회(informal consultation) 참여

. 결의안 초안위원회(drafting committee) 참여등

o 아국과 관련된 주요사안에 관한 결의안 제출대책 수립

마. 표결참여 대책

o 과거 3년간 총회에서 채택된 주요결의에 대한 각국의 표결내용 분석

o 기본 표결대책

- 세부사안에 대한 표결대책

o 유엔기구 이사국(또는 위원) 선거참여 대책수립

- 아국에 대한 지지요청내용 분석
- 지지국 선정
  . 금후 아국의 입후보시 지지획득 고려
- 표결 참여대책 수립
  . 공개 및 비공개투표 참여대책 별도 수립

3. 사무국 협조확보

o 사무국 협조체제 구축

- 주요 사무국 간부와 접촉강화

o 사무국의 분석자료 입수

o 총회개최전, 총회기간중 사무국으로부터 지원을 받아야 할 분야 발굴

4. 총회 참가대표단 구성

o 각 위원회 활동시 본부 및 재외공관 관련직원 출장 지원

o 타부처 또는 연구기관등의 전문가 파견 검토

o 행정요원 지원검토

- 타자수 포함

5. 총회 및 각 위원회 활동을 위한 소요예산 확보

* 지구촌 행사 및 장관 유엔참석 행사경비

- 별도 산정

o 총회 참가대표단 출장경비

- 대표단 구성 및 기간 확정후 산출
- 타부처 및 연구기관 참석자 지원여부 검토

o 우방국 및 사무국 직원과의 협조체제 구축을 위한 활동비

o 리셉션등 기타 행사경비

6. 제46차 총회 토의결과 분석(총회종료 직후)

o 주요의제에 관한 각국입장 분석

o 주요의제 토의내용 분석

o 주요결의 검토

- 결의의 쟁점부분 분석

- 각국의 표결내용 분석

유엔대표부 보강

o 인력 보강

- 인력보강에 대한 대표부 건의(안) : 별첨

o 청사구입 또는 신축

- 현 대표부청사는 협소(93년 임차계약 만료)

- 신청사 구입 또는 신축 추진

. 맨하탄 부동산시세 최근 폭락, 신청사 구입 적기

o 대사관저 이전

- 대사관저 협소로 각종행사(오.만찬, 리셉션등) 개최에 부적절

o 맨하탄내 직원주택 국유화(긴급상황 대처능력 제고)

- 국유화 대상직원

. 공사

. 안보리 및 제1위원회 담당 참사관

. 총무담당 서기관

. 외신관

- 직원주택 국유화에 따른 예산지원

. 자녀학비 보조수당(월 $1,000 내외)

. 차고임차비(월 $500 내외)

. 보험료(차량보험, 의료보험등 월 $200 추가소요)

o 차량지원

- Mini Van 1대, 의전차량 1대, 행정차량 1대 추가지원

o 예산 증액편성

중장기 대유엔정책 수립

1. 국제기구외교 수행능력 제고

o 신규채용자에 대한 교육과정 대폭강화

o 국제기구 전문가 양성

o 관계부처와의 유엔대책 협의 정례화

o 국제기구에 대한 직원파견 확대

o 우방국, 비동맹, 동구권 국가와 국제기구국장회의 정례화 추진

- 현재 한.일 유엔국장회의 교대 개최중

o 사무국 인사초청, 회의외교 실무교육 실시

- 국제기구업무 담당직원 대상

o 유엔자료실 설치

- 유엔의 각종자료, 정보의 data base화

- 각종회의 참가보고서 축적

2. 국제기구소재 공관보강 및 신설

o 주비엔나 국제기구대표부 설치

o 제네바, 방콕, 나이로비등 국제기구 소재지 공관 인원보강

3. 유엔총회 의장단 및 안보리등 이사국 진출

o 유엔총회 의장단 진출

- 유엔총회 및 각 위원회 의장.부의장, 보고자 진출

o 안보리 이사국 진출

o 경사리 이사국 진출

o 총회 및 경사리 산하 위원회 이사국 진출

- 군축위원회, 인권위원회등

o 국제사법재판소 재판관 진출

* 상기 진출문제에 관한 종합적 추진계획 별도 수립

4. 사무국 직원 진출

o 아국인의 유엔사무국 요직 진출

- 사무차장 보급을 포함 전문직 약 20명 진출 목표

- 대상인사 선정, 유엔측과 교섭

유엔대표부 인원 보강(안)

(외무부 직원기준)

91. 6. 14.
국제연합과

1. 직 원

담 당 업 무	현 인 원	소요인원	보강인원
1. 공관장	1	1	0
2. 업무총괄(차석대사)	1	1	0
3. 정 무 o 국제안보, 군축, 평화유지, 국제법, 국제정보, 외기권, 지역문제, 남북한문제, 유엔 재정문제	o 공 사 1 o 참사관 3	o 공 사 1 o 참사관 3 o 서기관 3	o 서기관 3
4. 경 제 o 국제경제, 환경, 개발, 다국적기업 문제등	o 참사관 1 o 서기관 1	o 공 사 1 o 참사관 2 o 서기관 2	o 공 사 1 o 참사관 1 o 서기관 1
5. 사 회 o 인권, 여성, 아동, 마약, 사회문제등	o 참사관 1 o 서기관 1	o 참사관 2 o 서기관 2	o 참사관 1 o 서기관 1
6. 총 무 o 총무, 행정, 외신, 문서, 전산업무	o 서기관 1 o 외신관 2	o 참사관 1 o 서기관 1 o 행정관 1 o 외신관 3 o 전산관 1	o 참사관 1 o 행정관 1 o 외신관 1 o 전산관 1
계	o 공관장 1 o 차석대사 1 o 공 사 1 o 참사관 5 o 서기관 3 o 외신관 2	o 공관장 1 o 차석대사 1 o 공 사 2 o 참사관 8 o 서기관 8 o 행정관 1 o 외신관 3 o 전산관 1	o 공 사 1 o 참사관 3 o 서기관 5 o 행정관 1 o 외신관 1 o 전산관 1
	o 총인원 13	o 총인원 25	o 총인원 12

0033

2. 고용원

o 고용원 현원 : 12명

o 증원 소요 : 최소 5명

- speech writer : 1명

- 경제.사회관계 전문연구원 : 1명

- 기타 고용원 : 3명. 끝.

공 란

91
-3940

기 안 용 지

분류기호 문서번호	국연 2031-108	(전화:)	시 행 상 특별취급	
보존기간	영구·준영구. 10. 5. 3. 1	장 관		
수 신 처 보존기간				
시행일자	1991.6.24.			

보조기관		협조기관		문서통제
국 장	전결			1991. 6. 24
과 장				
기안책임자	송영완			발송인

경 유	주뉴욕총영사	발신명의		발송 1991. 6. 24 외무부
수 신	주유엔대사			
참 조				
제 목	유엔가입에 따른 제반조치사항			

1. 제46차 유엔총회 개막일(91.9.17) 아국의 유엔가입이 실현될 전망임에 따라 유엔가입과 관련된 제반 조치필요사항을 1차 검토하여 별첨자료를 작성한 바, 동 조치사항 점검표중 수정 또는 보완이 필요한 내용에 대한 귀견을 91.7.10한 본부 필착토록 송부하여 주시기 바랍니다.

0042 /계속/

(2)

2. 또한 별첨 점검표는 주로 본부에서 조치해야 할 사항을 중심으로 작성하였는 바, 귀 대표부에서 조치하여야 할 사항에 대한 별도 점검표 작성이 필요할 경우, 동 자료를 작성하여 상기 수정, 보완목록과 함께 본부로 송부하여 주시기 바랍니다.

첨부 : 표제 점검표 1부. 끝.

예고 19 91.12.31.일반 일반문서로 재분류

검토필(1991. 6. 30.)

0043

관리번호 91-4161

원 본

외 무 부

종 별 :

번 호 : UNW-1803 일 시 : 91 0711 1900

수 신 : 장 관(국연)

발 신 : 주 유엔 대사

제 목 : 유엔가입에 따른 제반조치사항

대:국연 2031-708 (91.6.24)

대호 점검표에 대한 수정 또는 보완사항을 우선 아래보고하며, 기타 수시 추보위계임.

I.1. 국내조치

2. 다. 유엔가입에 따른 회원국 분담금 예산 확보

0. 아국의 분담금율은 92-94 기간중 유엔예산의 0.24 프로-0.69 프로 예상

I.2. 유엔가입신청

2. 미국및 CG 와의 협의:7.22 시작주 CG 회의 개최(본직 귀임직후)

0. 안보리 가입신청서 처리 대책

-표결 또는 콘센서스 채택방식문제

-안보리 회의 심의시(결의안 통과후) 남북한 대표참가 발언여부(추가)

5. 가입신청서 제출

0. 본직이 사무총장에게 직접제출

-안보리 의장에게 사전통보

-CG , 중.소 에 사전통보

-북한에도 사전통보

I.3. 남북한 유엔대사 회담

1. 현상황및 기본입장

0. 북한의 남북대사급 회담 계속 불응에 따라 회담개최 가능성희박

-아국가입서 제출전 회담 재촉구

0. 북측의 향후 실무접촉 요청에 대한 아측입장 결정

2. 대사급 회담개최시 구체적 논의사항

국기국 장관 차관 1차보

PAGE 1 91.07.12 09:03

외신 2과 통제관 BS

0044

0. 가입신청서 처리방안

-결의안 형태(단일 또는 별개)

-결의안 채택방식(표결 또는 콘센서스)

-결의안 공동제안국문제

4. 기타

0. 회담 불개최시 미.중간 및 한. 중간 협의 채널 활용

-금후 안보리및 총회에서의 처리방안 협의

I. 4.1. 신청서 처리방향

0. 남북한 대표의 안보리 초청발언 대비(단, 가능성 희박)

0. 안보리 결의안 공동제안국 문제

-최근 관행은 공동제안국 없음.

0. 안보리 이사국 이외의 우방국의 지지, 우정발언 자원시 대책

-북측의 반대 가능성관련

2. 총회대책

다. 국명표기 조기 결정

0. 좌석배치 문제와 관련성 감안

-사무국앞 통보시한 감안

바. 가입결의 채택직후

0. 국기 게양식

-간단한 치사준비

사. 홍보활동

0. 안보리, 총회의 결의채택 과정

IV.2. 유엔대표부 보강

0. 대표부 직제 개편

-"주국제연합 대표부"를 "국제연합 상주대표부" 로 변경 (UNW-1782 호로 건의한 명칭과함께 본부검토 바람.)

-직원 재발령(주뉴욕 총영사관 겸직 발령해제)

0. 대표부 현판식 거행

-유엔가입 직후(91.9.17) 장관주재

0. 대사 상주대표 신임장 발급, 유엔사무총장에게 신임장제정

(공관장 직함도 상주대표로 할것인지 본부검토)

0. 대표부 도서.자료실 보강

-필요도서, 자료확보

0. 대표부 업무 전산화

-유엔 각종자료, 토의결과등

-유엔 사무국과 연계

0. 인력보강

-고용원(연설문작성, 자료조사 전문등) 대폭증강

0. 대표부 문서 양식등 변경

0. 대표부 직원 신분증, 공용및 직원개인차량 등록변경. 끝.

(대사 노창희-국장)

예고:91.12.31. 일반
의거 일반 ...

검토필(1991.6.30.)

PAGE 3

0046

공 란

공 란

「유엔外交」적극 전개

政府 96년까지 安保理비상임理事國 추진

동아 10.17 3면

정부는 오는96년까지 유엔안보리비상임이사국이되는 것을 목표로 외교활동을 전개중인 것으로 17일 알려졌다.

정부의 한 고위당국자는 이날 아시아지역에 배정되는 1개 안보리비상임이사국은 92~93년회기에 日本이 이미 결정됐고 94~95년은 오만이 강력한 후보로 나서고 있는 상태』라고 전하고 『정부는 96~97년 회기에 비상임이사국이 된다는 목표를 가지고 있다』고 말했다.

이 당국자는 『각 지역별로 1개국씩 배정되는 안보리비상임이사국이 되기 위해서는 적어도 3、4년전부터 해당지역의 국가들을 상대로 득표활동을 벌여야 한다』고 설명하고 『유엔내에서 우리의 위상제고를 위한 활동이 이미 시작됐다』고 덧붙였다.

이 당국자는 또 『정부는 적어도 내년총회에서 행정조정위원회 합동감사반 국제법위원회등 3、4개주요 위원회의 임원국에 선출되도록 할 방침』이라고 전했다.

0043

다자외교 전문가 육성방향

91. 10. 18.
국제연합1과

1. 다자외교 전문가 육성 기본방향

ㅇ 유엔가입을 계기로 우리의 다자외교 활동 영역이 급격히 확대됨에 비추어 다자외교 전문가 집중 육성방안 (단기방안)과 외무부의 다자외교 능력 함양을 위한 인적, 제도적 장치마련 (중장기 방안)을 병행 시행

ㅇ 다자외교 전문가 육성의 주안점

- 전문지식 축적
- 어학능력 함양
- 회의외교 주도능력 제고
- 타국 다자외교 전문가와의 인적교류 확대

2. 다자외교 전문가 육성 세부사항

가. 회의외교 직원 교육 강화 (단기방안)

1) 외교안보연구원 교육과정상 회의외교 교육 실시

ㅇ 신규채용자 교과목중 회의외교 업무를 추가하여 주요 국제현안별 학과 교육

* 현행교과목 편성 (6개분야) : 국제관계학, 지역연구, 직무학, 영어, 교양학, 개인연구
(총 59과목, 118학점, 1480시간)

0050

o 회의 외교업무 교육내용

- 주요 국제현안별 학과교육 : 군축, 환경, 경협, 인권, 국제법등 주요 국제현안에 관한 논의 동향, 각국입장에 관한 교육실시

2) 견습직원 제도 신설

o 신규채용자중 다자외교 분야를 지망하는 직원의 경우, 해외연수 대신 주유엔대표부 또는 주제네바 대표부의 견습직원으로 파견, 국제회의 참관 및 참여기회 확보

o 동 해외견습기간 종료후 본부 관련부서 (다자외교 담당부서)에 배치하여 근무토록 하고 재외공관 발령시 주유엔대표부, 주제네바대표부등에 우선 배치토록 함.

나. 다자외교 분야 전문가 양성을 위한 중·장기 인력관리 방안

1) 본부 인력관리

o 다자외교를 담당하는 부서(외교정책기획실, 국제기구국, 조약국, 국제경제국, 통상국) 근무직원은 2년이상 근무원칙 (5개부서간 또는 국내 타과 이동은 신축 운영)

- 상기 5개부서의 과장은 다자외교분야 2년이상 근무자로 보직

  * 국제경제국의 경우 과학환경과, 경제기구과, 통상국의 경우 통상기구과가 다자외교 담당부서에 해당되며 외정실의 경우 정책총괄과, 안보정책과가 해당됨.

o 재외공관 발령시 다자외교 담당공관에 배치토록 우선적 고려

o 다자외교 담당부서 직원 및 행정지원인력 보강

- 사서직원 배치 (각과 1명씩)

- 행정직직원 배치 (각과 1명씩)

- Speech writer 채용 (국단위로 1명씩)

0051

2) 재외공관 인력관리

o 다자외교 담당공관 (유엔, 제네바, 유네스코, 오스트리아, 태국, 케냐등)의 핵심직원 근무기간 연장 검토

- 현행 근무기간(3년)으로는 다자외교 분야에서 충분한 업무파악 및 적극적 활동을 기대하기 곤란 (4년으로 근무기간 연장 검토 필요)

o 공관근무 종료후 본부 전보시 관련부서에 우선적 배치

- 재외공관 전보시에도 순환근무 원칙 감안, 국제기구가 있는 국가(케냐, 태국, 필리핀등) 또는 주재국 외무부 국제기구담당 부서와의 업무협조가 많은 국가(ASEAN, 인도등)에 우선적 고려

  * 향후 다자외교에 있어 아주그룹국가와의 공동보조를 취하게 되는 사례 급증 예상

3) 국제기구담당 조직 재정비 (검토)

o 국제기구국에 타국의 예와 같이 경제기구과 및 과학환경과를 둠.

- 국제경제국 업무는 다개도국 경제협력 및 금후 OECD 가입을 대비, 동 업무를 전담토록 함. 끝.

0052

2. 신임장 제정

0053

협 조 문 용 지

분류기호 문서번호	국연 2031- 323	(2179-80)	결재	담 당	과 장	국 장
시행일자	1991. 8. 1.					
수 신	의 전 장	발신	국제기구조약국장 (서명)			
제 목	주유엔대사 신임장					

91.9.17(화) 아국이 유엔에 가입할 전망임에 따라 주유엔대사는 신임장을 유엔 사무총장에게 제출하여야 하는 바, 하기 참조, 주유엔대사 신임장을 작성, 주유엔 대표부에 송부하여 주시기 바랍니다.

- 아 래 -

1. 주유엔대사 직명 :

   H.E. Mr. Chang Hee ROE

   Ambassador Extraordinary and Plenipotentiary and Permanent Representative of the Republic of Korea to the United Nations

2. 유엔 사무총장 직명 :

   H.E. Mr. Javier PEREZ de CUELLAR

   Secretary-General of the United Nations

3. 비고 : 신임장 작성일자(필요시)는 91.9.17로 표기. 끝.

0054

가입조치사항

암호수신

외 무 부

종 별 :

번 호 : UNW-2304 일 시 : 91 0827 1800

수 신 : 장관(의전)

발 신 : 주 유엔 대사

제 목 : 신임장

대:WUN-2210

대호, 표제관련 사무국 의전실 접촉결과를 아래보고함.

-아래-

1. 신임장 발급자 명의:국가원수 , 정부수반 또는 외무장관

2. 신임장 접수자 직책, 성명: 유엔사무총장 페레스 데 케야르

3. 신임장 문안: 별첨참조

4. 신임장 발급자가 국가원수인 경우 국무총리 또는 외무장관 부서 불요

5. 신임장 원본 국문표기 불요

첨부 FAX:UNW(F)-467:1. 유엔 의전편람 신임장 관련부분,2. 말레이지아 신임장,3. 호주신임장 끝.

(대사 노창희-의전장)

의전장 국기국

0055

PAGE 1

91.08.28 08:32

외신 2과 통제관 BN

AUG 27 '91 16:16 KOREAN MISSION

P.1

#별첨

UNW(F)-467 10827 1800

(외전)

총7매

0056

I. ESTABLISHING A NEW MISSION IN NEW YORK

When a country has been admitted by the General Assembly as a State Member of the United Nations, it is expected that it will establish a permanent mission at United Nations Headquarters or at other major United Nations centres, such as Geneva or Vienna, and appoint a permanent representative. By its resolution 257 A (III), the General Assembly expressed its opinion that the presence of the permanent mission and the permanent representative of a Member State at the seat of the Organization would serve to assist in the realization of the purposes and principles of the United Nations and to keep the necessary liaison between the Member States and the Secretariat.

In conformity with international law and United Nations practice, the term "permanent representative" has a clear interpretation. At the United Nations, this term was institutionalized by the General Assembly in its resolution 257 A (III) wherein it recommended, *inter alia*, that credentials of newly appointed permanent representatives be issued by either the head of State or Government or minister for foreign affairs and that in the case of the temporary absence of the permanent representative from the seat of the Organization, the Secretary-General of the United Nations be notified of the name of the person who would be in charge of the mission as chargé d'affaires a.i.

From the foregoing, it is obvious that the term "permanent representative of a Member State to the

1

7-1

United Nations" defines a person of the appropriate diplomatic rank[1] who *permanently* (as distinct from temporarily) resides at the seat of the Organization and is the head of an established permanent representation (mission) with a postal address and a telephone number.

II. LETTERS OF CREDENTIALS

On 3 December 1948, the General Assembly adopted resolution 257 A (III) regarding permanent missions of Member States to the United Nations. The resolution reads as follows:

"*The General Assembly*,

"*Considering* that, since the creation of the United Nations, the practice has developed of establishing, at the seat of the Organization, permanent missions of Member States,

"*Considering* that the presence of such permanent missions serves to assist in the realization of the purposes and principles of the United Nations and, in particular, to keep the necessary liaison between the Member States and the Secretariat in periods between sessions of the different organs of the United Nations,

"*Considering* that in these circumstances the generalization of the institution of permanent missions can be foreseen, and that the submission of credentials of permanent representatives should be regulated,

"*Recommends*

"1. That credentials of the permanent representatives shall be issued either by the Head of the State or by the Head of the Government or by the Minister of Foreign Affairs, and shall be transmitted to the Secretary-General;

"2. That the appointments and changes of members of the permanent missions other than the permanent representative shall be communicated in writing to the Secretary-General by the head of the mission;

"3. That the permanent representative, in case of temporary absence, shall notify the Secretary-General of the name of the member of the mission who will perform the duties of head of the mission;

"4. That Member States desiring their permanent representatives to represent them on one or more of the organs of the United Nations should specify the organs in the credentials transmitted to the Secretary-General;

"*Instructs* the Secretary-General to submit, at each regular session of the General Assembly, a report on the credentials of the permanent representatives accredited to the United Nations."

The annex to the report of the Secretary-General to the General Assembly at its fourth session on permanent missions to the United Nations[2] gave a form of credentials which, in the light of the above resolution, appears to be satisfactory and which, accordingly, is

---

[1] It has become the standard for the Governments of Member States to appoint permanent representatives to the United Nations with the rank of Ambassador Extraordinary and Plenipotentiary.

[2] See *Official Records of the General Assembly, Fourth Session, Annex to the Summary Records of the Sixth Committee*, p. 17.

7-2

0057

reproduced below as a guide to the drafting of such instruments.

Standard form of credentials

"Whereas the Government of . . . has set up at the seat of the United Nations a permanent mission to maintain necessary contact with the Secretariat of the Organization,

"Now therefore we . . . [name and title] have appointed and by these presents do confirm as permanent representative to the United Nations His/Her Excellency . . . [name] . . . [title].

"His/Her Excellency . . . is instructed to represent the Government of . . . in the following organs: . . . He/She is also authorized to designate a substitute to act temporarily on his/her behalf after due notice to the Secretary-General.

"In faith whereof we have signed these presents at . . . on . . .

"...
"[Signature and title]
"[Head of State,
Head of Government
or Minister for Foreign Affairs]"

It should be noted that all letters of credentials must be addressed *by name* to the Secretary-General of the United Nations.

For practical reasons, most Governments of Member States prefer to accredit their newly appointed permanent representatives to *all organs of the United*

Nations, which has now become the accepted standard practice. In such cases, the beginning of the third paragraph of the letter of credentials is formulated as follows:

"His/Her Excellency . . . is instructed to represent the Government of . . . in all organs of the United Nations."

However, in accordance with a practice that has been followed for over 40 years, Member States elected to the Security Council, the Economic and Social Council or the Trusteeship Council are required under the relevant rules of procedure to submit separate credentials for their representatives in each of these organs.

III. APPOINTMENT OF A NEW PERMANENT REPRESENTATIVE

When a new permanent representative is appointed to the United Nations, it is requested that the permanent mission concerned submit, at the earliest opportunity, details of the permanent representative's arrival date, means of transport and port of entry into the United States of America to the United Nations Chief of Protocol so that the necessary customs and immigration clearances may be obtained from the United States authorities and arrangements made for extending to him/her, upon arrival, the usual diplomatic courtesies. The permanent representative should submit his/her curriculum vitae as soon as possible, before his/her meeting with the Chief of Protocol.

7-3

0058

Upon the arrival of the new permanent representative in New York, he/she should arrange an appointment with the Chief of Protocol in order to be briefed on the details of the established procedure for the *presentation of credentials* to the Secretary-General. On this occasion, the letter of credentials of the new permanent representative will be reviewed by the Chief of Protocol in order to ensure that it corresponds to the accepted standard.

The Chief of Protocol will then make the necessary arrangements, such as fixing the date and time, for the new permanent representative to present his/her letter of credentials to the Secretary-General.

The recommended attire for this occasion is a lounge/business suit, preferably dark, or national dress.

On the day and time agreed upon, the Chief of Protocol will escort the new permanent representative to the office of the Secretary-General for the ceremony of the presentation of credentials. He/she may be accompanied by one or two members of his/her delegation.

It is expected that, at the time of presentation of credentials, the new permanent representative will make a *brief* statement to the Secretary-General.

A special press release containing biographical data on the new permanent representative and announcing *his/her presentation of credentials* to the Secretary-General will be issued by the Department of Public Information on the same day. A photographer will

take an "official portrait" of the new permanent representative just before the presentation of credentials and will record the actual presentation.

The practice of leaving calling cards with the permanent representatives of Member States to the United Nations and senior officials of the Secretariat has been practically discontinued, thus leaving it to the discretion of each new permanent representative to act as he/she deems appropriate.

However, it is customary for a newly appointed permanent representative to call on the Presidents of the General Assembly, the Security Council and the Economic and Social Council and senior officials of the Secretariat. In addition, a new permanent representative usually informs all other permanent representatives in writing that he/she has presented his/her letter of credentials to the Secretary-General and assumed his/her duties. Apart from that, the Chief of Protocol sends out a memorandum informing all departments of the United Nations of the presentation of credentials of the new permanent representative.

As to the procedure of the accreditation of a permanent representative of a Member/observer State to the offices of the United Nations at Geneva, Vienna, Nairobi, Bangkok, Santiago, Addis Ababa and Baghdad, a letter of credentials should be addressed, *by name*, to the Secretary-General of the United Nations with copies to the respective director-general or executive secretary of a regional or United Nations office or commission and a mention of the office or specialized agency to which the new permanent representative/ob-

7-4

0053

server is accredited. If the permanent representative/observer is accredited to a United Nations office or specialized agency at Vienna, separate credentials should also be addressed to the Government of Austria. The new permanent representative should contact the executive head of the United Nations office concerned in order to arrange an appointment to present the original letter of credentials. The executive head will thus receive the credentials on behalf of the Secretary-General of the United Nations. However, specialized agencies such as the Food and Agriculture Organization of the United Nations, the International Atomic Energy Agency, the International Civil Aviation Organization, the International Fund for Agricultural Development and the United Nations Educational, Scientific and Cultural Organization receive credentials addressed to the executive heads of the body concerned and not to the Secretary-General of the United Nations.

IV. LETTERS AND NOTES VERBALES

All correspondence to the Protocol and Liaison Service at United Nations Headquarters should be addressed to the Chief of Protocol and signed by either the permanent representative or the chargé d'affaires, bearing his/her full signature. All diplomatic movements, appointments, promotions, departures, etc., as well as any personnel movements, should be announced in a letter addressed to the Secretary-General. Any official communication containing important information regarding the Governments of Mem-

8

ber States should also be communicated in a letter by the head of the mission.

Notes verbales addressed to the Protocol and Liaison Service should bear the official seal and the initials of the responsible officer. They are normally used to communicate routine administrative matters other than personnel.

V. REGISTRATION OF MEMBERS OF PERMANENT/OBSERVER MISSIONS

The names of all members of permanent missions, whether diplomatic or non-diplomatic, and of their families and household employees should, upon their arrival at Headquarters, be communicated to the Secretary-General in accordance with General Assembly recommendations. For this purpose, the following documents, as applicable, should be sent to the Protocol and Liaison Service.

(*a*) *Persons with diplomatic status*:

(i) A registration form (SG.5) signed by the applicant;

(ii) A letter (*not a note verbale*) addressed to the Secretary-General signed by the permanent representative or chargé d'affaires stating:

a. Name, diplomatic rank, functional title and date of appointment;

b. Request for privileges and immunities;

c. Order of precedence at the mission;

(iii) Six photographs for a diplomat, five for a spouse and none for children or household employees;

9

7-5

0060

SENATOR THE HON. GARETH EVANS Q.C.

MINISTER FOR FOREIGN AFFAIRS AND TRADE
PARLIAMENT HOUSE
CANBERRA A.C.T. 2600

18 OCT 1988

His Excellency Mr Javier Perez de Cuellar
Secretary-General of the United Nations
United Nations Headquarters
NEW YORK

Your Excellency

I have the honour to inform you that the Government of Australia has appointed Dr Peter Stephen Wilenski to be the Permanent Representative of Australia to the United Nations at New York, in succession to Mr Richard Woolcott.

In this capacity, Dr Wilenski will have the personal rank of Ambassador and is empowered to represent the Australian Government without limitation as to Session in all organs of the United Nations.

I request that Dr Wilenski be granted such facilities as may be necessary for the effective performance of his functions.

I avail myself of this opportunity to renew to Your Excellency the assurances of my highest consideration.

GARETH EVANS

7-6

0061

Ministry of Foreign Affairs,
Malaysia,
KUALA LUMPUR.

10 May, 1988.

Your Excellency,

I have the honour to inform you that His Majesty's Government has designated Dato' RAZALI bin ISMAIL, Ambassador Extraordinary and Plenipotentiary, as Permanent Representative of Malaysia to the United Nations in succession to Dato' MOHD. YUSOF bin HITAM.

Dato' RAZALI bin ISMAIL is instructed to represent His Majesty's Government in all organs of the United Nations. He is also authorised to designate a substitute to act temporarily on his behalf, whenever this becomes necessary, after due notice to you.

I have the honour to convey to Your Excellency the assurances of my highest consideration.

(DATO' HAJI ABU HASSAN BIN HAJI OMAR)
Minister of Foreign Affairs,
Malaysia.

His Excellency Javier Perez de Cuellar,
Secretary General of the United Nations,
NEW YORK.

7-7

TOTAL P.02

0062

외 무 부

종 별 :

번 호 : GVW-1772 일 시 : 91 0918 1600

수 신 : 장 관(의전,총인,연일,기법)사본:주유엔대사(중계필),박수길 (

발 신 : 주 제네바대사대리

제 목 : UN가입 후속주치

연: GVW-0430

아국의 9.17 UN 가입에 따른 당관의 지위변경등을 위한 제반 후속 조치 절차를 당지 유엔제네바 사무처 의전실과 협의한바 아래 관련사항에 대해 필요한 조치를 취하여 주시기 바람.

1. 당관이 UN 회원국 대표부로서의 지위를 갖기 위해서는 OBSERVER가 아닌 REPRESENTATIVE 로서의 당관 공관장의 유엔 사무총장앞 임명 통지서를 다시 제정해야 함.(당관의 지위변경 사실은 신임장 제정후 당관의 회람공한으로 당지 각대표부 및 국제기구에 통보예정임)

2. 이를 위해서는 뉴욕주재 아국대표부가 UN사무총장에게 주제네바 상주대표부의지위를 PERMANENT OBSERVER MISSION 에서 PERMANENT MISSION으로 변경코자 한다는 통 보조치를 취해야 하며, 이경우 유엔사무총장이 당지 대표부 지위 변경의사를 당지유엔사무초에 통보 한다함.

3. 당관의 명칭(국문 및 영문)은 연호로 건의한 명칭을 사용코자 하니 임명 통지서 작성시 참고바람.끝

(차석대사 김삼훈-실장)

의전장 1차보 총무과 기획실 국기국 의정실 분석관 청와대 안기부

PAGE 1 91.09.19 09:22 WH

외신 1과 통제관

0063

MINISTRY OF FOREIGN AFFAIRS
REPUBLIC OF KOREA

Seoul, September 17, 1991

Excellency,

I have the honour to inform Your Excellency that the Government of the Republic of Korea has appointed Mr. Soo Gil Park, Ambassador Extraordinary and Plenipotentiary, as Permanent Representative of the Republic of Korea to the United Nations Office and other International Organizations at Geneva.

I also wish to inform Your Excellency that the Representative is accredited to all organs of the United Nations in Geneva and to all meetings held in Geneva under the auspices of the United Nations and that he is authorized, if necessary, to designate a substitute to act temporarily on his behalf after due notice to Your Excellency.

I avail myself of this opportunity to renew to Your Excellency the assurances of my highest consideration.

Lee Sang-Ock
Minister of Foreign Affairs

His Excellency
Mr. Javier Perez de Cuellar
Secretary-General of the
United Nations
New York

0064

관리 번호 91-5051

외 무 부

종 별 : 지 급

번 호 : UNW-2828 일 시 : 91 0919 1630

수 신 : 장관대리(의전,총인,국연,기정,시애틀총영사관 경유 장관:직송필)

발 신 : 주 유엔 대사

제 목 : 신임장제정

대:의전 20110-33688

1. 본직은 9.19 케야르 유엔사무총장에게 대호 신임장을 제정하였는바, 요지아래 보고함.(오윤경공사 배석)

가. 신임장 제정, 기념촬영후 옵서버 임명장 제정시와는 달리 삼페인 축배,환담(12:50 부터 약 15 분간)

나. 환담요지

0. 사무총장

-한국의 유엔가입과 초대 상주대표직 수임을 축하함.

-종전보다도 더 활발히 유엔활동에 참여, 기여할것을 기대함.

-유엔가입으로 남북한 관계발전 및 통일을 앞당기는데 도움이 되기바람.

-남북한간 이산가족 교류등 절실한 인도적 문제부터 해결해 나가면 실마리가 풀릴것으로 보며, 유엔가입은 통일의 첫걸음이 될것으로 확신함.

0. 본직

-앞으로 유엔에서 우리 국력에 걸맞는 역할과 책임을 다할것을 다짐함.

-지난번 분담금 위원회에서 아국의 분담금율을 갑자기 3 배이상 인상할것을금차 총회에 건의하기로 결정하여 놀랐지만, 이에 응하기로 한것도 그러한 의지의 표시임.

-9.24 대통령 각하께서 유엔을 방문, 귀하와의 재회를 고대하고 계심.

-북한이 현재는 주저하고 있으나, 시간이 흐르면 결국 개방하는 방향으로 나갈것이며, 현재의 강경자세에서 보다 온건하고 현실적인 자세로 전환할 것으로보며, 향후 5-6 년후 양자관계는 기본적인 변화가 있을것임.

2. 북한대사 박길연도 동일 사무총장에게 신임장을 제정함.(12:30 부터 12:45 분간) 끝

의전장 장관 차관 1차보 2차보 총무과 국기국 분석관 청와대 안기부

PAGE 1 91.09.20 06:16

외신 2과 통제관 CE

0065

(대사 노창희-의전장)

관리 번호	91-1170

원 본

외 무 부

연일

종 별 : 지 급

번 호 : UNW-2848 일 시 : 91 0919 2030

수 신 : 장관대리(연일,정특,기정,해기,주시애틀경유 장관:직송필)

발 신 : 주 유엔 대사

제 목 : 남북한 대사의 신임장 제정

연:UNW-2828

1. 연호, 본직의 신임장 제정사실이 금일 오후 유엔 PRESS RELEASE 로 배포된바, 별첨 FAX 송부함.

2. 금일 오후 박길연 북한대사의 신임장 제정관련 유엔 PRESS RELEASE 도 아울러 송부함.

첨부:상기 프레스릴리스 각 1 매:UNW(F)-543 끝

(대사 노창희-국제기구국장대리)

예고:91.12.31. 까지

국기국 장관 차관 외정실 분석관 청와대 안기부 공보처

PAGE 1

91.09.20 10:05

외신 2과 통제관 BS

0067

United Nations

UNW(F)-543 10919 2030
(연일. 정특. 기정. 국기) 총 204

Press Release

Department of Public Information • News Coverage Service • New York

Biographical Note

BIO/2603
19 September 1991

NEW PERMANENT REPRESENTATIVE OF REPUBLIC OF KOREA PRESENTS CREDENTIALS

Chang Hee Roe, the Republic of Korea's first Permanent Representative to the United Nations, presented his credentials this afternoon to Secretary-General Javier Pérez de Cuéllar.

Mr. Roe has served as his country's Permanent Observer to the United Nations since March. Prior to that assignment, he served in his Government's Ministry of Foreign Affairs as Ambassador-at-large. From 1988 to 1990, he was the Senior Protocol Secretary to the President of the Republic of Korea.

Mr. Roe, who joined the Ministry of Foreign Affairs in 1960 and became its Director of Legal Affairs in 1968, served as a Minister in the Korean Embassy in Washington, D.C., from 1981 to 1984. He then served as his country's Ambassador Plenipotentiary to Nigeria until 1987, before returning to the Foreign Ministry.

Other overseas diplomatic posts held by Mr. Roe include those of First Secretary at the Korean Embassy in Ottawa in 1969, and Counsellor at the Korean Embassy in Stockholm from 1975 to 1978. Mr. Roe directed the Foreign Ministry's Treaties Division from 1973 to 1975, and was appointed its Director-General in 1980. He served as a Senior Research Officer at the Ministry's Institute of Foreign Affairs and National Security from 1972 to 1973.

Mr. Roe received a degree in economics from Seoul National University. Born on 25 February 1938, he is married and has two children.

* **** *

2-1

United Nations

Press Release

Department of Public Information • News Coverage Service • New York

Biographical Note

BIO/2602
19 September 1991

NEW PERMANENT REPRESENTATIVE OF DEMOCRATIC PEOPLE'S REPUBLIC OF KOREA

PRESENTS CREDENTIALS

Pak Gil Yon, the Permanent Representative of the newly elected Member State of the Democratic People's Republic of Korea to the United Nations, this afternoon presented his credentials to Secretary-General Javier Pérez de Cuéllar.

Mr. Pak has been his country's Permanent Observer to the United Nations since March 1985. Prior to that, he served as Deputy Minister for Foreign Affairs for more than a year.

Mr. Pak began his diplomatic career in 1964 as a senior desk officer in his Government's Ministry of Foreign Affairs. In 1969, he was appointed Vice-Consul to the Consulate General in Yangon, Myanmar, where he served until 1972. He then moved to his country's Embassy in Singapore as First Secretary.

In 1978, he became Deputy Director of Department in the Ministry of Foreign Affairs, and two years later was promoted to Director.

Mr. Pak is a graduate of the University of International Affairs in Pyongyang. He has been honoured with a number of medals and Orders of National Flag.

Born in 1943, in Chagang Province, Mr. Pak is married and has two sons and a daughter.

* **** *

2-2

4429P

For information media—not an official record

0063

외 무 부

암호수신

종 별 :

번 호 : AVW-1184 일 시 : 91 0920 1900

수 신 : 장 관(연일,국기)

발 신 : 주 오스트리아 대사

제 목 : 신임장 갱신

아국의 유엔가입에 따라 당지 유엔사무소(THE UNITED NATIONS OFFICE AT VIENNA)에 옵써버 자격으로 제출되어있는 본직의 신임장을 갱신하여 주시기바람.(외무장관 명의로 유엔 사무총장 앞으로 발급함).끝.

국기국 국기국

PAGE 1

91.09.21 09:41

외신 2과 통제관 EE

0070

분류번호	보존기간

발 신 전 보

번 호 : WUN-3094 910920 1122 ED 종별 : 암호타전

수 신 : 주 유 엔 대사.총영사

발 신 : 장 관 (의 전)

제 목 : 유엔가입 후속조치

연 : GVW-1772

아국의 유엔가입에 따라 주제네바대사 및 대표부의 지위를 정식회원국 자격으로 변경하는 절차에 관련 필요하니, 유엔사무국의 관련규정 및 주제네바대사의 신임장 견본등을 보고바람. 끝.

(의전장 장 선섭)

국제기구국장 : Chung

보안 통제	

앙 고 재	91년 9월 20일	의전과	기안자 성명		과 장	의전반	국 장	의전장	차 관	장 관
			이					전결		

외신과통제

0071

관리 번호	91-1132

	분류번호	보존기간

발 신 전 보

WAV-1041 910924 1742 DW

번 호 : 종별 :

수 신 : 주 오지리 대사. 총영사

발 신 : 장 관대리(연일)

제 목 : 신임장 갱신

대 : AVW - 1184

대호, 장관 귀임(10.6)후 의전과에서 조치 예정이니 참고바람. 끝.

(국기국장대리 금 정호)

보 안 통 제	

심의관

앙 고 재	91년 9월 24일	UN1과	기안자 성 명		과 장		국 장		차 관	장 관
							전결			

외신과통제

0072

	분류번호	보존기간

발 신 전 보

번 호 : WUN-3545 911014 1043 DU 종별 :

수 신 : 주 유 엔 대사.~~총영사~~

발 신 : 장 관 (의 전)

제 목 : 유엔가입 후속조치

연 : GVW-1772, WUN-3094

1. 아국의 유엔가입에 따른 주제네바 및 오지리 대사의 신임장(9.17자로 발급)을 금주 파편으로 해당 대사관에 각각 송부예정임.

2. 이에따라 주제네바 대사가 연호(GVW-1772) 2항으로 건의해 온 주제네바 대표부의 지위 변경을 통보하는 공한을 귀대표부 명의로 유엔사무총장에게 제출하고 결과 보고바람.

3. 또한 주오지리 대사에 대해서도 상기와 같은 후속조치가 필요한 경우 조치바람.

끝.

(의전장 장 선섭)

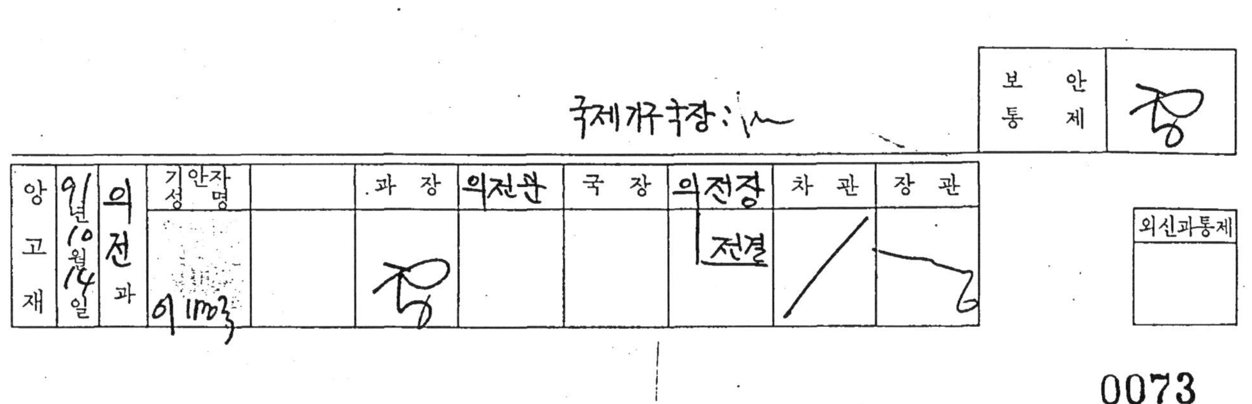

국제기구국장 :

보안 통제	

앙 고 재	91년 10월 14일	의전과	기안자 성명		과 장	의전관	국 장	의전장	차 관	장 관
								전결		

외신과통제

0073

외 무 부

종 별 :

번 호 : UNW-3490 일 시 : 91 1024 1200

수 신 : 장 관 (의전) 사본:주제네바대사(중계필)

발 신 : 주 유엔 대사

제 목 : 유엔가입 후속조치

대: WUN-3545, 3630

연: UNW-3428

주제네바 대사 신임장 제정과 관련, 10.23.유엔사무국 의전실 측은 연호 법률국견해와는 달리 본직명의 사무총장앞 서한을 통하여 주제네바 아국대표부의 지위 변경을 통보하여 주도록 요청해옴에 따라 동일 본직명의 서한을 발송하였음. 끝

(대사 노창희-국장)

의전장 미주국 국기국

PAGE 1

91.10.25 02:00 FN

외신 1과 통제관

0074

관리 번호 91-1364

외 무 부

종 별 :

번 호 : GVW-2197 일 시 : 91 1030 1900

수 신 : 장관(의전,연일)

발 신 : 주 제네바 대사

제 목 : 신임장 제정

대: 의전 20241-37477

연: GVW-1772

1. 본직은 금 10.30(수) 16:00 MARTENSON 주 제네바 유엔 사무처장에게 주 제네바 상주 대표로서의 신임장을 제정하였음.

2. MARTENSON 사무처장은 한국의 유엔가입과 이에 따른 본직의 지위변경을 진심으로 축하하며, 한국의 유엔 가입이 세계 평화에 도움이 될것으로 확신한다고 말함.

3. 한편, 신임장 제정에 이은 환담시 차기 유엔 사무총장 후임 선출 전망에 관해 의견 교환한바, 동 사무처장이 밝힌 견해를 아래 보고하니 참고 바람.

- 금번 사무총장 선출을 위요한 기본 흐름은 이번만은 아프리카 출신이 해야 할 차례라고 확신하는 아프리카 제국(50 여국) 및 이를 지지하는 라틴 아메리카 제국(20 여국)과 이에 맞서는 서구 선진제국간의 대결, 즉 남북간의 대결 양상을 보일 것으로 전망됨.(중국도 기본적으로 아프리카 후보 지지 입장인 것으로 관측)

- 이러한 상황하에서 가장 유력한 총장 후보는 GALI 이집트 부수상일 것인바, 그는 아프리카 대륙을 대표하며, 그 자신은 기독교 신자로서 부인은 유태인이므로 각종 유리한 조건을 겸비하고 있다고 봄.

(다만, 연령이 69 세로서 너무 나이가 많다는 것이 단점임)

또한 아프리카 제국은 서구 선진제국이 비아프리카 후보를 내세울 경우 설령 안보리에서 추천된다하더라도 총회에서 부결시킬 것이라는 입장을 분명히 밝혀두고 있으므로 비아프리카 출신의 총장 선출은 상당히 어려울 것으로 보임.

- 한편, 같은 아프리카 출신 후보인 CHEZERI 탄자니아 경제기획장관의 경우는 MARXIST 국가 출신이라는 점에서 지지를 받기가 어려울 것이며, AGHA KAHN 의 경우는

의전장 국기국

PAGE 1 91.10.31 05:55

외신 2과 통제관 FM

0075

이란 여권을 소지하고 있고 현실적으로 특별히 그를 지원해줄 그룹이 없어 힘들것으로 보고 있음.

- 그러나 총장 선출 당시 의장국의 권한도 무시할수 없으므로 실제 사무총장 선거가 시행될 12 월의 의장국이 소련임에 비추어 소련이 현 케야르 총장의 선출 경위처럼 예상밖의 인물을 추천하여 그가 선출될 가능성도 배제할수 없을 것인바, 현재로서는 속단은 금물이라함. 끝

(대사 박수길-의전장)

예고 91.12.31. 까지

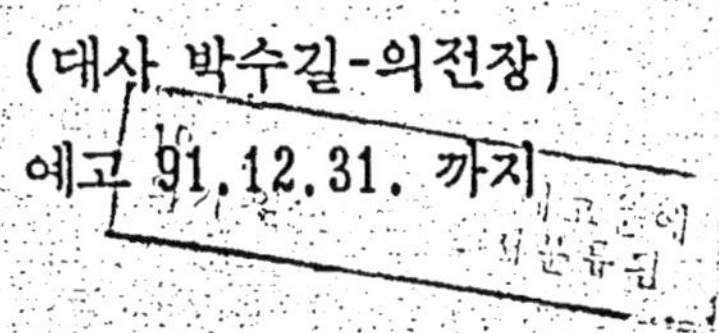

PAGE 2

0076

외 무 부

종 별 :

번 호 : AVW-1432 일 시 : 91 1031 1830

수 신 : 장 관(의전,국연일)사본:주유엔, 제네바대사)직송필

발 신 : 주 오스트리아대사

제 목 : 신임장 제출

대:의전20241-37477

당관은 금 10.31(목) 오전, 별도의 의식 절차없이 아국의 유엔가입에 따른 본직의 새 신임장을 당지의 유엔사무소장 앞 본직 공한을 첨부하여 제출하였음.끝.

의전장 국기국

PAGE 1 91.11.01 09:16 WH

외신 1과 통제관

0077

3. 예산·인력 추가 확보

0078

유엔가입 추진관련 인력 보강계획(안)

91. 3. 11.
국제연합과

1. 기본방향

   o 금년내 유엔가입 실현을 위한 효과적 계획수립 및 집행을 위한 인력보강
   o 비교적 용이하게 시행할 수 있는 단기방안 및 본부 인력보강 중심 검토

2. 추가 인력 소요 판단

   가. 유엔업무담당 현인력(7명) : 과장, 4급 1, 5급 3, 5급시보 1, 7급 1

   나. 추가인력 소요분야 : 문서작성, 가입관련 국내절차 준비

      1) 문서작성 분야

단계별 업무	시기구분	소요인력	대 상 직 원 (안)
1단계 o 가입지지용 메모랜덤 및 성명문 작성	91.3월-7월	3급1, 5급1	o 3급직원 : 별첨 참조 o 5급직원 : 영어 2급 취득자 (별첨 참조)
2단계 o 연설문 (가입 수락연설, 총회 기조연설) 작성	91.6월-7월 (2개월)	연구위원 1, 3급 1	o 추후 별도 선정

      2) 국내절차 분야(국무회의 심의, 국회비준 동의) :

         조약심의관 책임하에 국제법규과 중심으로 별도 구성

첨 부 : 유엔가입 추진관련 업무담당 대상직원 (안)

0073

(첨 부)

유엔가입 추진관련 업무담당 대상직원(안)

1. 심의관급(3급) 직원

성 명 (연 령)	직 급 (현직급승진일)	주 요 경 력	비 고
이 양 (47)	3급 (85.10)	주유엔 1등, 안보, 북미과장, 주독일 참사관	
이 량 (50)	3급 (87.7)	주유엔 1등, 국제기구과장, 주제네바 참사관	
최 영 진 (43)	3급 (87.10)	국제기구과장, 주미참사관	

2. 5급 직원 (영어검정 2급 취득자)

성 명 (연령)	직 급 (입부일자)	연수.공관 경력 (현 소속)	현 소속부서 구 성	비 고
조태용 (35)	5급 (80.8)	영국연수, 주유엔 2등, 주이락 2등 (중동 1과)	과장, 4급 2, 5급 4 (7)	영어검정 (통합) 2급
조병제 (35)	5급 (81.12)	영국연수, 주미 2등 (안보과)	과장, 4급 3, 5급 3, 7급 1(8)	"
김창범 (31)	5급 (81.12)	미국연수, 주일 2등 (동북아 1과)	과장, 4급 1, 5급 6, 7급 1(9)	"
김은석 (33)	5급 (80.8)	미국연수, 주불, 카메룬 2등 (마그레브과)	과장, 4급 1, 5급 2, 7급 1(5)	영어작문 2급
허 철 (37)	5급 (81.12)	미국연수, 주 U.A.E. 2등 (북미과)	과장, 4급 2, 5급 3, 7급 2(8)	"

* 상기 대상인사중 선정 불가능시 어학연수 이수 귀국 직원(91.6월)중 선정

0080

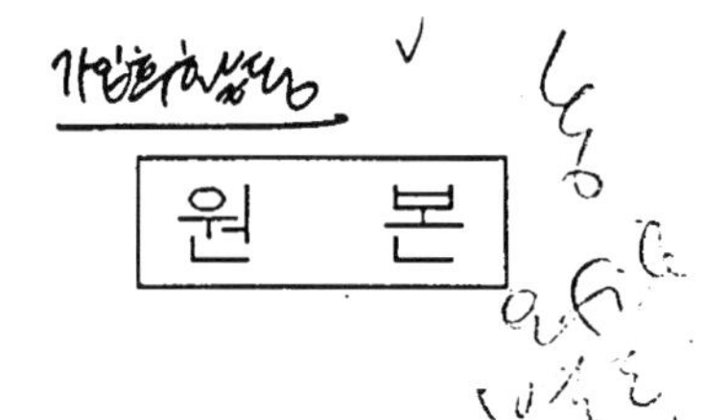

관리 번호	91 -3733

외 무 부

원 본

종 별 : 지 급

번 호 : UNW-1439 일 시 : 91 0601 0100

수 신 : 장관(문동석 국제기구조약국장)

발 신 : 주 유엔 대사

제 목 : 업연(대표부 활동강화)

대:WUN-1567,1557

대호관련 우선 아래사항을 참고바람.

1. 대표부 체제강화

가. 인원

0. 현재의 기능및 지역별 담당관제도를 기능별 과단위로 확대개편, 가입후 각종 유엔회의(연 120 여개 개최)에 임해야 할것임.

0. 특히 지금까지의 정무위주활동에서 환경, 과학, 사회, 경제, 분야등으로활동영역을 넓혀 국익을 반영시킬수 있도록 하여야할것임.

-정무

담당업무:국제안보, 평화유지, 군축, 국제법, 국제정보, 외기권, 지역문제,남북한문제, 유엔재정문제등

최소인원:공사 1, 참사관 3, 서기관 3

-경제

담당업무:국제경제, 환경, 개발, 다국적기업 문제등

최소인원:공사 1, 참사관 2, 서기관 2

-사회

담당업무:인권, 여성, 아동, 마약사회. 문제등

최소인원:참사관 2, 서기관 2

-총무

담당업무:총무, 행정, 외신, 문서, 전산업무

최소인원:참사관 1, 서기관 1, 외신관 3, 행정관 2 (전산관포함)

0. 상기 인원은 향후 대 유엔활동을 원활히 하기위한 최소한의 외무부직원 (대사및

국기국

91.06.01 14:31

외신 2과 통제관 CH

0081

차석대사 제외) 인원수로서 주재관수는 포함치 않고있는바, 과학, 여성,문제등 분야는 관계부처 전문가들의 별도상주도 고려할수 있을것임.

0. 고용원

-현재 청사 고용원 12 명은 공관인원 증가규모에 맞추어 대폭 증원되어야 하는바 , 전문 SPEECH WRITER 1 명, 경제. 사회관계 전문연구원 1 명등 고급두뇌2 명을 포함한 5 명정도의 증원이 긴급함.

나. 예산

0. 현 대표부 기본운영에 필요한 도급경비 예산은 년 40 만불 (상용잡급및 임차료 제외)에 불과, 91 년 상반기 예산은 3 월경 이미 소진된 실태인바, 현 시점에서 최소 50 프로 증액, 아울러 공관인원이 증원될경우, 이에상응하는 예산증액(활동비 포함)이 절실함.

0. 아울러 각종 유엔회의를 COVER 하기 위해서는 일부직원(안보리담당, 외신관등)의 맨하탄 이주가 필요한바, 이경우 주택임차료 (월 5,000 불이상)및 자녀교육수당(1 인당 최소 월 1,500 불)등 제반 경비지원을 고려해야 됨.

2. 시설확충

가. 사무실및 관저

0. 현재 대사관저, 청사 모두 면적및 기능상 많은 문제가 있어 청사이전및 관저이전 매입 모두 추진해야될 실정인바(기보고 주국련 2031-204 91.3.28 , 참조: 기획관리실장 참고요망), 관저후보지로 적절한 건물 구입에는 최소 1,800 만불이 예상되며 , 적절한 규모의 독립청사 구입에는 최소 2,500 만불이 소요될 것으로 보임.

0. 또한 현 대사관저는 내부를 일부수리 (200-300 만불 소요)하여 차석대사용으로, 현 차석대사용 관저는 공사용으로 전환함을 아울러 검토요망함.

나. 차량

0. 현재 당관 공용차는 문서수발용 차량포함 5 대에 불과하여 , 각종행사 활동에 극히 어려움이 많은바, VIP 용 승용차 및 VAN 각 1 대의 증차 필요성이 절실함.

3. 기증품및 민속공연등

가. 기증품

0. 기증품은 회원국이 기증의사를 유엔에 통보하면 사무총장실 산하 UN ARTCOMMITTEE 에서 기증품의 종류, 규모, 위치할 장소등 관련사항을 토의한다고함.

0. 기증품은 박물관 전시품 수준을 희망하고있으나, 각국에서 제공하는 수준은

대부분 그에 미치지 못하고 있다함.

0. 기증품을 일방적으로 결정, 제공하면 유엔으로서도 거절하기가 곤란함으로 일단 받아들이지만 기증품 품목여하에 따라서는 아예 전시되지 않거나 전시에오랜 시일이 소요되는 경우가 많다함.(소련이 기증한 조각동상은 설치합의에 3 년이 걸렸다함.)

0. 그간 비공식적으로 거론된바 있던 88 올림픽때의 대고, 또는 유엔구내 놀이터 시설은 간단히 결정하기 어려운 면들이 있다고 보이므로 기증품 선정문제는 좀더 시간을 두고 검토할 필요가 있다고봄.

나. 민속공연등

0. 최근 신규회원국 가입후 유엔내 민속공연 또는 예술품 전시등 사례는 없었던 것으로 알려져 있는바, 상세 추후 파악되는대로 회보함.

4. 기타

참고로 유엔 분담금 문제도 사전 검토해야될 사항인바, 동건관련 사항은 기보고(주국련 2031-263 ,91.4.18)를 참조바람. 끝

(신기복)

예고:91.12.31. 일반

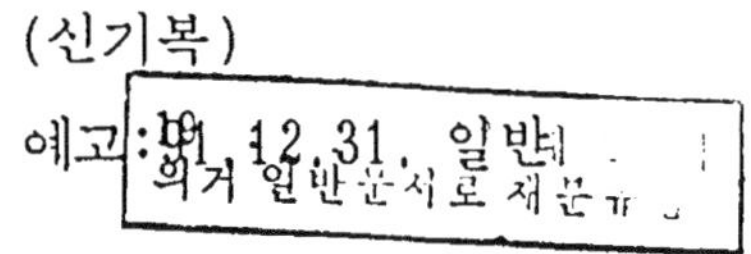

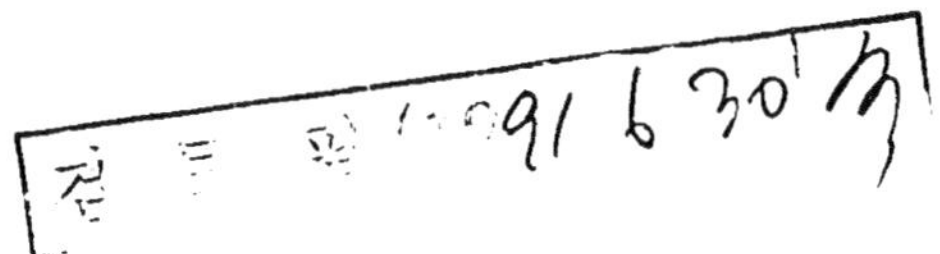

PAGE 3

0083

관리 번호	91 -618

외 무 부

종 별 : 지 급

번 호 : USW-2954 일 시 : 91 0613 2300

수 신 : 장관(기법,미일)

발 신 : 주 미 대사

제 목 : 유엔 관계 국무부 조직

대 WUS-2485

대호 주재국 국무부의 유엔 관계 업무 담당 부서의 조직등에 대해 하기 보고함.

1. 개괄

0 국무부의 유엔 관련 조직은 국제기구국의 일부로 조직되어 있음.

0 국무부의 유엔 관련 조직은 유엔 본부및 미국의 유엔 대표부가 뉴욕에 소재하고 있어 본부와 대표부간 업무 협조가 수월하고 또한 행정적 업무 부담이 타국 외무부 유엔 관계 조직보다는 적다는 이점을 갖고 있으며, 따라서 상대적으로소규모의 본부 조직으로 유엔 관계 업무를 처리하고 있음.

2. 유엔 관계 조직(별전 국제 기구 조직표 참조)

0 국제 기구국에는 1 명의 차관보가 있으며, 동 차관보는 2 명의 보좌관및 1명의 정책 기획관을 두고 있으며, 특별 사업이 있을 경우 특별 사업 담당 보좌관을 설치할수 있음(현재는 아프카니스탄 문제 조정관이 있음)

0 차관보 밑에는 1 명의 수석 부차관보와 2 명의 부차관보가 있고, 각 차관보 밑에는 기능별로 각과가 있음.

0 3 명의 부차관보와는 별도로 차관보 밑에는 유엔 행정담당관(UN SYSTEM ADMINISTRATION)과 국 행정 담당관(EXECUTIVE DIRECTOR)이 있고 그 밑에는 각과를 두고 있음.

3. 유엔 관계 하부 조직내 기능 분장및 인원 현황

가. 수석 부차관보 관할(정무관계)

0 수석 부차관보는 유엔 정무관계일을 담당하며, 그밑에 유엔 정무과와 다자문제 조정과(MULTILATERAL PROGRAM COORDINATION)이 있음.

0 유엔 정무과는 가장 핵심적인 유엔 정무 업무를 담당하고 있으며, 과장 밑에 2

기획실 미주국 국기국

PAGE 1 91.06.14 15:25

외신 2과 통제관 BA

0084

명의 부과장을 두고, 담당직원은 통상 7 명으로 구성됨. 담당직원은 지역별 및 기능별로 소관 업무를 맡고 있음.

0 다자 문제 조정과는 유엔 정무과의 기능을 도와주며(각 관련 지역국과의 업무 협조및 조정 역할)유엔총회 준비, 사무총장 인선등 통상적인 지역, 기능 업무가 아닌 정무 관계일을 담당함(통상 직원 3-4 명)

나. 국제 원조및 전문기구 담당 부차관보 관할

0 동 부차관보는 IPU, IAEA 등 전문기구를 담당하는과, UNDP 등 후진국 개발 사업 분야를 담당하는과, 유엔의 경제 제제문제, 경제국과 업무 협조및 조정 역활등을하는 경제 정책과, 유엔및 유엔 전문기구 사무국등 유엔 조직에 미국인을 충원하는 기능을 하는 유엔 조직 충원과등 4 개과를 관장하고 있음.

0 통상 각과는 과장과 직원 4 명으로 구성되어 있음.

다. 사회 및 인권 문제 담당 부차관보 관할

0 동 부차관보는 인권(UNHRC) 및 여성 문제 담당과, 난민 문제(UNHCR)담당과등 실무 담당 부서와 공보과, 의회 담당과, 국제회의 준비과(미국 유치 국제 회의 준비및 국제회의 참석 국무부 직원에 대한 협조 제공0등 국제 기구국 전체를 위한 기능 부서를 관장함.

0 각과는 통상 과장 및 3-4 명의 담당 직원으로 구성됨.

라. 기타 행정 담당 부서

0 유엔 행정 담당 부서는 대 유엔 예산 문제 담당과와 유엔 조직의 전반적 기능에 대한 평가를 하는 유엔 조직 조정과가 있음.

0 국제 기구국 전체의 행정담당 부서는 행정지원을 담당하는 3 개의 과로 이루어져 있음.

0 상기 행정 담당 부서는 과장및 3-4 명 정도의 직원으로 구성되어 있으며,업무 성격상 상당수 직원이 행정직(CIVIL SERVICE)으로 보해져 있음.

4. 여타국과의 업무 분장 기준

0 국무부 유엔 조직은 여타 국가의 유엔 관계 조직과같이 타부서와의 업무 협조및 조정에 큰 비중을 두고 있으며, 각 부차관보내에 유관부서와의 업무 협조및 조정을 담당하는 부서를 두고 체계적으로 업무 협조 및 조정을 추진함.

0 또한 유엔 관계 업무 담당관은 항상 담당 직원 차원에서 유관부서 담당관과 업무 협조및 조정을 하면, 통상 지역(기능)국 담당관및 정무(경제) 차관실 담당보좌관과

유기적인 업무 협조 체제를 유지하고 있음.

5. 유엔 관련 조직내 인원 배정

0 미국의 공무원 조직은 아국과 달리 하부 조직에 대한 정원 배정을 하지 않고 주어진 시점에서 주어진 인원을 배정하는 식으로 이루어짐(정원 개념 없음)

0 국무부 유엔 조직내 인원은 미국의 대외 정책에서 유엔이 차지하는 비중에 따라 크게 달라져 왔으나, 최근 NEW WORLD ORDER 논의에서 유엔의 역할이 크게 강조됨에 따라 향후 크게 인력이 보강될 전망임.

(대사 현홍주-실장)

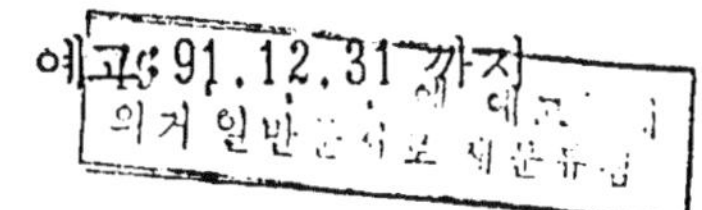
예고: 91.12.31 까지

검 토 필 (1991.6.30.)

PAGE 3

0086

가입후 대책

유엔대표부 인원 보강(안)

(외무부 직원기준)

91. 6. 14.
국제연합과

1. 직 원

담 당 업 무	현 인 원	소요인원	보강인원
1. 공관장	1	1	0
2. 업무총괄(차석대사)	1	1	0
3. 정 무 o 국제안보, 군축, 평화유지, 국제법,국제정보, 외기권,지역문제, 남북한문제, 유엔 재정문제	o 공 사 1 o 참사관 3	o 공 사 1 o 참사관 3 o 서기관 3	o 서기관 3
4. 경 제 o 국제경제, 환경, 개발, 다국적기업 문제등	o 참사관 1 o 서기관 1	o 공 사 1 o 참사관 2 o 서기관 2	o 공 사 1 o 참사관 1 o 서기관 1
5. 사 회 o 인권, 여성, 아동, 마약, 사회문제등	o 참사관 1 o 서기관 1	o 참사관 2 o 서기관 2	o 참사관 1 o 서기관 1
6. 총 무 o 총무, 행정, 외신, 문서, 전산업무	o 서기관 1 o 외신관 2	o 참사관 1 o 서기관 1 o 행정관 1 o 외신관 3 o 전산관 1	o 참사관 1 o 행정관 1 o 외신관 1 o 전산관 1
계	o 공관장 1 o 차석대사 1 o 공 사 1 o 참사관 5 o 서기관 3 o 외신관 2	o 공관장 1 o 차석대사 1 o 공 사 2 o 참사관 8 o 서기관 8 o 행정관 1 o 외신관 3 o 전산관 1	o 공 사 1 o 참사관 3 o 서기관 5 o 행정관 1 o 외신관 1 o 전산관 1
	o 총인원 13	o 총인원 25	o 총인원 12

0087

2. 고용원

o 고용원 현원 : 12명

o 증원 소요 : 최소 5명

- speech writer : 1명

- 경제.사회관계 전문연구원 : 1명

- 기타 고용원 : 3명. 끝.

0088

관리 번호	91 —4082

외 무 부

종 별 :

번 호 : UNW-1761 일 시 : 91 0708 2130

수 신 : 장 관(기재,기예,국연)

발 신 : 주 유엔 대사

제 목 : 공관예산 증액 긴급요청

1. 당관 각종예산은 특히 도급경비경우, 90 년이래 계속 거의 동일한 액수가배정되어 공관운영에 막대한 어려움을 겪어왔는바 (주국련 2031-224 :91.4.11 참조), 유엔가입에 따른 최근의 업무량증대 및 금번 직원증원(3 명)등을 고려할때 현예산으로는 당장의 기본적인 공관운영경비 충당에도 크게 부족한 실정임.

2. 더구나 앞으로 대표부 기능강화에 따른 업무량 폭증을 생각할때 예산상 압박이 더 심각해 질것으로 보이는바, 이런점을 감안, 하반기 배정액과는 별도로금년도 도급경비 및 활동비 예산을 아래와같이 긴급증액, 추가지원하여 주실것으로 강력 건의하오니 적극 반영하여 주시기 바람.(동 증액 예산요구액은 지구촌행사 및 9 월 유엔총회 아국대표단 방문관 관련된 예상 소요경비는 제외한 액수임.)

가. 도급경비 (추가증액:$571,500 불)

1)예산증액 요청개요

가)수용비

증액:$100,000

0. 사유:

-유엔가입에 따른 유엔문서 컴퓨터 관리를 위한 기재임차 (또는 구입)

-인원 증원에 따른 복사기, FAX, 타자기 등 사무기재 임차(또는 구입) 및 각종자료, 간행물, 물품구입

나)공공요금

0. 증액:$80,000

0. 사유

-공관전화 추가설치, 차량및 이동전화 증설

-파우치 및 우편물량증대

기획실 기획실 국기국

PAGE 1

91.07.09 10:53

외신 2과 통제관 BS

0083

다)자산취득비

0. 증액:$170,000

0. 사유

-직원증원에 따른 사무기재 구입 및 노후화 가구교체 ($100,000)

-외빈차 1 대 (링컨:$30,000), 행정용 승용차 ($20,000)및 VAN ($20,000) 각 1 대 추가 구입

라. 제세공과금

0. 증액:$50,000

0. 사유

-관저보험료, 차량보험료 (대당 $5,000) 인상및 차량추가 구입에 따른 보험료 증액

-차석대사 관저에 대한 보험 신규가입

마)차량비

0. 증액:$35,000

0. 사유

-인원증원 및 차량추가 구입에 따른 각종차량 유류대 증액

바)기판비

0. 증액:$20,000

0. 사유

-유엔가입에 따른 각종 대표단 방문증대 관련 제반 지원

사)특판비

0. 증액:$50,000

0. 사유

-유엔가입에 따른 각종 대외활동 증대

아)기타 예산항목 증액

0. 국외여비:$10,000 , 시장비:$50,000 , 연료비:$6,500

0. 사유

-공관강화에 따른 예산소요

2)상기 요청사항중 차량관련, 현재 당관에는 91 WAGON 및 87 OLSSMOBILI 승용차 등 2 대의 차량이 있는바, 특히 87 년형 승용차가 최근 노휴화에 따른 각종문제를

야기, 외빈탑승중 도로상에서 운행이 정지되는 사례가 빈발하는등 안전상의 문제가 발생하고 있어 교체구입이 시급함. 본부 예산사정상 일시불 구입이 어렵다면 3 년정도의 장기임대 (LEASING: 이경우 월임대료 링컨 :$600-650 불, 일반승용차 $400 불선) 도 가능한바, 차량 감가상가등을 고려할때는 장기적인 관점에서 검토할만한 방안으로 사료됨.

3)상기 도급경비 증액요청은 상용잡급및 임차관련 예산은 제외한 것이며, 현재 직원 증원에 따른 당관 사무실 부족으로 청사면적의 추가임차가 불가피한 실정인바, 이에관한 사항은 추가 건의예정임.

(대사 노창희-실장)

예고:91.12.31. 일반
의거 일반문서로 재분류됨

검토필(1991 . 6 . 30.)

PAGE 3

0091

관리 번호	91 -767

외 무 부

종 별 :

번 호 : UNW-1900 일 시 : 91 0723 1930

수 신 : 장관(기재,국연)

발 신 : 주 유엔 대사

제 목 : 도급경비 증액

연:UNW-1761

연호 예산 증액요청중 도급경비관련, 주요항목에 대한 상세내역을 재차 보고하오니, 동경비 증액지원 ($571,500 불)이 급박한 실정임을 고려, 적의 반영되도록 조속 조치하여 주시기 건의함.

1. 수용비

0. 증액:$100,000

0. 사유

-유엔가입에 따른 모든 공용문서, 초청장, 봉투등 신규제작:$20,000

-방대한 유엔문서의 컴퓨터 관리를 위한 기재임차 또는 구입:$10,000

-인원증원에 따른 복사기($6,000 X 2 대), FAX ($4,000), 파기기 ($2,000), 타자기 ($700 X 3 대) 구입 또는 임차

-간행물 구독증가:$5,000

-각종 유엔자료구입:$15,000

-제반 사무용품 및 공관운영 기본 물품구입:$30,000

2. 공공요금

0. 증액:$80,000

0. 사유(예시)

-공관전화 추가설치(대당 $400 X 10 대), 전화회선증설 및 이에따른 사용요금 증가 ($15,000), 차량(대당 $1,000) 및 이동전화(대당 $1,000) 증설

파우치 요금증액:$10,000

-우편요금 증액:$10,000

-FAX 요금 증액:$10,000

기획실 국기국

PAGE 1 91.07.24 10:30

외신 2과 통제관 BS

0092

3. 자산취득비

0. 증액:$170,000

0. 사유

-직원증원관련 사무기재 구입 (책상, 가구등 기본사무기재:1 인당 $5,000 X4 인)

-노후화 가구교체(현재 직원 17 명 대부분이 소파등 기본사무집기 조차 구비치 못하고 있는바 대사제외 15 명에 기본가구 구입 :$30,000)

-회의실 탁자 및 의자 (25 명분) 구입:$20,000

-대사실 응접세트 교체:$10,000

-기타 기본 사무실 집기등 구입$20,000

-외빈차 (링컨:$30,000), 행정용 승용차(FORD LTD:$20,000)및 VAN (DODGEVAN:$20,000)구입

4. 제세공과금

0. 증액:$50,000

0. 사유(예시)

-차석대사 관저 화재보험 등 가입:$11,000

-차량증가에 따른 보험료증액:(대당 $5,000)

-상반기 정기지원 부족액:$8,000

5. 시설장비 유지비

0. 증액:$50,000

0. 사유

-현 청사 회의실은 12 명만 수용가능, 인원증가에 따른 직원수를 수용키 불가하므로 확장수리

6. 차량비

0. 증액:$35,000

0. 사유

-직원증원에 따른 실 유류비지원 및 차량증가에 따른 유류대, 수리비증액

7. 특판비

0. 증액:$50,000

0. 사유

-가입에 따른 각종위원회, 회의활동비 ($15,000), 공관장 활동강화 위한

사교클럽가입비 ($20,000), 각종 화한, 선물비 ($15,000)

8. 기판비

0. 증액:$20,000

0. 사유

-총회 개회후 회원국으로서의 각종대표단 지원 (최소 20 회 예상:20 회 X $500) 및 총회, 각위원회, 각종회의 참석에 따른 특. 야근 식대($10,000) .끝.

(대사 노창희-국장)

예고:91.12.31. 일반

관리 번호	91 -769

외 무 부

종 별 :

번 호 : UNW-1898 일 시 : 91 0723 1930

수 신 : 장 관(기재,국연)

발 신 : 주 유엔 대사

제 목 : 고용원증원

1. 현재 당관내 청사근무 고용원수는 총 12 명인바, 직원수(17 명)및 업무량에 비해 그간 심각한 보조인력의 부족현상을 겪어 왔음.

2. 더구나 향후 유엔가입에 따라 각종 업무가 질적, 양면에서 폭증됨과 아울러 직원수도 크게 늘어나고 있는 상황을 고려할때, 최소한 아래규모의 고용원증원이 절박한 실정이오니, 적극검토, 승인하여 주시기 바람.

가.SPEECH WRITER 및 RESEARCH ASSISTANT 채용

-향후 각종 연설문및 대외문서의 품위및 통일성을 유지케하고 직원업무를 보조할수있는 RESEARCH 능력을 가진 미국인 전문가 각 1 명 채용

-이같은 WRITER 는 영어를 모국어로 하지 않는 일본등 많은 국가의 대표부에서도 전문인력을 고용하고 있는바, 최소한 수준을 가진 인원채용에는 최저 연봉 4 만불 정도 소요됨.

나. 업무보조원 및 운전원 증원

-인원 증원및 업무량 배가에 따른 공관의 제반 활동을 보조할수 있도록 최소한 업무보조원 3, 전산원 1, 타자원 2, 운전원 2 명 (각각 최저 월봉급 $1,500수준)증원이 불가피함. 끝.

(대사 노창희-실장)

예고:91.12.31. 까지

19 . . . 에 예고문에 의거 일반문서로 재분류됨

기획실 국기국

PAGE 1

91.07.24 10:15

외신 2과 통제관 BS

0095

관리 번호	91-4678

외 무 부

종 별 :

번 호 : UNW-2175　　　　　일 시 : 91 0816 1830

수 신 : 장 관(기법,국연)

발 신 : 주 유엔 대사

제 목 : 통일원 주재관 신설의견

대:WUN-2163

1. 대호 아국통일정책홍보, 남북관계와 관련된 사항은 당관의 주요한 고유업무로서 당관에서는 관련업무를 정무.경제. 홍보.정보등의 각분야 담당관이 분담하여 왔는바, 별도 주재관 파견시에는 업무성격상 중복이 불가피하고 대외접촉상 혼선이 없지 않을것이므로 대호 주재관 신설건은 장기적인 관점에서 시간을 두고 신중히 검토함이 바람직할 것으로 사료됨.

2. 참고로 당관은 현재 인원으로도 사무실이 크게 부족하여 일부인원이 사무실 통로에서 집무해야 할 형편이므로 당관 수용능력에도 문제가 있음. 끝.

(대사 노창희-실장)

예고: 91.12.31. 일반

기획실　　국기국

PAGE 1　　　　　91.08.17 09:37

외신 2과 통제관 BS

0096

관리번호	91-4333

외 무 부

종 별 :

번 호 : UNW-2261 일 시 : 91 0823 1830

수 신 : 장 관(기법,국연,해서,기정)

발 신 : 주 유엔 대사

제 목 : 공보관 증원요청

1. 당지 북한대표부는 앞으로 유엔을 무대로 불가침선언, 한반도 비핵지대화등 그들의 선전활동을 강화하고 N.Y.T. , C.F.R, 컬럼비아대학등 미국 언론.학술. 문화계 침투를위한 활발한 접촉활동이 예상됨.

2. 또한 아국 유엔가입으로 유엔상주 특파원등 대규모 뉴욕주재 외신(500 여명)의 관심증대로 인간 각종문의, 회견등 접촉이 쇄도하고 있으며 아국특파원 증파등으로 취재활동 지원을 위한 유엔공보실 등 유엔기구과의 협조업무도 폭증할 것으로 전망됨.

3. 이와관련 당관 공보관의 증가되는 업무처리와 북한의 선전책동에 대한 사전정보 파악및 적시대응등 효율적인 홍보활동강화를 위해 공보관 1 인의 증원이 시급한것으로 판단되니 조속 선처하여 주시기 건의함. 끝

(대사 노창희-차관)

예고:91.12.31. 일반

기획실 국기국 안기부 공보처

PAGE 1

91.08.24 08:02

외신 2과 통제관 BS

0097

관리 번호	91 -4714

분류번호	보존기간

발 신 전 보

유엔가입문제 관련문

번 호 : WUN-2244 910820 1605 FH 종별 :

수 신 : 주 유엔 대사. 총영사 (국연)

발 신 : 장 관

제 목 : Speech Writer 채용

대 : UNW-1898

대호, 유엔가입 계기 주요행사 및 제46차 총회 토의참여와 관련, 귀관의 각종연설문 및 주요문서 작성을 보조하기 위한 Speech Writer 의 채용이 시급하다고 판단되니 ~~을 검토코자 하니~~ 소요예산과 채용대상자 기확보시 인적사항도 보고바람. 끝.

(장 관)

예 고 : 1991.12.31. 일반

보안 통제	

앙 고 재	91년 8월 19일	과	기안자 성명		과 장	심의관	국 장		차 관	장 관

외신과통제

0098

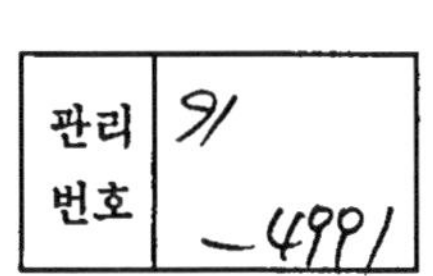
관리 번호 91-4991

원 본

외 무 부

종 별 :

번 호 : UNW-2719　　　　일 시 : 91 09161 200

수 신 : 장관(국연,기재)

발 신 : 주 유엔 대사

제 목 : SPEECH WRITER 채용

연:UNW-2467

46 차 유엔총회가 9.17 개회되는 만큼 연호 SPEECH WRITER 임시 채용건 지급 송인 바람. 끝

(대사 노창희-국장)

~~예고:91.12.31 일반~~

19 . . . 에 의거 일반문서로 재분류

국기국　기획실

PAGE 1　　　91.09.17 07:42

외신 2과 통제관 BW

0093

관리 번호	91 -5022

원 본

외 무 부

종 별 : 지 급

번 호 : UNW-2783 일 시 : 91 0918 0200

수 신 : 장관대리(연일 이규형 과장)

발 신 : 주 유엔(국기국장 문동석)

제 목 : 업연

대:WUN-2914

1. 수고가 많겠음.

2. 대표부 SPEECH WRITER 건은 장관님께도 말씀드렸으니, 예산과 관계없이 "채용하라" 는 지시를 차관까지 결재 맡아 타전하기 바람.

3. 이디오피아 외상면담건은 일단 자료를 준비하는 것이 좋겠음. 끝.

예고:91.12.31. 일반

의거 일반문서로 재분류됨

국기국 차관

PAGE 1

91.09.18 15:40

외신 2과 통제관 BN

0100

관리 번호	91 -5040

	분류번호	보존기간

발 신 전 보

번 호 : WUN-3060 910919 1835 FN 종별 : 지 급

수 신 : 주 유엔 대사.총영사

발 신 : 장 관 대리 (연일)

제 목 : Speech Writer 채용 허가

대 : UNW-2719

1. 대호, Speech Writer 임시채용을 승인함.

2. 동인의 이력서 파편 송부바람. 끝.

(차 관 유종하)

예고 ~~91.12.31.일반~~

19 . . . 에 예고문에 의거 일반문서로 재분류됨

보 안 통 제	

앙 고 재	91 년 9 월 18 일	과	기안자 성 명		과 장	심의관	국 장	1차관보	차 관	장 관
							전결		전결	

외신과통제

0101

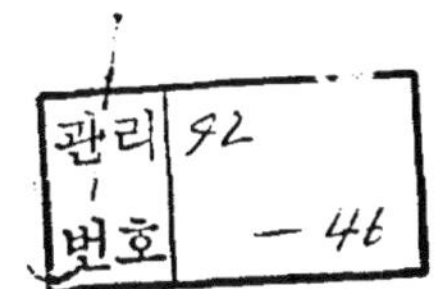

	분류번호	보존기간

발 신 전 보

번 호 : WUN-0094 920114 1754 ED 종별 : ~~암호송신~~

수 신 : 주 유엔 대사. ~~총영사~~ (김중재 참사관)

발 신 : 장 관 (이규형 배)

제 목 : 업 연

대 : UNW-0064 (92.1.8, Speech Writer 보수, 처우)

1. 대호건, 기획관리실측과 협의한바, 예산 및 타공관과의 형평문제로 어려움이 있음. 동건 재협의코자 하니 동인의 status를 Speech Writer 대신 유엔문제 Consultant로 공전 재건의하여 주시기 바람. (이력서등은 별도 불필요하며 담당업무등을 전문적 시각에서 기술·타전바람.)

2. 또한 차관님께서 관심을 갖고 계시는바, 서울에서 관심을 표해 둘만한 행정적 사안(고용원, 예산, 관저, 청사, 차량등 관련)을 차제에 정리하여 소제앞 업연으로 ~~건의해~~ 알려 또는 서한 주시기 바람. 끝.

예고: 1992.6.30. 일반

보안통제	

앙고재	92년 1월 14일	UN1과	기안자 성명		과 장		국 장		차 관	장 관

외신과통제

0102

4. 주유엔 대표부 현판 제작

0103

심의관

협조문용지

분류기호 문서번호	국연 2031-275	(2179-80)	결재	담 당	과 장	국 장
시행일자	1991. 7. 12.			(서명)	(서명)	(서명)
수 신	기획관리실장	발신	국제기구조약국장			(서명)
제 목	재외공관 현판 제작					

유엔가입에 따라 주유엔대표부 현판이 새로 필요하오니 아래 문안에 따라 재외공관용 표준 현판(동판)을 제작, 주유엔대표부로 송부해 주시기 바랍니다.

- 아 래 -

주국제연합 대한민국 대표부

Permanent Mission of the Republic of Korea to the United Nations. 끝.

0104

심의관

협조문용지

분류기호 문서번호	국연 2031-276	(2179-80)	결재	담 당	과 장	국 장
시행일자	1991. 7. 12.			(서명)	(서명)	(서명)
수 신	기획관리실장	발신	국제기구조약국장			(서명)
제 목	유엔대표부 명칭					

주유엔 대표부는 유엔가입에 따라 현재의 동 대표부 정식명칭을 변경하는 문제(예컨대 "주국제연합 대표부"에서 "국제연합 상주대표부"로)에 대하여 검토해 줄것을 요청해 왔는 바, 이에대한 귀실 의견을 회보하여 주시기 바랍니다. 끝.

0105

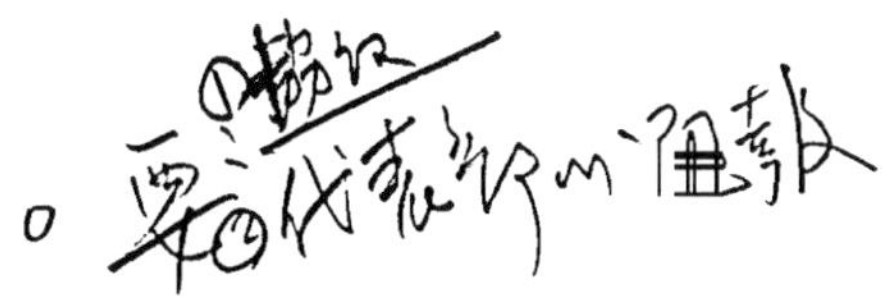

분류기호 문서번호	기법2031- 207	협 조 문 용 지 (720-2946)	결재	담 당	담당관	조정관
시행일자	1991. 7. 20.					
수 신	국제기구조약국장	발 신 기획관리실장 (서명)				
제 목	국제연합 대한민국 대표부 명칭					

대 : 국연 2031 - 276

1. 대한민국 재외공관 설치법 제1조는 재외공관의 종류를 대사관, 공사관, 대표부, 총영사관 및 영사관으로 규정하고 있으며, 외무부와 그 소속기관 직제(별표5 참조)에도 주국제연합 대한민국 대표부를 포함한 4개의 국제기구 주재 상주공관을 대표부로 표시하고 있습니다.

2. 또한 관행상으로도 '대표부'가 상주공관을 의미하는 것으로 볼수 있는 바, 상기 법규정과 관행에 비추어 주국제연합 대한민국 대표부의 명칭은 현행대로 두는 것이 좋다고 사료됩니다. 끝.

0106

27506

기안용지

분류기호 문서번호	국연 2031-	(전화:)	시행상 특별취급	
보존기간	영구·준영구. 10. 5. 3. 1	장	관	
수신처 보존기간				
시행일자	1991. 7. 25.			

보조기관	국 장	전결	협조기관		문서통제 1991. 7. 26 통제관
	심의관				
	과 장				
기안책임자		송영완			발송인 발송 1991. 7. 외무부

경 유 수 신 참 조	주유엔대사	발신명의	
제 목	대표부 명칭 검토		

대 : UNW-1803

대호, 하기사유로 귀대표부 국문 명칭을 기존대로 주국제연합 대한민국 대표부로 하는 것이 바람직하다고 판단됨을 참고하시기 바랍니다.

- 아 래 -

1. 재외공관 설치법 제1조는 재외공관의 종류를 대사관, 공사관, 대표부, 총영사관 및 영사관으로 규정하고 있으며, 외무부와 그 소속기관 직제에도 주국제연합

/계속/

0107

(2)

대한민국 대표부를 포함한 4개의 국제기구 주재 상주

공관을 대표부로 표시하고 있음.

2. 또한 관행상으로도 "대표부"가 상주공관을 의미하는

것으로 볼 수 있음. 끝.

0108

관리 번호	91 -4285

	분류번호	보존기간

발 신 전 보

WUN-2299 910822 1733 FN

번 호 : 종별 :

수 신 : 주 유엔 대사.총영사

발 신 : 장 관 (국연)

제 목 : 대표부 현판 송부

대 : UNW-1803

대호, 귀대표부 현판을 금파편 송부한 바, 9.17(화) 아국의 유엔가입 승인후 대표부에서 본직 참석하에 현판식을 거행토록 할수 있도록 준비바람. 끝.

(국제기구조약국장 문동석)

예고 : 91.12.31 일반

보안 통제	

앙 고 재	91년 8월 22일	유엔과	기안자 성명		과 장	심의관	국 장		차 관	장 관
			송영완							

외신과통제

0103

5. 유엔사무국 게양 태극기 제작

0110

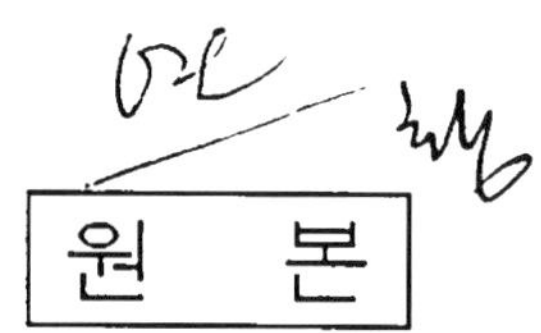

원 본

외 무 부

종 별 :

번 호 : UNW-1945 일 시 : 91 0726 1830

수 신 : 장 관(국연)

발 신 : 주 유엔 대사

제 목 : 국기제작 자료

1. 유엔사무국측은 아국 유엔가입 관련, 아국 국기제작 방법을 문의하여 왔는바, 태국기 제작방법을 최대한 상세히 설명한 영문자료, 당관에 송부바람.

2. 참고로 유엔은 회원국 국기가 필요한 경우에는 자체제작을 하므로 아측에서 태국기를 특별히 제작, 지원할 필요는 없다고함. 끝.

(대사 노창희-국장)

국기국

PAGE 1

91.07.27 09:38 WG

외신 1과 통제관

0111

	분류번호	보존기간

발 신 전 보

번 호 : WUN-2009 910729 1713 DQ 종별 :

수 신 : 주 유엔 대사. 총영사

발 신 : 장 관 (국연)

제 목 : 국기제작자료

대 : UNW-1945

1. 대호, 총무처에서 작성한 영문자료(책자발간용으로 작성한 초안)를 별첨 FAX 송부함.

2. 총무처 관계관에 의하면 만약 태극의 빨강 및 파랑색에 대한 구체적인 질의가 있을 경우에는 진홍색과 아청색이라고 답할수 밖에 없다 함.

첨부 : FAX. 끝. (WUNF-0120)

(국제기구조약국장 문동석)

보안 통제	

앙 고 재	91년 7월 29일	연 과	기안자 성명		과 장	심의관	국 장		차 관	장 관

외신과통제

0112

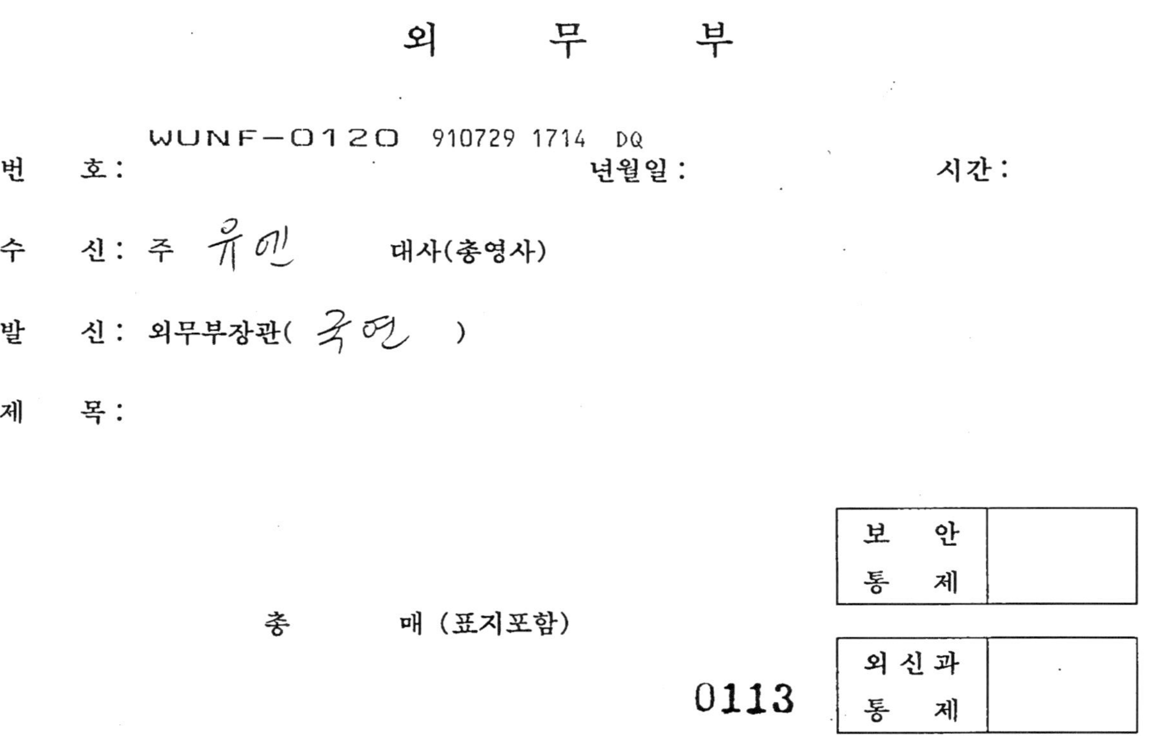

외 무 부

WUNF-0120 910729 1714 DQ

번 호: 년월일: 시간:

수 신: 주 유엔 대사(총영사)

발 신: 외무부장관(국연)

제 목:

총 매 (표지포함)

보 안 통 제	

외신과 통 제	

0113

*Specifications of the Korean National Flag

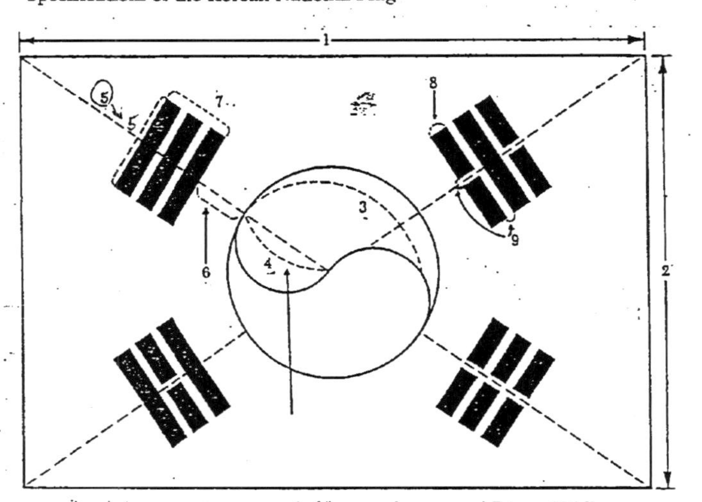

1. Length: Diameter × 3
2. Width: Diameter × 2
3. Diameter (Width × ½)
4. Radius (Width × ¼)
5. Diameter × ½ (Width × ¼)
6. Diameter × ¼ (Width × 1/8)
7. Diameter × ⅓ (Width × 1/6)
8. Diameter × ⅓ × ¼ (Width × 1/24)
9. Diameter × ⅓ × ¼ × ½ (Width × 1/48)

* Taegŭk circle COLOR Identification

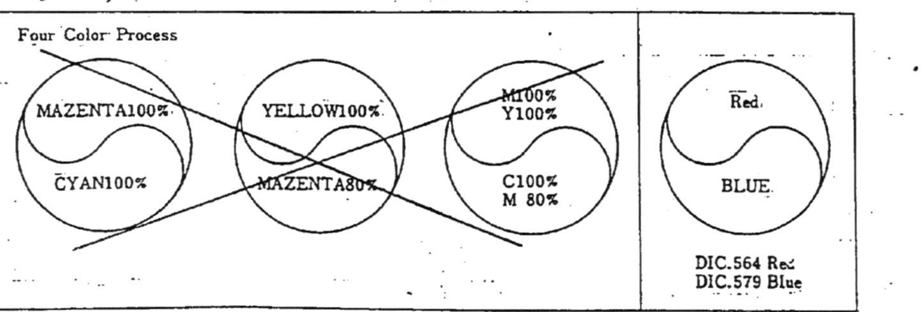

④

4. Standard Sizes of the Flag

The Korean National Flag is produced in sizes specified in the table below. As need arises, the Flag may also be made in other sizes, but always in the same proportion, three by two.

Size No.	Sizes (Length × Width)
S	Over 300cm × over 200cm
1	270cm × 180cm
2	210cm × 140cm
3	150cm × 100cm
4	105cm × 70cm
5	90cm × 60cm
6	60cm × 40cm
7	45cm × 30cm
8	30cm × 20cm

*Sizes S and 1 are for flagpoles in front of, or on top of, buildings. Sizes 3, 4 and 5 are for use at the outside of private homes.

5. The National Flag in Black and White

When the Korean National Flag is printed in black and white, the field and the upper section of the circle are left in white or the same color as the background material, and the lower section of the circle and the trigrams are printed in black.

0114

①

2. Meaning of the Flag

The Korean National Flag, as the symbol of the dignity and pride of the Republic of Korea, is named "T'aegŭkki."
The name was derived from the circle in the center, called *t'aegŭk.*

> The circle is divided equally and in perfect balance. The red upper section represents the *yang* and the blue lower section stands for the *yin*. The two symbolize the great cosmic forces, contrasting but achieving perfect harmony and balance according to the traditional Oriental philosophy.

The *t'aegŭk* circle* stands for creation and development by expressing the everlasting principle of formation and transitions of all beings in the greater universe through the harmonious interplays of all pairs of opposites, such as light and dark, male and female, positive and negative, etc.

The four trigrams surrounding the circle, represents the detailed conditions of ceaseless interactions between the *yin* and *yang* undergoing changes in quality and growth in volume.

The white ground of the Korean National Flag symbolizes the purity of the Korean people who, from time immemorial, have loved to wear white clothes, and their peace-loving spirit.

The Korean National Flag, as a whole, highlights the ideal of the Korean people aspiring to advance forever along with the great universe.

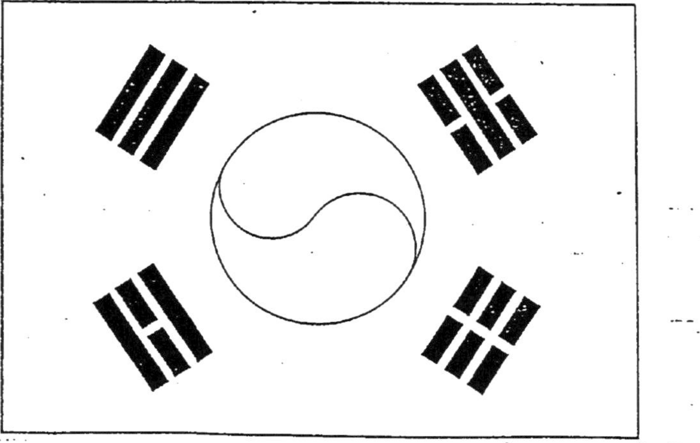

DESIGN OF THE KOREAN NATIONAL FLAG

②

3. How to Draw the Flag

The Korean National Flag is in the proportion three by two, and has a white field. Its design consists of a *t'aegŭk* circle in the center and four trigrams, one between the circle and each of the four corners of the flag.

The circle is placed exactly in the center of the flag, and its diameter is one-half of the width of the flag. The "S" line dividing the circle begins at the point where the diagonal line crossing the flag from its left top to the right bottom first meets the circumference of the circle, and ends at the point precisely opposed to it. Each curve of the "S" character should form half of the circumference of a smaller circle, the diameter of which is exactly half of that of the big circle. The upper section of the divided circle is red, and the lower section is blue.

The four trigrams are placed between the circle and the four corners of the flag so as to surround the circle in the center—*kŏn* (☰) at the upper left, *kon* (☷) at the lower right, *kam* (☵) at the upper right, and *i* (☲) at the lower left. The length of the trigrams should be half of the diameter of the circle, or one-fourth of the width of the flag. Their width is one-third of the diameter of the circle, or one-sixth of the width of the flag. Distance between the circle and the trigrams is one-fourth of the diameter of the circle, or one-eighth of the width of the flag, and the centers of the trigrams should coincide with the diagonal lines crossing the flag. The width of each bar forming the trigrams is one-fourth of the width of the trigrams, or 1/24 of the width of the flag. Distance between the bars is one-half of the width of the bars, or 1/48 of the width of the flag. The bars are all black.

* Four Trigrams Color Identification

All Black

Kŏn　　Kon　　Kam　　i

0115

태 극 기

—제작·게양및관리요령—

총무처 / 1989

0116

생활속에 함께하는 태극기로

국기는 나라의 상징이며 민족의 전통과 이상이 담겨져 있으므로 우리나라 국기인 태극기를 소중히 하고 태극기에 대한 예절을 지켜 존엄성을 높이는 일은 바로 국가와 민족에 대한 자존심을 지키는 일이며, 국민으로서 마땅히 하여야 할 도리라 하겠습니다.

이번에 정부에서는 태극기에 대한 존엄성을 높이는 일과 함께 국민이 일상생활속에서 자연스럽게 태극기를 가까이 하고 친근감을 느낄 수 있도록 하기 위하여 태극기의 게양 및 관리에 관한 사항중 일부를 자율화하였습니다.

우리 모두가 태극기를 아끼고 사랑하는 것이 바로 나라와 겨레를 위하는 길이라는 인식을 함께 하여 우리의 이웃에서부터 태극기 사랑운동을 펌으로써 선진문화국민으로서의 자긍심을 높여 나아가야 하겠습니다.

1989. 3. 10

총 무 처 장 관

0117

국기제정약사

○1882. 8.	(음)	박영효가 수신사로 일본에 갔을 때 최초로 사용하였다 함.
○1883. 1.	(음)	고종 20년 태극 4괘가 그려진 기를 국기로 사용토록 왕명으로 공포하였으나, 정확한 제작·사용방법 등을 규정하지 않음.
○1949. 1.		대통령 특명으로 "국기시정위원회"를 구성한 이후 수차에 걸친 회의 끝에 현행 국기를 확정.
○1949. 10.		"국기제작방법"공포 (문교부고시 제2호)
○1950. 1.		"국기게양방법"공포(국무원고시 제8호)
○1966. 4.		"국기게양방법에관한 건" 공포 (대통령고시 제2호)
○1984. 2.		"대한민국 국기에관한 규정" 제정 공포(대통령령 제11361호)
○1987. 4.		"대한민국 국기에관한 규정" 개정 (대통령령 제12148호) ※ 국기강하시각 변경
○1989. 3.		"대한민국 국기에관한 규정"개정 (대통령령 제12642호) ※국기의 실내게양방법 등 개선

0118

대한민국국기

○태 극 기 : 우리나라의 상징인 국기로서 태극 도형을 중심으로 구성하였기 때문에 태극기라 함.

○깃 면 : 길이(가로)와 너비(세로)를 3 : 2의 비례로 하며 흰색바탕으로 함.

○태극도형 : 태극원안의 상단부는 빨강색(진홍색)으로 하고, 하단부는 파랑색(아청색)으로 하며 빨강색부분은 양(陽), 파랑색부분은 음(陰)이라고 함.

○4괘 (卦) : ☰(건)·☷(곤)·☵(감)·☲(이)로 구성하며 모두 검정색으로 함.

0113

태극기에 담긴 뜻

○흰색 바탕은 백의민족의 순결성과 전통적으로 평화를 애호하는 민족성을 표상하고

○태극도형과 4괘는 음(陰)과 양(陽)의 상호 작용에 의하여 우주만물이 생성·발전하는 대자연의 이치를 나타낸다고 할 수 있음.

○따라서 태극기는 민족의 이상과 우주관이 담겨진 나라의 상징으로서 이는 우주와 더불어 길이 길이 발전하고자 하는 우리 겨레의 이상을 집약·표상하고 있다고 하겠음.

0120

차 례

Ⅰ. 국기에 대한 예절

□ 국기에 대한 경의표시 방법

▷ 오른손을 펴서 왼편 가슴에 대면서 국기를 주목함.

▷ 군인·경찰 등 제복을 입은 사람은 국기를 향하여 거수경례

※ 평복에 모자를 쓴 사람은 오른손으로 모자를 벗어 왼편 가슴에 대면서 국기를 주목하며, 모자를 벗기 곤란한 경우에는 모자를 쓴 채로 오른손을 펴서 왼편 가슴에 대면서 국기를 주목함.

□ 국기에 대한 맹세

▷ 맹세문

나는 자랑스런 태극기 앞에 조국과 민족의 무궁한 영광을 위하여 몸과 마음을 바쳐 충성을 다할 것을 굳게 다짐합니다.

▷ 맹세를 하여야 하는 경우

- 각종 의식에서 "국기에 대한 경례"를 할 때
- 국기의 게양식 및 강하식

※ 게양식 등에서 애국가 주악을 생략하는 경우는 맹세 생략

0122

Ⅱ. 국기의 제작방법

□ 깃면의 구성

▷ 국기의 깃면은 그 바탕을 흰색으로 하고 그 깃면의 길이(가로)와 너비(세로)는 3 : 2의 비례로 함.

▷ 국기의 깃면은 태극도형(太極圖形)과 4괘(卦)로 구성함.

□ 태극도형의 작도

▷ 깃면의 두 대각선이 서로 교차하는 점을 중심으로 깃면 너비의 2분의 1을 지름으로 하는 원을 그림

▷ 두 대각선중 왼쪽 윗모서리에서 오른쪽 아랫모서리로 그어진 대각선상의 원의 지름을 2등분하여, 왼쪽부분에 원의 지름의 2분의 1 (깃면너비의 4분의 1)을 지름으로 하는 반원을 대각선의 아랫부분에 그리고, 그 오른쪽 부분에 원의 지름의 2분의 1(깃면 너비의 4분의 1)을 지름으로 하는 반원을 대각선의 윗 부분에 그림

▷ 반원으로 연결된 원의 윗부분은 빨강색(진홍색)으로, 그 아랫부분은 파랑색(아청색)으로 함.

□괘의 작도

▷ 4괘는 건(乾 :☰)·곤(坤 :☷)·감(坎 : ☵)·이(離 :☲)로 하되, 깃면의 왼쪽 윗부분에 건을, 오른쪽 아랫부분에 곤을, 오른쪽 윗부분에 감을, 왼쪽 아랫부분에 이를 각각 배열함.

▷ 괘의 길이는 태극지름의 2분의 1(깃면 너비의 4분의 1)로 하고, 괘의 너비는 태극지름의 3분의 1(깃면 너비의 6분의 1)로 하며, 괘와 태극사이는 태극지름의 4분의 1(깃면너비의 8분의 1)을 띄움

▷ 괘의 길이 중심을 깃면의 두 대각선상에 두되, 그 길이는 두 대각선과 각각 직각을 이루도록 함.

▷ 괘의 구성부분은 효(爻)로 하되, 그 효의 너비는 괘너비의 4분의 1(깃면 너비의 24분의 1)로 하고, 효와 효사이 및 끊어진 효의 사이는 효너비의 2분의 1 (깃면 너비의 48분의 1) 로 함.

▷ 괘는 검정색으로 함.

- 8 -

0124

※ 깃면의 제작방법

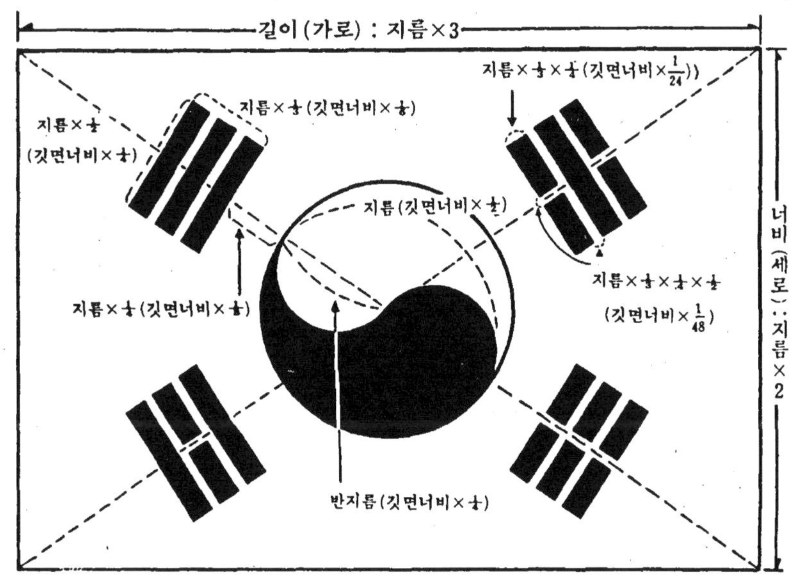

※ 국기의 호수별 표준규격은 다음과 같으며 필요한 경우에는 깃면의 길이와 너비의 비례 (3 : 2)를 지켜 그 크기를 달리 제작할 수 있음.

□ 국기의 호수별 표준규격

호수	깃면의 표준규격 (길이×너비)	비 고
특호	300cm이상×200cm이상	• 건물게양대용 : 특호·1호 및 2호 • 일반가정의 옥외게양용 : 3호·4호 및 5호
1 호	270cm×180cm	
2 호	210cm×140cm	
3 호	150cm×100cm	
4 호	105cm× 70cm	
5 호	90cm× 60cm	
6 호	60cm× 40cm	
7 호	45cm× 30cm	
8 호	30cm× 20cm	

□ 국기의 검정색 표시

▷ 깃면을 흑백으로만 인쇄하여야 하는 부득이한 경우에는

- 깃면의 바탕과 태극의 윗부분은 인쇄물등의 바탕색으로
- 태극의 아랫부분과 4괘(卦)는 검정색으로 나타냄.

□ 금실의 부착

▷ 금실을 부착할 수 있는 경우는 다음과 같으며, 이때의 금실의 폭은 깃면 너비의 1/7 ~ 1/8로 하고 깃대와 닿는 부분에는 달지 아니함.

- 국가를 대표하는 사람의 승용차에 다는 경우
- 의전용으로 쓰이는 경우
- 실내에서 게양하는 경우
- 각종 국제회의시에 탁상용으로 쓰이는 경우

□깃봉 및 깃대의 제작

▷깃 봉

- 깃봉의 모양은 꽃받침 5편이 있는 둥근 형태의 무궁화 봉오리 모양임.
- 깃봉의 색은 전부 황금색으로 함.
- 깃봉의 지름은 국기 깃면 너비의 1/10로 함.

▷깃 대

- 깃대는 대나무·쇠 등 견고한 재질로 만듬.
- 깃대의 색은 대나무색 또는 대나무색과 비슷한 색으로 함.

  *깃대의 색을 흰색으로 할 수 있는 경우

  ┌건물 등에 고정된 깃대
  ├의전용 및 탁상용 깃대
  └실내게양용 깃대

- 12 -

0128

※ 깃봉의 제작방법

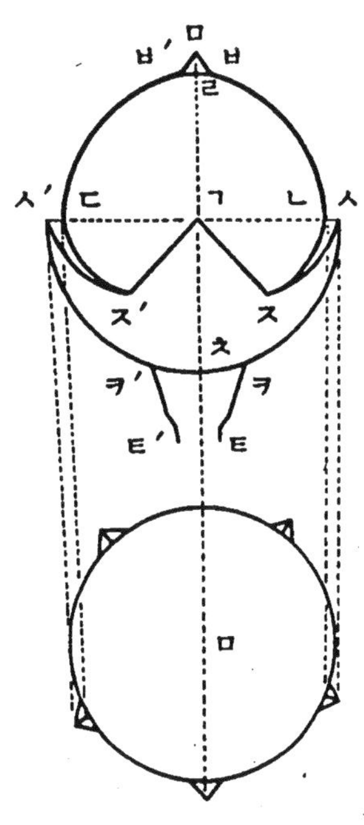

- ㄴㄷ은 깃봉의 지름임 (깃면 너비의 1/10)
- ㄱㄴ : ㄱㄹ=7 : 8로 하여 ㄴㄹㄷ의 반타원을 이룸
- ㄹㅁ · ㄹㅂ은 각 ㄱㄹ의 1/8
- 꽃받침 첨단의 부피는 ㄱㄴ의 1/10
- ㄱ을 중심으로 하여 ㅅㅊㅅ′의 반원을 그려 꽃받침을 이룸
- ㅈ은 ㄱㅊ, ㄱㅅ의 각 중간점에서 수평 수직된 선의 교차점임.
- ㅊㅋ은 ㄱㄴ의 1/3
- ㅋㅌ은 ㄱㄴ의 2/5

0123

Ⅲ. 국기의 게양

□국기를 전국적으로 게양하는 날

▷경 축 일

- 1월 1일
- 3월 1일 (3·1절)
- 7월 17일 (제헌절)
- 8월 15일 (광복절)
- 10월 1일 (국군의 날)
- 10월 3일 (개천절)
- 10월 9일 (한글날)

▷조의를 표하는 날(조기게양일)

- 6월 6일 (현충일)
- 국장기간
- 국민장일

▷기타 정부가 따로 지정하는 날

□연중 국기를 게양하여야 하는 기관

▷국가와 지방자치단체 및 공공단체의 청사

▷각급 학교

- 14 -

0130

□국기의 게양 및 강하시각

▷ 비 또는 눈이 내리지 않는 날의 낮동안 게양함.

▷ 국기의 게양 및 강하를 전국적으로 통일하기 위하여 정한 시각은 다음과 같음.

('87. 5. 10시행)

기 간	게양시각	강하시각
3월~10월	07 : 00	18 : 00
11월~다음해 2월	07 : 00	17 : 00

※ 비 또는 눈이 오거나 다시 개거나 하는 때에는 일기에 따라 수시로 강하 또는 게양함.

▷ 재외공관의 국기게양 및 강하시각은 주재국의 관례에 따름.

□국기의 게양식 및 강하식

▷ 대상기관 : 연중 국기를 게양하여야 하는 기관

0131

▷ 식의 거행방법

- 애국가주악 (국기에 대한 맹세 포함)은 자체 방송(녹음) 시설을 이용하되 주악시간과 게양·강하시간이 일치되도록 함.
- 애국가주악은 건물안과 경내에서 들을 수 있도록 함.
- 일기변동으로 정해진 시간외에 게양 · 강하할 때에는 식을 생략함.
- 국기게양식의 경우에는 근무자 등이 없는 시간이므로 애국가 주악(국기에 대한 맹세 포함)을 생략할 수 있음.

▷ 국기와 다른 기의 게양 · 강하순서

- 국기와 다른 기를 게양할 때에는 국기와 다른 기를 동시에 게양하거나 먼저 국기를 게양한 후 다른 기를 게양하여야 하며, 강하할 때에는 국기와 다른 기를 동시에 강하하거나, 국기보다 다른 기를 먼저 강하하여야 함.

0132

▷ 게양식 및 강하식 때의 경의표시 방법

• 건물 밖에 있는 사람

  - 국기를 볼 수 있는 사람은 국기를 향하여 경례

  - 주악만을 들을 수 있는 사람은 그 방향을 향하여 차렷자세

• 건물안에 있는 사람은 국기를 향하여 선 채로 차렷자세

• 경내의 차량에 탑승하고 있는 사람은 차량을 정지하고 앉은 채 차렷자세

□ 국기의 게양방법

▷ 경축일 및 평일의 게양방법은 아래 그림과 같이 깃봉과 깃면의 사이를 떼지 아니함.

- 17 -

0133

▷ 조의를 표하는 현충일·국장기간·국민장 등의 날에는 아래 그림과 같이 깃봉과 깃면의 사이를 깃면 너비만큼 내려 담.

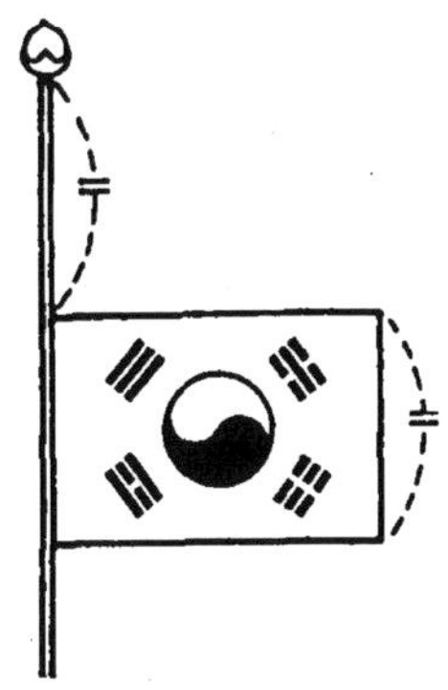

▷ 경축행사 등의 경우에 국기 깃면을 늘여서 다는 방법은 아래 그림과 같이 깃면 길이의 흰부분만을 길게 하여 이괘(離卦)가 왼쪽 위로 오도록 함.

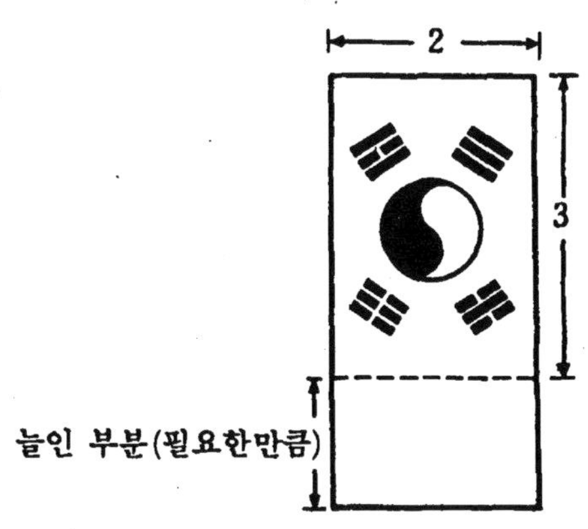

□게양대의 설치

▷상업지역 안에서 폭 15미터 이상의 도로에 연한 2층이상의 건축물

- 옥상의 전면 중앙 또는 현관의 차양시설에는 7미터이상, 2~3층건물은 5미터이상
- 전면지상에는 10미터이상

※ 건축법시행령 제60조 참조

▷주　　택

- 건물의 미관상 알맞는 높이로 게양대를 고정 설치하거나 조립식(이동식) 깃대를 꽂는 시설을 설치
- 집밖에서 바라본 설치장소

┌단독주택 : 대문의 왼쪽
└공동주택 : 앞쪽 베란다의 왼쪽

▷2개이상의 게양대를 설치할 경우, 게양대와 게양대 사이는 게양하는 깃면의 길이보다 넓게 하여야 함.

- 19 -

0135

□국기의 게양위치

— 집이나 건물의 밖에서 바라다 본 위치 —

▷ 옥외게양

• 일반가정의 경우

*단독주택(대문 왼쪽에 게양)

*공동주택(앞쪽 베란다의 왼쪽에 게양)

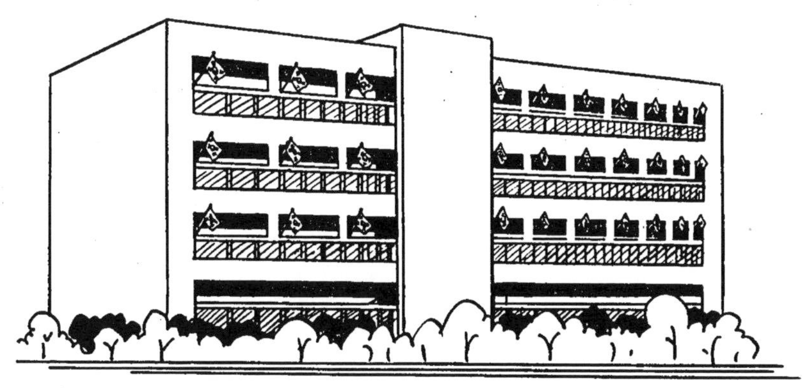

0136

• 건물의 경우

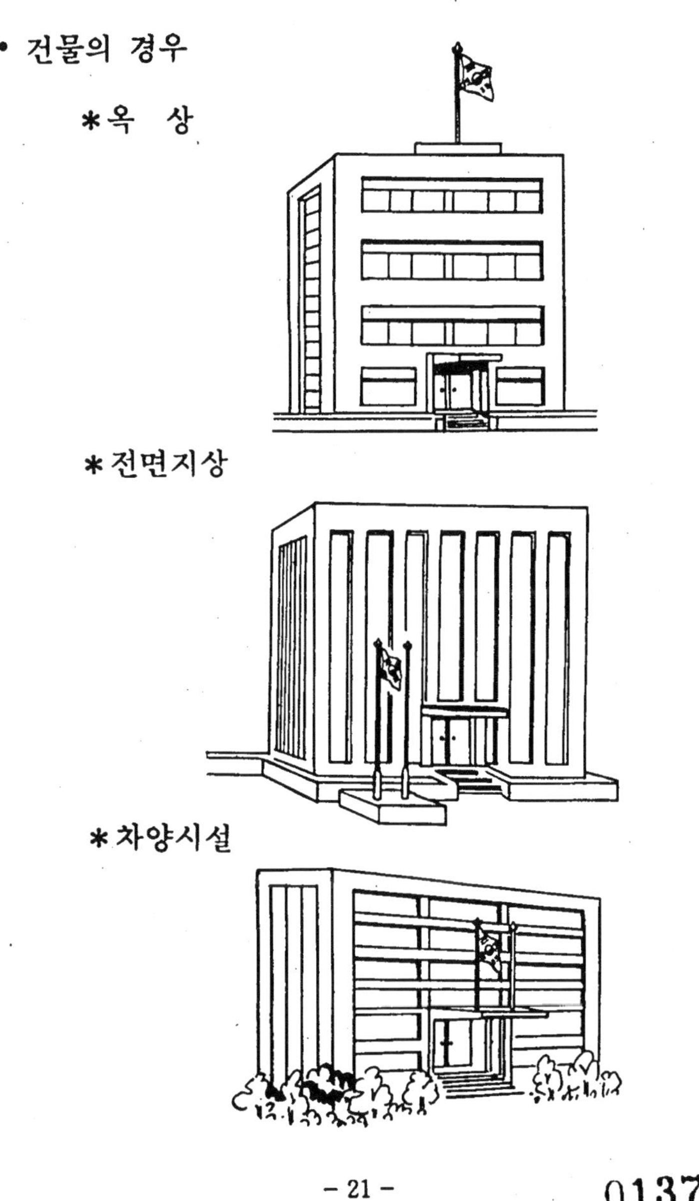

- 21 -

0137

▷ 옥내 게양

• 사무실 등에서는 탁상용 기 또는 실내게양용 기(깃봉·깃대 포함)를 비치하든가 깃면만을 벽에 게시하는 방법중 실내환경에 맞게 국기의 크기 및 게양위치를 선택함.

• 회의장 · 강당 등에 국기를 깃대에 달아서 세워놓거나 게시할 때에는 전면의 중앙 또는 왼쪽에 국기가 위치하도록 함.

▷ 차량의 경우

• 각종 차량에는 전면을 밖에서 보아 왼쪽에 국기를 게양함.

▷ 국기와 다른 기를 함께 게양하는 경우

• 국기와 다른 기를 게양할 때에는 게양하는 기의 수가 홀수인 경우와 짝수인 경우로 구분하여 다음 그림과 같이 위치하도록 함.

- 22 -

0138

(홀수인 경우)

(짝수인 경우)

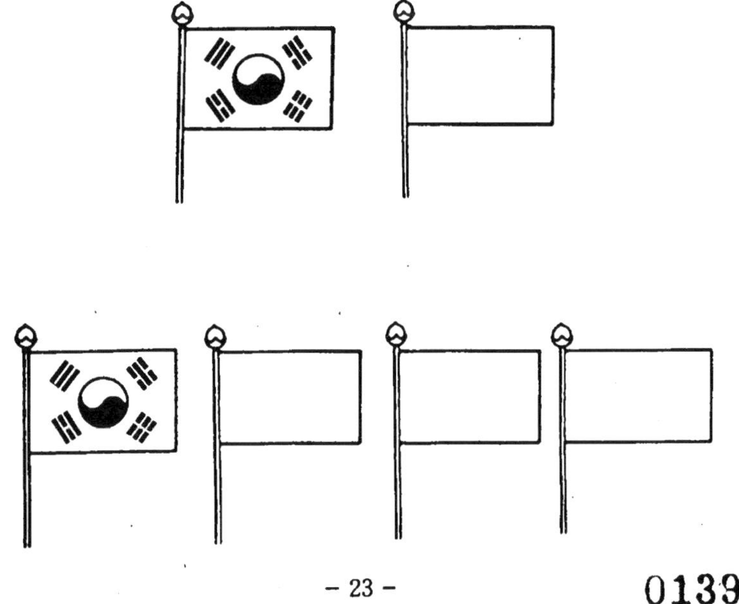

- 23 -

0139

□국기와 외국기의 게양

▷ 우리나라를 승인한 나라의 국기에 한하여 게양하는 것이 원칙임.

▷ 미수교국 국기게양

미수교국 국기를 게양할 필요가 있는 경우 사전에 총무처장관의 협의를 거쳐 게양할 수 있음.

▷ 국기와 외국기를 함께 게양할 경우에는 그 크기 및 높이가 같아야 함.

▷ 국기와 외국기를 함께 게양할 때에는 국기를 가장 윗자리에 게양하고 외국기의 게양순위는 외국 국가명칭의 알파벳 순서에 따르되, 게양하는 기의 수가 홀수인 경우와 짝수인 경우로 구분하여 아래 그림과 같이 게양함.

(홀수인 경우)

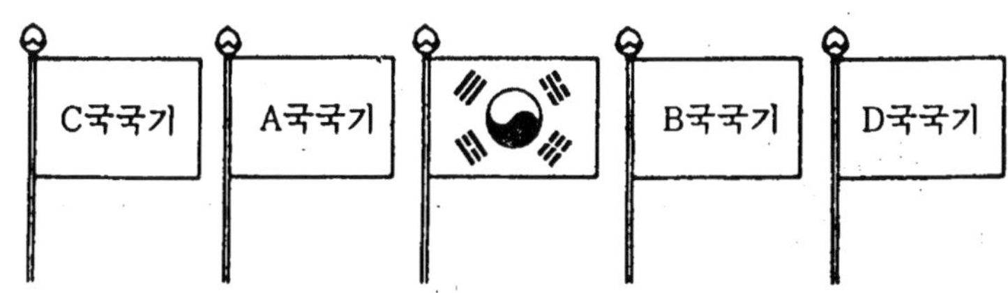

0140

(짝수인 경우)

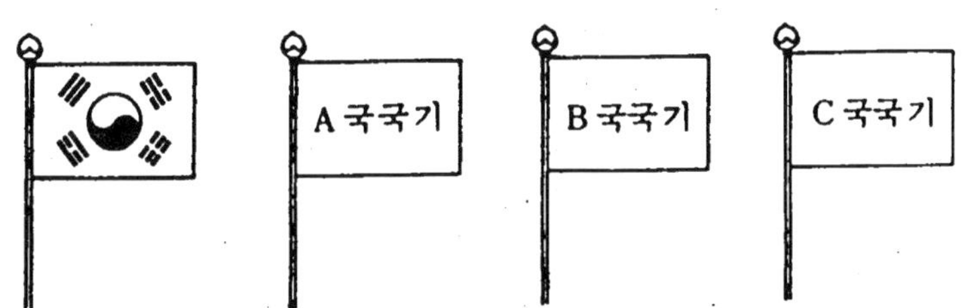

▷ 국기와 외국기를 교차시켜 게양하는 방법은 아래 그림과 같이 밖에서 보아 국기의 깃면이 왼쪽에 오도록 하고 국기깃대가 외국기의 깃대 앞쪽으로 오도록 함.

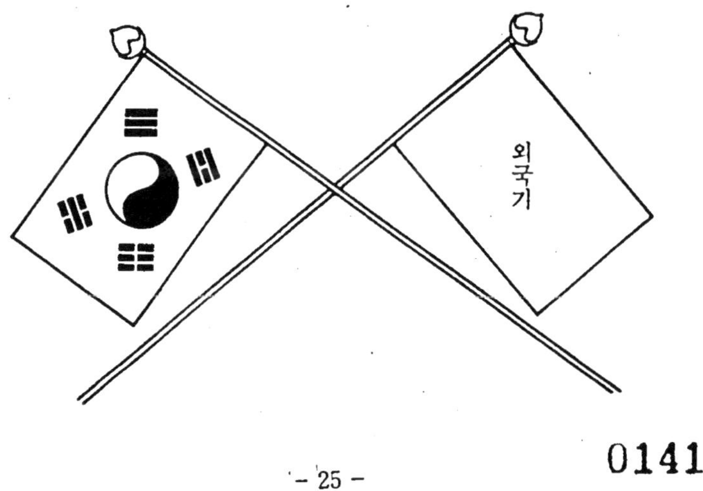

0141

Ⅳ. 국기의 관리

□ 국기의 세탁 사용

▷ 국기가 훼손된 때에는 이를 방치하거나 다른 용도에 사용하지 말고 깨끗하게 소각하여야 함.

▷ 때가 묻었거나 구겨진 경우에는 이를 세탁하거나 다려서 다시 사용할 수 있음.

□ 수기의 관리

▷ 여러사람이 모이는 집회 등 각종 행사에서 수기(手旗)를 사용할 경우에는 행사주최측은 수기의 집중관리를 통하여 행사후 국기가 함부로 버려지는 사례가 없도록 함.

□ 영구에 덮는 국기의 관리

▷ 영구(靈柩)에 국기를 덮을 때에는 영구의 덮개를 위에서 바로 내려다보아 덮개의 윗부분 오른쪽에 건괘(乾卦)부분이, 왼쪽에 이괘(離卦)부분이 오도록 함.

▷ 이때에 국기 깃면이 땅에 닿지 않도록 하여야 하며, 국기는 영구와 함께 매장할 수 없음.

0142

국기관련법규

○ 대한민국 국기에관한 규정

국기의 제작·게양 및 관리 등에관한사항을 규정

- 대통령령 제11361호로 제정('84. 2. 24)
- 대통령령 제12148호로 개정('87. 4. 29)
- 대통령령 제12642호로 개정('89. 3. 10)

○ 건축법시행령 (제60조)

국기게양대 설치에 관한 사항을 규정

○ 상표법 (제 9 조)

國旗·國章 등은 상표로 등록할 수 없음.

○ 국기에 관한 벌칙

- 형법 제105조 (國旗·國章의 冒瀆)
- 형법 제106조 (國旗·國章의 誹議)
- 형법 제109조 (외국의 國旗·國章의 冒瀆)

태 극 기

– 제작·게양 및 관리요령 –

1989. 9 . 10. 발행

편집 : 총무처 의정과

(720 – 4335～6)

발행 : 총 무 처

(비매품)

0144

發行人 金炳琯
編輯人 權五琦
印刷人 金琓熙
論說主幹 李埰柱
編輯局長 洪仁根
서울鍾路區世宗路139㊉110-715
電話案內 721-7114
編輯局 721-7241
廣告局 721-7755
購讀申請 配達事故 721-7575
出版局 文化센터 781-0114
購讀料 月定 5,000원 1部 200원
本報는 新聞倫理綱領 및 그 實踐要綱을 遵守한다.

한반도統一 새기틀 마련

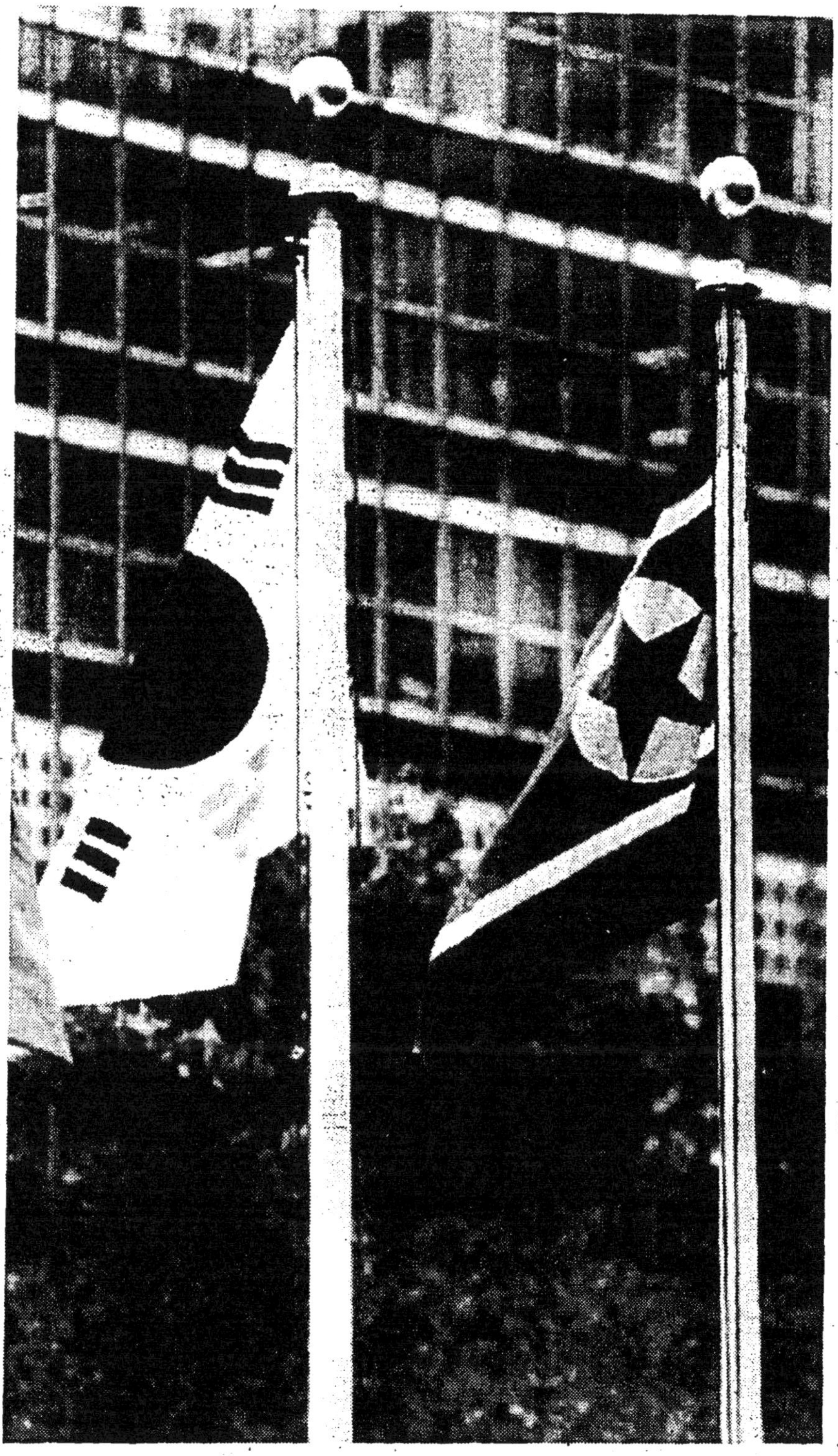

나란히 오른 南北韓旗 大韓民國의 태극기와 조선민주주의인민공화국의 인공기가 18일 오전7시(韓國時間) 뉴욕 유엔본부앞 회원국 국기 게양대에 올려졌다. <유엔본부AP聯>

오늘의 紙面

유엔加入안
國政감사
國有地임
경찰銃에

0145

연일

총 무 처

의 정 01600-2126 736-4494 1991. 9. 24.

수 신 외무부장관

참 조 국제기구국장

제 목 사실확인 조사 의뢰

우리나라의 유엔 가입에 따라 뉴욕 유엔본부 앞 회원국 국기게양대에 게양된 태극기가 잘못 제작되었다는 여론이 있는 바, 사실 여부를 확인하여 그 결과를 통보하여 주시고, 시정할 사항이 있으면 조속히 개선·조치하여 주시기 바랍니다. 끝.

총 무 처 장

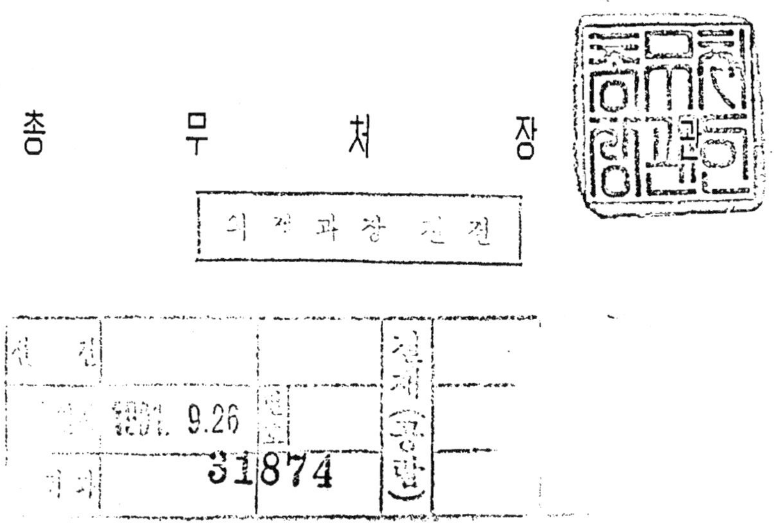

의정과장 전결

선 전			처리과	
접수	1991. 9.26			
처리	31874			

0146

분류번호	보존기간

발 신 전 보

WUN-3260 910926 1559 FH

번 호 :

종별 :

수 신 : 주 유엔 대사. 총영사

발 신 : 장 관 (연일)

제 목 : 태극기제작 오류확인

연 : WUNF - 0120

1. 총무처는 태극기제작과 관련, 괘의 구성부분인 효의 넓이를 괘너비의 4분의 1(깃면너비의 24분의 1)로 하고, 효와 효사이 및 끊어진 효의 사이를 효너비의 2분의 1(깃면너비의 48분의 1)로 하여야 하나 9.17. 국기 게양식시 사용된 유엔제작 태극기는 괘의 너비와 효와 효사이의 너비가 동일한 것으로 보여진다고 지적하여 왔음.

2. 동건관련, 태극기 제작상의 오류여부를 확인(국내 TV 및 신문에 나타난 바로는 오류여부가 분명치 않음)하고, 사무국이 연호 태극기 제작에 관한 설명서대로 태극기을 제작치 않았을경우 동 사유가 사무국내 국기 제작에 관한 별도 지침이 있기때문인지 여부 및 특별한 사유가 없이 단순한 제작상의 오류일 경우 태극기를 새로 제작, 게양토록 조치하고 결과 보고바람.

끝.

~~(국장)~~

(국제기구조약국장대리 금정호)

보 안 통 제	

앙 고 재	91년 9월 24일	과	기안자 성명		과 장	심의관	국 장		차 관	장 관

외신과통제

0147

발 신 전 보

분류번호	보존기간

번 호 : WUN-3483 911008 1832 ED 종별 : 지급

수 신 : 주 유엔 대사. 총영사

발 신 : 장 관 (연일)

제 목 : 태극기 제작오류확인

연 : WUN - 3260

1. 연호, 태극기 제작오류여부 지급확인 회보바람.

2. 동건관련, 신문보도(동아, 10.6자) 내용 별첨 FAX송부함.

첨부 : FAX - 끝.

WUNF-184

(국제기구국장 문동석)

보안 통제	

앙 고 재	91년 10월 8일	과	기안자 성명		과 장	심의관	국 장		차 관	장 관
							전결			

외신과통제

0148

외 무 부

WUNF-0184 911008 1832 ED 21

번 호 :

수 신 : 주 UN 대사 (총영사)

발 신 : 외무부장관(연일)

제 목 : 태극기 제작오류 확인

총 2 매 (표지포함)

0149

東亞日報

1991. 10. 6. 日, 14면

유엔게양 太極旗 잘못 제작됐다

卦구성 爻사이폭 틀려…외무부 조사착수

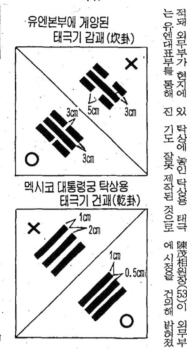

지난달 17일(이하 현지 시간)미국 뉴욕의 유엔본부앞 국기게양대에 북한의 인공기옆에 게양된 태극기가 잘못 제작된것으로 지적돼 외무부가 현지에 있는 유엔대표부를 통해 진상조사에 나섰다.

이와 함께 지난달 25일 盧泰愚대통령과 멕시코 살리나스대통령과의 정상회담때 멕시코 대통령궁의 탁상에 놓인 탁상용 태극기도 잘못 제작된 것으로 밝혀졌다.

이같은 사실은 지난 20여년 동안 태극기의 올바른 제작및 게양을 위해 힘써온 한국국기선양연구원 陳茂相원장(53)이 외무부에 시정을 건의해 밝혀졌다.

陳원장은 『로이터통신을 통해 타전돼 국내외 신문등에 보도된 유엔본부앞 태극기 사진을 살펴본 결과 괘(卦)를 구성하는 효(爻)의 폭과 효사이의 간격이 잘못돼있음을 확인했다』고 말했다.

현재 태극기작도법을 규정한 대통령령(제11361, 12148호)에는 「효와 효 사이의 간격은 효폭의 2분의1로 함」이라고 돼있다.

그러나 이번 유엔본부국기게양식 사진에 나온 태극기의 감괘(坎卦·태극기 우측상단 괘)에 그려진 효와 효사이를 사진에 찍힌 상태에서 실측한결과 효사이는 3㎝와 5㎝로 서로 달랐다.

멕시코 대통령궁의 탁상용 태극기의 경우는 효너비가 1㎝이므로 효와효사이가 규정상 0.5㎝가 되어야 하는데도 사이가 모두 규정의 네배인 2㎝씩으로 실측되는등 우스꽝스러운 모양으로 제작돼 있다.

陳씨는 이같은 사실을 최근 외무부와 총무처에 알려주었으며 외무부는 유엔대표부에 연락, 태극기의 제작상태를 확인중이다.

외무부는 유엔본부에 게양된 태극기는 국내에서 제작해 보낸 것이 아니라 유엔본부가자체제작한것이며 멕시코대통령궁의 탁상용 태극기도 멕시코정부가 제작해 사용중인것이라고 밝혔다.

외무부의 한 관계자는 『유엔본부 사무국으로부터 태극기 제작방법을 알려달라는 요청이 와 총무처로부터 영문으로 된 제작서를 받아 건네 주었다』면서 『태극기가 유엔에서 제작돼 게양된후 제대로 제작됐는지 여부는 현지에서 어느누구도 확인해 보지않았을 것』이라고 말했다.

한편 陳원장은 『태극기는 나라의 상징이자 4천만의 얼굴이라 할 만큼 중요한 것이어서 대통령령으로 제작방법을 규정하고 있다』면서 『그런데도 현지 대사관이나 유엔대표부, 대통령을 수행한 그많은 공직자들이 역사적인 유엔본부의 태극기게양식에 가서 제나라 국기가 제대로 만들어졌는지조차 확인해보지도 않고 있었다는 것은 부끄러운 일』이라고 지적했다. 〈趙誠夏기자〉

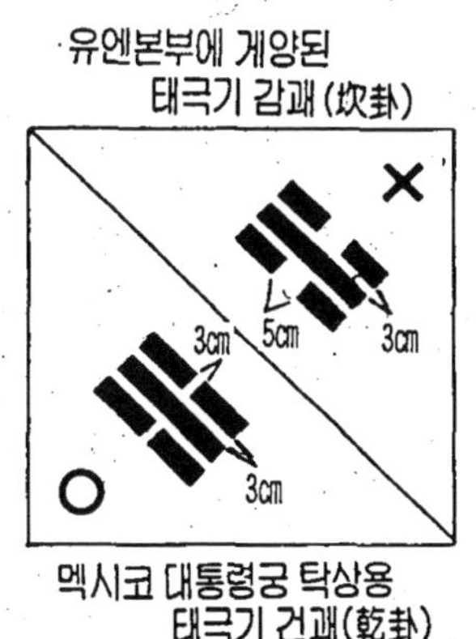

유엔본부에 게양된 태극기 감괘(坎卦)

멕시코 대통령궁 탁상용 태극기 건괘(乾卦)

1㎝ 2㎝ 1㎝ 0.5㎝

0150

원 본

외 무 부

종 별 :

번 호 : UNW-3241 일 시 : 91 1008 1600

수 신 : 장 관 (연일)

발 신 : 주 유엔 대사

제 목 : 태극기 제작 오류 확인

대: UNW-3483,3260

1. 대호건 유엔 국기제작 담당관인 유엔경비실 MR. CAUFIELD 를 면담, 현재 게양된 태극기를 직접 점검한바, 효와 효사이의 간격은 효너비의 2분의 1로 되었으나, 끊어진효의 사이는 대호 지적대로 규격보다 넓은 간격으로 제작되어 있음을 확인하고, 즉시 이의 시정을 요청하였음.

2.동인은 한국을 포함한 신규회원국의 국기를 급히 제작하는 과정에서 이와같은 오류가 발생하였음을 시인하고, 태극기를 다시 제작, 게양하겠다고 한바, 추후 확인 보고 예정임.동인은 또한 제네바 및 비엔나 유엔사무소에 기발송한 태극기도 새로 제작하는 태극기로 교체하겠다고 하였음. 끝

(대사 노창희-국장)

국기국

PAGE 1 91.10.09 09:17 WG

외신 1과 통제관

0151

분류기호 문서번호	감사 01254- 363	협 조 문 용 지 (720-2315)	결 재			
시행일자	1991. 10. 11					
수 신	국제기구국장	발 신	감 사 관 (서명)			
제 목	민원서류 송부 (마대복)					

1991. 10. 10 자로 총무처로 부터 이송된 별첨 민원서류는 귀국 소관사항으로 사료되어 송부하오니 필요한 조치를 취하여 주시고 그 결과를 우리실에도 통보하여 주시기 바랍니다.

첨 부 : 1. 총무처 공문 사본 1부.

2. 민원서류 사본 1부. 끝.

0152

1505 - 8 일 (1)
85. 9. 9 승인 "내가아낀 종이 한장 늘어나는 나라살림" 190mm×268mm(인쇄용지 2급 60g/m²)
가 40-41 1987. 11. 26.

'91.10
605

총 무 처

의 정 01254-2181 736-4494 1991. 10. .

수 신 수신처참조

제 목 민원서류 이첩

우리처에 접수된 별점 민원서류를 이첩하오니 귀부 관련사항을 검토한 후 조치하여 주시기 바랍니다.

첨부 : 민원서류사본 1부. 끝.

총 무 처 장 관

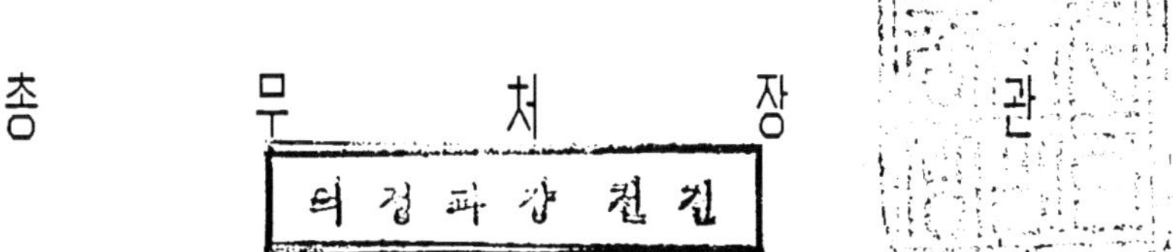

수신처 외무부, 국방부.

33506

0153

총 무 처

의 정 01254-218/ 736-4494 1991. 10. 8.

수 신 서울시 구로구 구로2동 390-42 마 대 복 귀하

제 목 민원회신

1. 귀하께서 우리처에 제출하신 "정규격 국기사용" 건의에 대한 회신입니다.

2. 우리처에서는 귀하께서도 아시다시피 각종매체를 통하여 올바른 규격의 국기 제작방법을 지속적으로 홍보하고 있으나 아직도 일부기관에서는 국기의 제작 및 게양관리를 소홀히 하는 사례가 있는 바, 귀하께서 지적하신 사항을 외무부, 국방부 등에 사실 확인 후 시정할 사항이 있으면 개선·조치토록 하겠사오니 그리 아시기 바랍니다. 귀댁내 건강과 행운이 깃들길 빕니다. 끝.

총 무 처 장

0154

정직 · 질서 · 창조

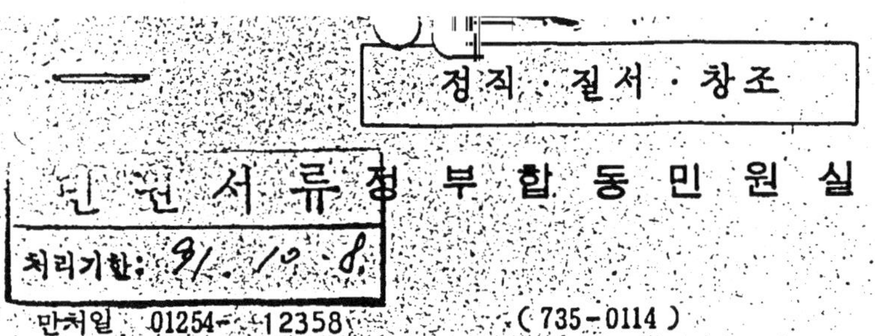

민원서류 처리기한: 91. 10. 8.

정 부 합 동 민 원 실

민처일 01254-12358 (735-0114)　　　1991. 9. 25. (5년)

수 신 총무처장관

참 조 의정국장

제 목 민원사안 처리요청

1991. 9. 25. 당실에 접수된 별첨 민원사안은 " 규격에 맞는 태극기를 사용하여 달라는 " 내용인 바, 이는 귀(부·처·실·청·시·도·국)에서 직접 처리함이 타당하다고 판단되어 정부합동민원실운영규정 제10조 제2항에 의거, 처리 요청하오니 민원사무처리규정 등 관계규정이 정하는 바에 따라 조사·처리하시고 그 결과를 민원인에게 회신하여 주시기 바랍니다.

첨 부 민원서류 1부. 끝.

선결	과장	(서명)	결재(공람)		
접수일시	1991. 9. 30	번호 14208			
처리과	이주열	-		사무관	(서명)

정 부 합 동 민 원 실 장

0155

공보관실 담당자 귀하

우리나라의 UN가입을 다 함께 축하 합니다.
UN본부에 태극기 게양을 보며 한없이 기뻐하고 박수를 보냈습니다.
그러나 게양된 태극기가 규격에 틀린 국기였을 보았을때 착잡한 심정으로 이글을 올립니다.

◎ 틀린부분은 효와 효사이의 넓이 입니다.
국기 규격을 보면 효는 1푼으로 하고 효와 효사이는 반푼(0.5푼)으로 한다로 되어 있습니다.
UN본부에 게양된 태극기는 효와 효사이가 1푼으로 되어 있으니 한눈에 보아서도 틀렸음을 알수 있습니다.
시정을 요합니다.

◎ L.A시 언덕에 우정의 종각 앞에 게양된 태극도 위와 같이 잘못 제작된 태극기로 게양 되었음을 금번 8월에 확인 하였습니다.
그런 종류의 태극기는 1948년 우리나라 국회에서 제정 공포되기 전의 태극기 규격입니다

◎ 한미 국방부 장관 연례 회의시 양국 국방장관이 국기 경례를 할때도 위와 같은 잘못된 태극기 였습니다

그 원인을 알고 보니까 일본에서 제작하여 세계 각국에 배포된 만국기 책자에 우리 태극기가 잘못 되어 있기 때문에 그 만국기 책자를 보고

0156

제작할 경우엔 틀린 태극기로 제작 되는 것으로 알고 있습니다.
올바른 태극기 제작과 더불어 우선 위의 몇가지 시정을 바랍니다. 거듭 부탁을 드립니다.

1991. 9. 18

마 대 복 드림

연락전화 858-5281

＊규격에 맞지 않는 태극기

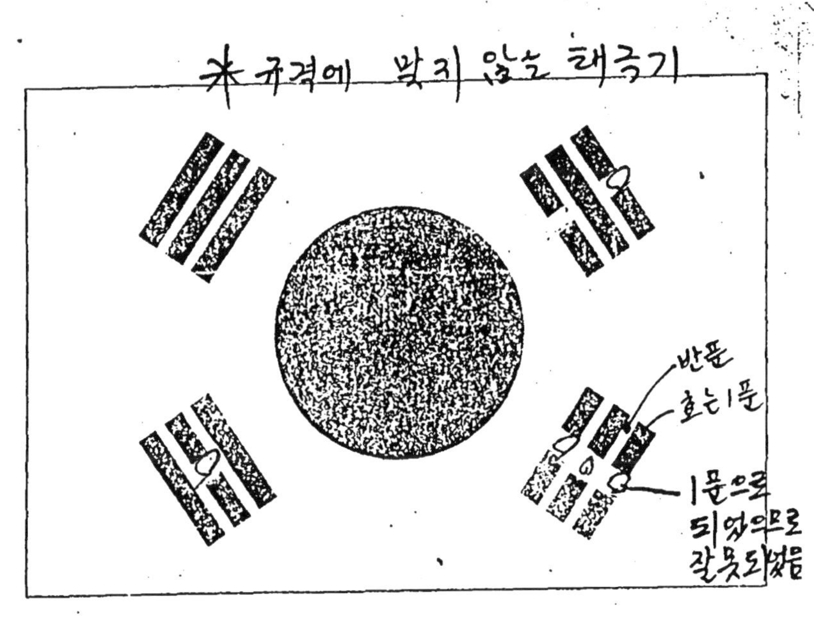

0157

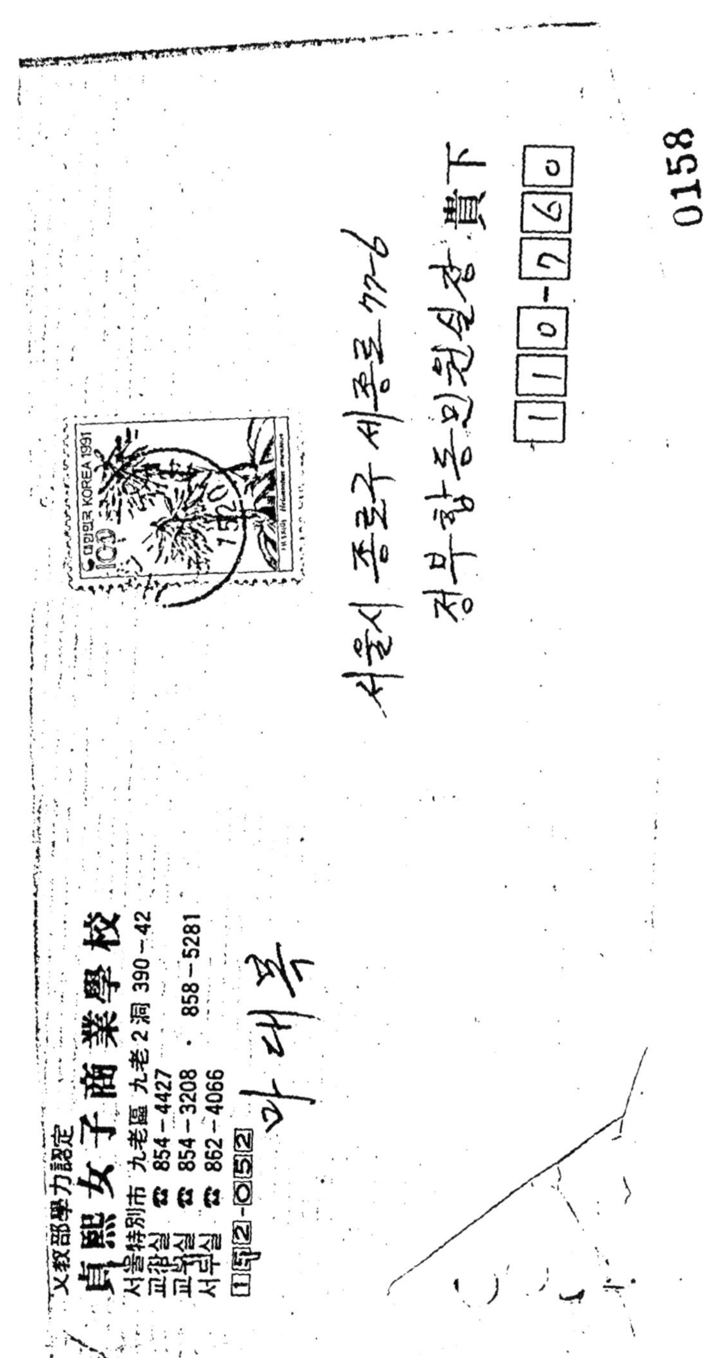

文敎部學力認定
貞熙女子商業學校
서울特別市 九老區 九老2洞 390-42
교장실 ☎ 854-4427
교무실 ☎ 854-3208 · 858-5281
서무실 ☎ 862-4066
152-052

박태주

서울시 종로구 세종로 77-6
정무장관실장 貴下
110-760

0158

심의관 (서명)

협조문용지

분류기호 문서번호	연일 2031-469	(2179-80)	결재	담 당	과 장	국 장
시행일자	1991. 10. 19.			(서명)	(서명)	(서명)
수 신	감 사 관	발신	국제기구국장			(서명)
제 목	민원서류 (마대복)					

대 : 감사 01254-363

1. 대호, 유엔본부에 게양된 태극기는 당국이 송부한 태극기 제작 설명서를 기초로 하여 유엔이 자체 제작한 것인바, 동 제작상의 오류를 기지적, 시정조치중에 있음을 알려드립니다. (주유엔대사의 관련보고 전문 별첨)

2. LA의 우정의 종각앞에 게양된 태극기 및 한미 국방부장관 연례회의시 게양된 태극기 문제는 당국소관 사항이 아님을 알려드립니다.

첨 부 : 1. 주유엔대사 보고전문 1부.

2. 민원서류 사본 1부. 끝.

0159

발 신 전 보

분류번호	보존기간

번 호 : WUN-0371 930205 1729 DS 종별 :

수 신 : 주 유엔 대사. 총영사

발 신 : 장 관 (연일)

제 목 : 태극기 시정 확인

연 : WUN-3260

대 : UNW-3241

92.12월 현재 잘못제작된 태극기가 유엔본부 회원국 국기게양대에 계속 게양되고 있다는 민원을 접수한바, 대호건 유엔사무국측의 시정조치여부를 확인 보고바람.

(국제기구국장 금정호)

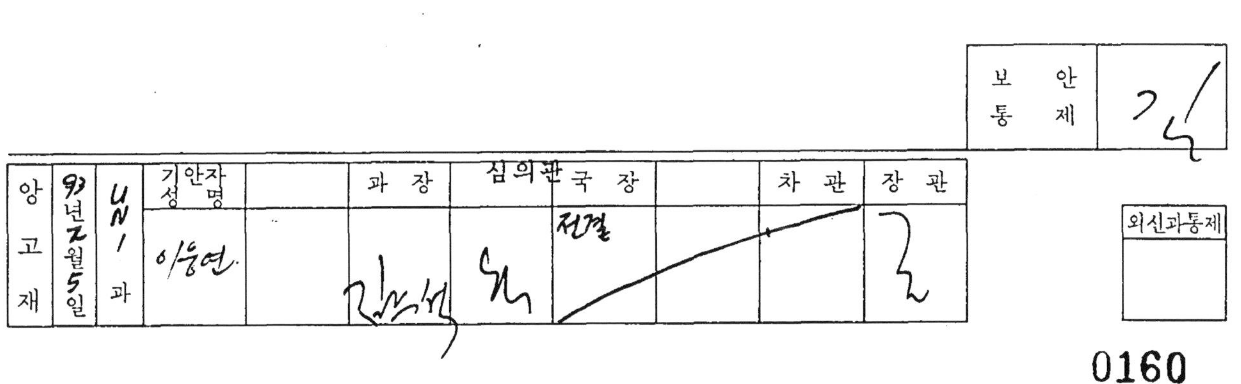

보안통제	

앙고재	93년 2월 5일	UN1과	기안자 성명		과 장	심의관	국 장		차 관	장 관
			이동연				전결			

외신과통제

0160

원 본

외 무 부

종 별 :

번 호 : UNW-0327 일 시 : 93 0208 1900

수 신 : 장 관(연일)

발 신 : 주 유엔 대사

제 목 : 태극기 시정 확인

대: WUN-0371

연: UNW-3241

1. 2.8 대호관련 유엔사무국 국기관계 담당관인 MR. CAUFIELD 를 면담하고 태극기를 직접 점검한 바, 연호 태극기 제작 오류사항이 상금 시정되지 않고 있음을 확인하였음(즉 끊어진 효사이의 간격이 규격보다 넓은 간격으로 제작)

2.이와관련 당관은 IGOR NOVICHENKO 유엔의 전장보를 면담, 태극기 제작 오류사항이 시정되지 않고 있는데 대해 유감을 표명하고 최단 시일내에 시정해 줄 것을 다시요청하였음. 이에 대해 동인은 금일 당장 태극기를 다시 제작하도록 주문하겠으며 태극기 완성후 아측에게 바로 통보해 줄것을 약속한 바, 추후 결과 보고 예정임(동인에 의하면 국기제작에 약 6주가 소요된다고 함)

(대사 유종하-국장)

국기국

PAGE 1 93.02.09 10:25 WH

외신 1과 통제관

0161

원 본

외 무 부

종 별 :

번 호 : UNW-0357 일 시 : 93 0210 2030

수 신 : 장관(연일)

발 신 : 주 유엔 대사

제 목 : 태극기 시정 확인

대 : WUN - 0371(1), WUNF - 0120(2)

연 : UNW - 0327

1. 2.10. 최홍기 서기관이 유엔사무국 국기관계담당관인 MR. CAUFIELD 로부터3 X 5 SIZE 의 태극기 (UN 본부에서는 4 X 6 및 3 X 5 FEET 두종류 SIZE 의국기를 사용하는데 이중 유엔본부앞 게양용은 4 X 6 라고 함)가 우선 새로 제작이되어 도착됐다는 통보를 받고 동인사무실을 방문.점검한 바, 대호(2) 본부송부 태극기 제작 규격 표준에 맞게 제작되었음을 확인하였음. (대호(1) 오류사항 시정 포함)

2. 아직 제작이 완료되지 아니한 유엔본부앞 게양용기(4 X 6 SIZE) 는 도착하는대로 다시 통보해 주겠다고 하는바, 추후 결과 보고 예정임.

3. 금일 유엔사무국의 국기검사과정에 대해 아울러 설명을 들었는바, 제작사로부터 국기가 완성 도착되면 먼저 국기담당과에서 1차 점검한후 유엔 도서관에 소속되어 있는 국기 검사관(동인은 지도검사도 한다함)이 국기의 이상유무를 최종 확인한후게양이 된다고 함. 이번에 새로만든 3 X 5 SIZE 태극기도 동 검사관의 검사를 필한것이라고 함. 끝

(대사 유종하 - 국장

국기국

PAGE 1 93.02.11 11:58 BH

외신 1과 통제관

0162

원 본

외 무 부

종 별 :

번 호 : UNW-1349 일 시 : 93 0427 2000

수 신 : 장관 (연일)

발 신 : 주 유엔 대사

제 목 : 태극기 시정 확인

대 : WUN - 0371

연 : UNW - 0357

1. 4.26 MR.CAUFIELD 유엔사무국 국기관계담당관으로 부터 유엔본부 게양용 연호 태극기가 새로 제작, 접수되었다는 통보를 받고 동인 사무실을 방문, 점검한 바,본부 송부 태극기 제작 규격표준에 맞게 제작되었음을 확인하였음

2. 아측은 유엔본부앞 게양 태극기를 새로 제작된 태극기로 즉시 교체하는 한편동 태극기를 제네바 및 비엔나 유엔사무소에도 송부하여 줄것을 요청하였음. 이에 대해 동인은 바로 조치하겠으며 유엔의전관례에 따라 구태극기는 소각하겠다고 함.

3. 당관은 4.22 NOVICHENKO 유엔의전장보에게 새로운 태극기 제작이 늦어지고있음을 지적하고 조속한 조치를 촉구한바 있음. 끝.

(대사 유종하 - 국장)

국기국

PAGE 1

93.04.28 10:19 BD

외신 1과 통제관

0163

정리보존문서목록

기록물종류	일반공문서철	등록번호	2020110155	등록일자	2020-11-27
분류번호	731.12	국가코드		보존기간	영구
명 칭	남북한 유엔가입, 1991.9.17. 전41권				
생 산 과	국제연합1과	생산년도	1990~1991	담당그룹	
권 차 명	V.36 유엔가입 기념품 기증, 1991-92				
내용목차	* 유엔가입 기념 기증품으로 월인천강지곡 선정 - 월인천강지곡 금속활자판틀 및 영인본 * 사후관리 내용 포함				

0001

관리 번호	91-550

	분류번호	보존기간

발 신 전 보

번 호 : WUN-1557 910530 1958 FL 종별 :

수 신 : 주 유엔 대사. 총영사

발 신 : 장 관 (국연)

제 목 : 신규가입국 기증품

1. 아국의 유엔가입 관련 업무에 참고코자 하니, 신규가입국의 가입을 전후한 민속공연, 예술품 전시, 기증품 제공등에 관한 유엔내 관행이 있는지 여부와 구체적 사례를 은밀히 파악.보고바람.

2. 또한 아국의 가입을 전후하여 상징적인 조형물 또는 시설등을 유엔에 기증품으로 제공할 경우 기증품(시설) 품목, 소요예산등에 관한 귀견을 시간을 두고 보고바람. 끝.

(국제기구조약국장 문동석)

19**91.12.31**.에 예고문에 의거 일반문서로 재분류됨

보안 통제	

앙 고 재	91년 5월 30일	과	기안자 성명		과 장		국 장		차 관	장 관
							전결			

외신과통제

0002

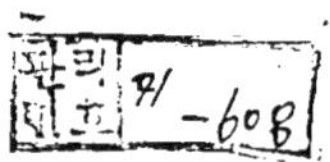

	분류번호	보존기간

발 신 전 보

번 호 : WUN-1668 910611 1906 DU 종별 :

수 신 : 주UN대표부 대사 대사. 총영사

발 신 : 장 관 (문정, 국련)

제 목 : 예술작품 기증

연 : WUN-1653 ~~WNY-0916~~

1. 문화부는 국무총리실 주재하에 외무부, 공보처 등 관계부처 회의결과 UN가입 계기로 아국 예술작품을 UN본부에 기증할 것을 적극 추진키로 결정하고 다음 품목을 기증코자 고려하고 있음.

o 88서울올림픽 개폐회식 사용 큰북 (용고)

- 지름 130Cm, 두께 155Cm (즉시 발송가능)

o 한국 민족문화를 상징하는 대형 벽장식물 (대형벽화 또는 수직제품)

- 제작시간 수개월 소요

2. 상기 기증관련 현지 의견을 조속 회신바라며, 기증시 설치장소, 시기 및 기증 기념행사 개최 여부등을 교섭후 보고바람.

(문화부 문화정책국장 신 현 웅)

19 91. 12. 31. 에 예고문에 의거 일반문서로 재분류됨

보 안 통 제	72

앙 고 재	91년 6월 11일	문화협력과	기안자 성 명	담 당	과 장		국 장		차 관	장 관
				오동일	72		전결			

외신과통제

0003

주 국 련 대 표 부

주국련 20313- 479 1991. 6. 13.

수신 장 관

참조 국제기구조약국장, 해외공보관장, 문화협력국장, 문화부 문화정책국장

제목 유엔가입(기증품)

1. UNW - 1549 의 관련입니다.

2. 연호관련 각국대표부등이 제공 유엔에 전시한 기증품 목록이 수록된 자료를 별첨과 같이 송부합니다.

첨 부 : 동 자료 1부. 끝.

주 국 련 대 

선 결			결재(공람)		
접수일시	1991.6.17	번호			
처리과	/33821				

0004

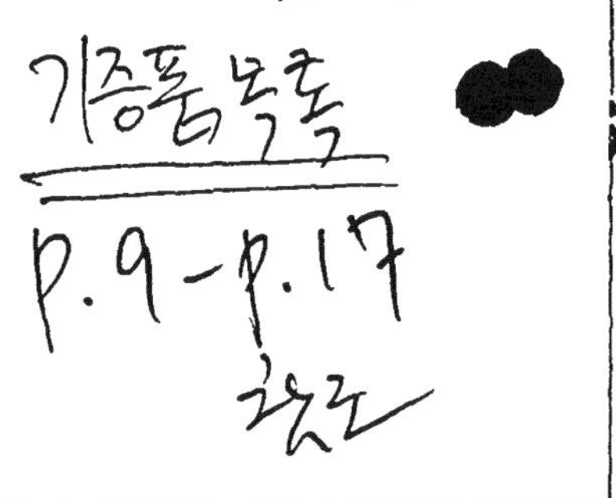

Department of Public Information
Press Section
United Nations, New York

Press Feature No. 217
September 1986

UNITED NATIONS HEADQUARTERS

The Headquarters of the United Nations stands on the eastern shore of Manhattan island, on the banks of New York City's East River. To its 18 acres come representatives of the earth's 5 billion people, to discuss and decide issues of peace, justice and economic and social well-being. Here, also, men and women of the United Nations staff, or Secretariat, work to carry out these decisions. The tall glass façade of the Secretariat Building and the low-slung, subtly curved General Assembly edifice, together with the United Nations' blue and white flag, have become the instantly recognizable symbols of the world Organization.

It is not just symbols, however, but a workshop that the visitor sees when crossing United Nations Plaza to enter this international enclave. Two distinct types of work are carried out at the Headquarters. The delegates deliberate in the General Assembly Building and the adjoining Conference Building, while most of the international staff of the United Nations service meetings, collect information and prepare reports in the 39-storey Secretariat Building.

The United Nations Headquarters was designed to serve four major groups: delegations, who now represent 159 Member States and who send more than 3,000 persons to New York each year for the annual sessions of the General Assembly; the Secretariat, numbering about 7,075 persons in New York out of a total of over 18,917 throughout the world; visitors, who average 1,413 a day; and journalists, of whom more than 450 are permanently accredited while twice that number are present during major meetings.

To accommodate those groups efficiently, there are separate facilities for each. The staff enter through the Secretariat Building at East 43rd Street; delegates have an entrance at the west side of the General Assembly Building at 44th Street; and visitors have access to the complex through the north end of the Assembly Building, between 45th and 46th Streets. The general public may attend open meetings, for which admission tickets are made available without charge. They may visit public areas in the General Assembly Building and may tour other areas with United Nations guides.

(more)

3808P
86-21978

For information media — not an official record

0005

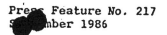

The site of the Headquarters is bounded on the north by 48th Street, on the south by 42nd Street, on the west by United Nations Plaza (a stretch of First Avenue) and on the east by the East River. The official address is United Nations, New York 10017, United States of America.

Selecting New York

The decision to locate the United Nations near New York City was made in London by the General Assembly at its first session on 14 February 1946, after offers and suggestions for permanent sites had been received from many parts of the world. On 10 December 1945, the Congress of the United States had unanimously resolved to invite the United Nations to establish its permanent home in that country.

Following selection of the United States, a special United Nations site committee looked over possible locations during the latter half of 1946 in such places as Philadelphia, Boston and San Francisco. While consideration had been given in the first place to areas north of New York City, crowded Manhattan had not been seriously studied. But a last-minute offer of $8.5 million for the purchase of the present site, by John D. Rockefeller, Jr., was accepted by a large majority of the General Assembly on 14 December 1946. New York City completed the site parcel by additional gifts of property.

The site chosen by the United Nations was a run-down area of slaughterhouses, light industry and a railroad barge landing. Trucks rumbled up and down First Avenue on one side, and automobiles sped along the East River Drive -- since renamed for Franklin Delano Roosevelt -- skirting the waterfront.

Planning Headquarters

Once the site had been settled upon, the next task was to design the Headquarters for the world Organization. Rather than hold an international competition, the United Nations decided that its new home should be the result of collaboration among eminent architects of many countries.

Wallace K. Harrison of the United States was appointed chief architect, with the title of Director of Planning. To assist him, a 10-member Board of Design Consultants was selected, composed of architects nominated by Governments.

The members of the Board were N.D. Bassov (Soviet Union), Gaston Brunfaut (Belgium), Ernest Cormier (Canada), Charles E. Le Corbusier (France), Liang Ssu-cheng (China), Sven Markelius (Sweden), Oscar Niemeyer (Brazil), Howard Robertson (United Kingdom), G.A. Soilleux (Australia) and Julio Villamajo (Uruguay).

The Director and the Board began their work early in 1947, at an office in Rockefeller Center -- a group of commercial buildings in New York City for which Mr. Harrison had served as one of the principal architects. Some 50 basic designs were created, criticized, analysed and reworked. The planners took into account the structure of the United Nations, with its General Assembly, three main Councils and permanent Secretariat. They had to integrate the needs of delegation and Secretariat personnel.

(more)

0006

Because the area was relatively small, a tall building would be required to house offices. The presence of firm bedrock near the surface -- the Manhattan schist on which most New York skyscrapers rest -- would facilitate construction, the planners determined. (The bedrock dips to 60 or more feet below sea level between 46th and 47th Streets, where Turtle Bay stretched inland from the East River in the last century -- an area which now lies beneath the broad lawn to the north of the General Assembly Building.)

It was decided to locate the Secretariat Building at the south end of the site to facilitate access to and from public transport systems along 42nd Street, which is the primary artery of midtown Manhattan. The structure's north-south orientation was selected partly for reasons of appearance and partly because a tall building on an east-west axis would have thrown its shadow over much of the site.

The designers conceived of a park-like plateau, from First Avenue to the river's edge, from which the buildings would rise. To utilize the area right up to the river, they decided that the landscaped area and the Conference Building would be cantilevered over the Franklin D. Roosevelt Drive.

Although the United Nations was not bound to comply with local ordinances, the Headquarters was planned in compliance with New York City building regulations, since the City is responsible for fire protection. Water, electricity, steam and other utilities are purchased at commercial rates.

The buildings as originally planned were estimated to cost nearly $85 million. At the direction of Secretary-General Trygve Lie, however, the designers cut the cost by $20 million, largely by reducing the height of the Secretariat Building from 45 to 39 storeys, by reducing the size of the conference areas and by utilizing an existing building on the site for the United Nations Library. The $65 million plan was approved by the General Assembly on 20 November 1947.

To finance construction, the United States Government made an interest-free loan of $65 million to the United Nations. Of this amount, the last instalment of $1 million was paid in 1982.

Construction of Buildings

With the plans approved, action to carry them out moved ahead quickly. The 270 residential tenants were relocated at United Nations expense, the meat packers and bargemen departed, and the existing buildings were demolished. The construction contract was awarded in January 1949 to a combination of four large New York building firms. Nineteen months later, on 21 August 1950, the first of the Secretariat workers moved into their new offices.

The major first addition to the Headquarters complex since then was the Dag Hammarskjöld Library, completed in 1961.

(more)

Over the years, the interiors of the buildings have been altered to accommodate the many States that have joined the Organization since its inception. In 1947, when construction plans were drawn up, there were 57 Member States and provision was made for an increase in membership to 70. This anticipated increase had been exceeded by 1955. A $3 million expansion programme, affecting mainly the meeting areas, was completed in 1964. It provided space for a membership of 126.

To accommodate the greatly expanded membership of the United Nations, the General Assembly in 1976 approved a set of major alterations to enlarge the seating capacity and otherwise refurbish the General Assembly Hall and all the large conference rooms. The reconstruction and remodelling cost about $15 million. Alterations in all large conference rooms and the Trusteeship Council Chamber as well as the work in the Assembly Hall were completed in September 1980. Alterations were also made to the Security Council office and lounge area.

Two other construction projects expanded Headquarters facilities. The first, a modern documents reproduction plant, built at a cost of $25.6 million and completed in June 1981, centres around a small sunken atrium filled with dogwood, honey locust and crabapple, and occupies two levels beneath the broad lawn north of the Assembly Building. The second project, which cost $8.7 million, was finished the following year: a 750-seat cafeteria for staff and delegates, located in a two-storey building at the south-east corner of the Secretariat Building overlooking the East River. The lower storey of the cafeteria annex contains meeting rooms for language classes and interpreters' offices.

Since the growth of the staff could not be accommodated in the existing Secretariat Building, it has been necessary to rent office space in adjacent buildings. A large number of staff, including the personnel of the United Nations Development Programme (UNDP), now work in two buildings of the United Nations Development Corporation, located across First Avenue on 44th Street. The Corporation is a public benefit, non-profit organization created by New York State to provide facilities for the United Nations and related organizations. The multi-use buildings also house a luxury hotel, an apartment hotel and a health club on floors not occupied by the United Nations. A third building being erected by the Corporation, to house the United Nations Children's Fund (UNICEF), is expected to be completed by early 1987.

<u>Secretariat Building</u>

The exterior facings of the 550-foot tall Secretariat Building are exclusively of aluminium, glass and marble. Wide areas of green-tinted glass are unbroken by conventional set-backs. In contrast, the windowless north and south facades of the building are faced with 2,000 tons of Vermont marble. In addition to the 39 storeys above ground, there are three basement levels connecting with the three basements of the Conference Building. Facilities

(more)

below street level include maintenance shops, a fire-fighting unit, receiving and loading platforms, a pouch dispatch unit, security offices, storage space, a three-level garage, an automobile service station and a refrigeration plant for air-conditioning.

Within the building, while some modern conveniences are provided for efficient functioning of the staff, there is nothing elaborate and offices are generally small, with no wasted space. The glass in the aluminium-framed windows, letting in a maximum of light over the 20 acres of office space, is specially designed to help retain solar heat. This, coupled with 4,000 under-the-window air-conditioning units, offers comfortable working conditions.

Movable steel partitions, which attach to brackets on the superstructure, can be shifted quickly and easily to meet changing requirements for office space. Ducts under the floors provide telephone, electric and signalling connections at six-foot intervals. An integrated system of electric dumb-waiters and conveyors speeds the movement of documents and mail throughout the building.

General Assembly Building

The General Assembly Building is a sloping structure with concave sides, 380 feet long and 160 feet wide, topped with a shallow dome containing light fixtures for the hall inside. The north end, opening onto a landscaped plaza, is the main public entrance to the Headquarters complex. It is faced with specially designed translucent glass panels set into marble piers designed to give the public lobby a subdued, cathedral-like lighting. The east and west walls of the building are faced with English limestone, with panels and trimmings in marble matching the north and south ends of the Secretariat Building. At the south end is a huge plate-glass window, 53.5 feet high, set in a deeply recessed marble frame, through which the delegates' lobby overlooks the Secretariat plaza.

The main visitors' entrance to the Headquarters is through the lobby of the Assembly Building, with its clean, modern lines of cantilevered balconies and soft lighting. Beyond the lobby to the right is the small Meditation Room, whose focal point is a massive block of iron ore dimly spotlighted from above. Suspended from the ceiling above the stair landing connecting the lobby with the second-floor ceremonial entrance to the General Assembly Hall is the Foucault pendulum, a gift of the Netherlands Government, offering visual proof of the rotation of the earth.

In the north-west part of the building's lobby, next to the Meditation Room entrance, is a 15-by-12 foot stained-glass panel by Marc Chagall, symbolic of man's struggle for peace. Dedicated to the memory of Secretary-General Dag Hammarskjöld and 15 others who died with him in a plane crash in 1961, the panel was paid for by contributions from United Nations staff members. Adjacent to the Chagall window, four bronze plaques commemorate "military observers and members of the Secretariat who died in the line of duty while serving the United Nations on its missions of observation, mediation and conciliation". Facing the Meditation Room, on permanent display, is a facsimile of the United Nations Charter. (The original is preserved in the United States Archives in Washington, D.C.)

(more)

0009

The blue, green and gold General Assembly Hall -- 165 feet long by 115 feet wide with a 75-foot ceiling -- occupies the second, third and fourth floors. Representatives of Member States sit behind leather-covered tables facing a raised speakers' rostrum and podium. At the podium sits the President of the General Assembly, with the Secretary-General of the United Nations to his right and the Under-Secretary-General for Political and General Assembly Affairs to his left.

The Assembly Hall was remodelled during 1979 to accommodate a maximum of 182 delegations. Each delegation has six seats -- three behind tables for full delegates and three in back of them for alternates. These 1,092 places fill the floor of the Hall and three stepped platforms rising from the rear. Behind them, there are places for 476 alternates, representatives of specialized agencies and other senior officers. At the sides are 187 seats for alternates, observers and others. In a balcony above is a row of 53 places for news media and 280 seats in five rows for the public. Chairs for 24 staff members who service the meetings are located at the sides of the podium.

All 2,103 seats are equipped with earphones, allowing the listener to "tune in" either to the language being spoken on the floor or to interpretations into any of the Assembly's six official languages -- Arabic, Chinese, English, French, Russian and Spanish. The interpreters sit in glass-walled booths overlooking the Hall. Similar booths are occupied by television and film cameramen, broadcasters and other information personnel, and official verbatim reporters.

Above and behind the speakers' rostrum are large panels listing the Member States of the Organization, where the results of votes are displayed. Delegates signal their countries' votes for or against a resolution, or their decision to abstain from a vote, by pressing green, red or yellow buttons on the tables in front of them.

The General Assembly first met in this Hall at the opening of its seventh regular annual session on 14 October 1952.

On two lower levels of the building are a large conference room, four smaller conference rooms, radio and television studios, sound-recording facilities and a master control room, which is the centre of a communications system serving the entire Headquarters. For visitors, there is a public area containing the United Nations Bookshop, a United Nations stamp sales counter, a gift centre, a souvenir shop, a coffee shop and other facilities.

Conference Building

The Conference Building, which connects the General Assembly and Secretariat Buildings, extends along the waterfront for 400 feet and is cantilevered over the Franklin D. Roosevelt Drive. Its narrow top level (fourth floor) contains the delegates' dining room (open to the public by reservation), private dining rooms, a staff cafe, a wall of vending machines for the use of staff members working night shifts and holidays, and a kitchen. More than half a mile of teak railing from Burma runs along three sides of an outside terrace on three levels of the Conference Building.

(more)

0010

On the second and third floors are the three Council Chambers, each of which is 72 feet wide, 135 feet long and 24 feet high.

The Security Council Chamber was furnished by Norway and designed by the Norwegian Arnstein Arneberg. A large mural by Per Krohg of Norway, symbolizing the promise of future peace and individual freedom, covers most of the east wall. There are 232 seats for the public and 118 for the press.

The Trusteeship Council Chamber, next door, was furnished by Denmark and designed by Finn Juhl, a Dane. Against one wall is a nine-foot statue of a woman with arms upraised, carved from teak by Henrik Starcke, also of Denmark. The Chamber, its seating capacity for delegations expanded in 1978, has 164 seats for the public and 30 for the press. It is also used by Main Committees of the General Assembly, which are composed of all United Nations Members.

The Economic and Social Council Chamber lies between the Trusteeship Council Chamber and the north delegates' lounge, whose large glass wall faces north overlooking the gardens. The Chamber was designed by Sven Markelius of Sweden and furnished by that country. It was rearranged in 1974 to accommodate the expanded membership of the Council, which doubled from 27 to 54 in 1973. Its galleries have 336 seats for the public and 40 for the press.

On the second floor, there is a large delegates' lounge in the north end, adjacent to the Economic and Social Council Chamber, and a smaller delegates' lounge at the south end, near the Security Council Chamber.

Beneath the Council Chambers are three large conference rooms designed for the Assembly's Main Committees, and six smaller conference rooms with no public accommodation.

Library Building

At the south-west corner of the United Nations grounds, and linked to the Secretariat Building, is the Dag Hammarskjöld Library, dedicated on 16 November 1961 in honour of the late Secretary-General. The building was erected to meet the Organization's growing demands for library services and its construction was made possible by a gift of $6.6 million from the Ford Foundation. The structure measures 219 feet by 84 feet and consists of six storeys -- three above ground and three below.

On the three floors above ground are collections of United Nations, specialized agencies and League of Nations documents, as well as general reference materials and maps. Visible from the plaza is the white pine-ceilinged, two-storey tall Woodrow Wilson Reading Room on the second floor. Below ground are a 195-seat auditorium, a periodicals library and additional book stacks. The library staff of about 160 have offices in the building.

The Library houses approximately 400,000 volumes in its general collection and, in addition, has several million United Nations documents. Its map section contains more than 80,000 maps. In 1985, the periodicals library had 10,445 official government publications and 4,400 non-official periodicals. It also had 330 daily newspapers and 225 government gazettes from 189 countries and Territories.

(more)

Grounds and Furnishings

A colourful approach to the Headquarters is provided by the flags of the 159 United Nations Members, flying in a wide curve of more than 500 feet long along United Nations Plaza.

A circular pool in front of the Secretariat Building with a fountain in its centre was built with a $50,000 gift from the children of the United States. The wavy pattern on the floor of the pool is formed by alternating bands of crushed white marble and black pebbles. The black stones were gathered from the beaches of Rhodes by the women and children of that Greek island and donated to the United Nations.

A bronze sculpture in memory of late Secretary-General Hammarskjöld was set at the edge of the pool in 1964. The abstract sculpture, entitled "Single Form", is the work of the English artist Barbara Hepworth and was donated by Jacob Blaustein, a former United States delegate to the United Nations. Some 21 feet high, it stands on a granite plinth.

A bronze statue by Henry Moore, "Reclining Figure: Hand", is placed on the landscaped area north of the Secretariat Building.

A Japanese bell and pagoda, donated by the United Nations Association of Japan, is located just west of the Conference Building, between the Secretariat and Assembly Buildings. Its base and surrounding floor are faced with stone quarried from the hills of Jerusalem and presented by Israel.

A monumental staircase, presented by the State of New York in memory of late Secretary-General Hammarskjöld, leads from the plaza in front of the public entrance of the General Assembly Building to the United Nations gardens. In these gardens, overlooking the East River, are a memorial to Eleanor Roosevelt and sculptures presented by Brazil, the German Democratic Republic, the Soviet Union and Yugoslavia.

Tons of topsoil and fertilizer were brought to the landscaped areas of the grounds to provide soil for trees, shrubs and flowers. Some 1,000 prize-winning rose bushes, 170 flowering cherry trees, 45 dwarf fruit trees and 25,000 daffodil bulbs, as well as a fine group of hawthorns, sweet gum, pin oaks, sycamores and honey locust trees, have helped transform the area from stone and steel to a green garden. Lining the asphalt walks are ilex, wisteria, rambler roses and a ground cover of English ivy and grass. Many of the plantings were donated by groups or individuals.

In keeping with the international character of the Organization, materials for the Headquarters were selected from many lands. Limestone for the facings of the Assembly and Conference buildings came from the United Kingdom, marble from Italy, office furniture and shelving from France, chairs and fabrics from Czechoslovakia and Greece, carpets from England, France and Scotland. In addition, tables were purchased from Switzerland and various woods for interior finishings from Belgium, Canada, Cuba, Guatemala, the Philippines, Norway and Zaire.

The only artwork at Headquarters commissioned by the General Assembly is the painting entitled "Titans", by the United States artist Lumen Martin Winter. It commemorates the 1970 World Youth Assembly, held at Headquarters, and is located on the third floor in the passage connecting the Conference and General Assembly Buildings. It was paid for by surplus voluntary funds donated for the Youth Assembly.

(more)

0012

Gifts at Headquarters

Following is a list of gifts accepted by the United Nations and on display at Headquarters:

From Governments

Donor	Description	Location
Argentina	"Todos Hombres del Mundo", a sculpture grouping of male heads by Martha Minujin	South-west foyer, 2nd floor outside General Assembly Hall
	"Silence in White", mixed-media painting by Marcelo Bonevardi	2nd floor corridor outside west foyer, General Assembly Building
Argentina and Sweden	Portrait of Dag Hammarskjöld by Celina D.M. de Mundin Schaffter	Main Reading Room, Library Building
Australia	Lace-wood panelling	Reception room and two offices of executive suite, 2nd floor, General Assembly Building
Austria	Tables and chairs	Coffee bar outside Conference Room 4, first basement, General Assembly Building
Belgium	Mural tapestry, "Triumph of Peace" (43.5 x 28.5 feet), one of the largest ever woven	Delegates' lobby, General Assembly Building
Brazil	Two murals, "War" and "Peace", oil on cedar plywood by Candido Portinari	Delegates' lobby, General Assembly Building
	Stainless steel sculpture, "Roots and Ties for Peace", by Yolanda d'Augsburg Ulm	North garden
Bulgaria	Replica of a Byzantine fresco depicting Bulgarian ruler Sebastocrator Kaloyan and his wife Desislava	2nd floor neck area, between Conference and General Assembly Buildings
Burkina Faso	Burnished cowhide	33rd floor of Secretariat
Byelorussia	Oil painting, "Vechar" ("Evening")	Delegates' dining room
Canada	Seven nickel and bronze ornamental metal doors	North entrance, General Assembly Building
Chile	Oil painting, "Corazón de los Andes" ("The Heart of the Andes"), by Nemesio Antuñez	First basement between Conference Rooms 5 and 6, General Assembly Building
China	Tapestry, "The Great Wall"	Delegates' north lounge
	Ivory carving, the "Chengtu-Kunming Railway"	3rd floor neck area, between Conference and General Assembly Buildings

(more)

0013

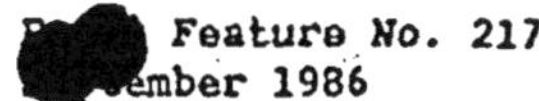
Feature No. 217
...ember 1986

Donor	Description	Location
Colombia ✓	Mural painting, "Sunrise in the Andes", by Alejandro Obregón	Delegates' north lounge
Cyprus	Amphora of white painted ware (700-600 B.C.)	2nd floor corridor of Conference Building, opposite Trusteeship Council Chamber
Denmark	Contribution for design and furnishing of Chamber, teakwood sculpture by Henrik Starcke	Trusteeship Council Chamber
Dominican Republic	Sculpture, "El Abrazo de Paz" ("The Embrace of Peace")	Delegates' lobby, General Assembly Building
Ecuador	Two rugs, hand-woven by the indigenous people of the Andes	First basement neck area, between General Assembly and Conference Buildings
Egypt	Gilded bronze statuette of the god Osiris (700 B.C.)	Delegates' lobby outside General Assembly Hall, 2nd floor
Ethiopia ✓	Ivory model of ancient stele	South-east foyer, 2nd floor, General Assembly Building
Finland	Stainless steel sculpture, pre-study of a detail of monument to composer Jean Sibelius in Helsinki, by Eila Hiltunen	East side of the visitors' plaza
France	Tapestry, "Le Ciel", by Matisse	Secretary-General's office
	Two paintings, "Bord de la Rivière by Albert Marquet and "Vue de Saint-Maximin" by Andre Derain, on loan from Museum of Modern Art, Paris, since 1965	Secretary-General's office
German Democratic Republic	Bronze sculpture, "Die Aufsteigende" ("The Rising Man"), by Fritz Cremer	North garden, adjacent to playground
Federal Republic of Germany	Room design and furnishing	Security Council delegates' lounge
Ghana	Wall hanging of kente cloth (hand-woven), entitled "One Head Cannot Go into Council" by Tikro Noko Adjina	South-east foyer, 2nd floor, General Assembly Building
Greece	Cast of statue of Poseidon, Greek god of the watery element	Public lobby, General Assembly Building
	Black pebbles from Rhodes	Fountain pool, Secretariat plaza
Guinea	"Nimba" figure of the Baga tribe	Delegates' entrance to General Assembly Building

(more)

0014

Donor	Description	Location
Holy See	Framed ceramic sculpture, "Embrace of Peace", by Angelo Biancini	Secretary-General's office in Security Council Chamber
	Mosaic reproduction, "Dove of Peace", from the Constantinian Basilica of Saint Peter's Church	South-east wall, General Assembly public lobby
Hungary	Hand-painted china vase showing Hungarian House of Parliament and United Nations Headquarters	Corridor between Security Council and Trusteeship Council Chambers, 2nd floor, Conference Building
India	Rugs	Outside Conference Room 1, first basement, Conference Building
	Black stone sculpture of sun god Surya (Pala dynasty, 11th century A.D.)	2nd floor neck area, between General Assembly and Conference Buildings
Indonesia	Two carved wooden figures, "Peace" and "Prosperity"	South-west foyer lounge, 2nd floor, General Assembly Building
Iran	Persian carpet	South-east foyer, 2nd floor, General Assembly Building
	Replica of clay tablet "Edict of Cyrus" (original dated 539 B.C.)	2nd floor corridor outside Economic and Social Council Chamber
Iraq	Replica of original stele (dated 1750 B.C.) enumerating laws of Hammurabi, the oldest written legal codes	2nd floor corridor, Conference Building
Israel	880 slabs of Jerusalem stone, forming base of Japanese Peace Bell structure	Landscaped area north-west of Secretariat Building
Latin American Group	Green marble plaque honouring Benito Juárez, by Angela Gurnia	West foyer lounge, 2nd floor, General Assembly Building
	Bronze plaque by Marisol Escobar commemorating 150th anniversary of Amphictyonic Congress of Panama and paying tribute to Simón Bolívar, Liberator	South-east corner of plaza in front of Secretariat Building
Liberia	Wood table with elephant tusks and ivory inlay of maps of Africa and Liberia and the United Nations seal	Public lobby outside Conference Room 4, General Assembly Building
Mali	Painted cotton "Dansa" wall hanging	Secretary-General's executive office, 38th floor
	Carved ebony antelope headdress	End of corridor within Security Council offices

(more)

0015

Donor	Description	Location
Malta	Abstract painting by Emanuel V. Cremona	2nd floor corridor outside west foyer, General Assembly Building
Mexico	Copy of stone head of Mayan priest	Secretary-General's reception room
	Painting, "Brotherhood", by Rufino Tamayo	Public lobby, General Assembly Building
	Brass armillary form on tan onyx base	Reception area on 37th floor
Morocco	Mosaic panel, with inscription from United Nations Charter on tiles	2nd floor neck area, between General Assembly and Conference Buildings
Netherlands	Foucault pendulum, which gives visual proof of earth's rotation	Public lobby, General Assembly Building
New Zealand	Rimu panelling	Delegates' lobby, 1st floor, General Assembly Building
Nigeria	Bronze sculpture, "Anyanwu" ("Sun"), by Ben Enwonwu	Outside Trusteeship Council Chamber, 2nd floor corridor
Norway	Contribution for design and furnishing, mural by Per Krohg	Security Council Chamber
Oman	Sterling silver coffee pot and enclosure	Delegates' dining room entrance
	Silver incense urn; contribution for decor and furnishing	2nd floor corridor, between Economic and Social Council and Trusteeship Council Chambers
Pakistan	Paintings by Chugtai	Delegates' dining room
Peru	Ceremonial burial mantle (2,000-3,000 years old)	South-west foyer lounge, 2nd floor, outside General Assembly Hall
Philippines	Abstract wood sculpture, "Goodbye to the Lateral Thrust", by Abueva	Delegates' entrance to General Assembly Building
Poland	Granite bust of Polish astronomer Nicolaus Copernicus, by Alphonse Karny and Z. Debniak	1st floor passage to Library Building
	Three picture cut-outs of ornamental birds	Delegates' dining room
	Stained-glass panel, "Sleeping Child", created after a drawing by painter Stanislaw Wyspianski	2nd floor, outside Security Council Chamber
Portugal	Tapestry, "Mar e Terra", by Camarinha	Delegates' private dining room, 4th floor, Conference Building
Romania	Mural tapestry, "Ode to Man", by Ion Nicodim	Delegates' north lounge, Conference Building

(more)

0016

Donor	Description	Location
Saudi Arabia	"Kiswa", a black silk curtain embroidered in silver and gold, formerly curtain of door of Holy Kaaba in Makkah	South-west foyer, 2nd floor, outside General Assembly Hall
Senegal	Tapestry, "Maaggala Tuubaa" ("Pilgrimage to Touba"), by Papa Ibra Tall	South-west foyer lounge, 2nd floor, General Assembly Building
Singapore	Scroll painting	Security Council President's office 2nd floor, Conference Building
Spain	Bronze bust of Padre Francisco de Vitoria, international law figure	North-west area of garden
Sri Lanka	✓ Oil painting, "Rice Cultivators of Ceylon", by Senaka Senanayake	East entrance to General Assembly Hall, 2nd floor
Suriname	Mahogany sculpture, "Woman as Mother Deep in Thought", by Johan H.A. Pinas	Secretary-General's small reception room, General Assembly Building
Sweden	Contribution for design and furnishing of the Chamber	Economic and Social Council Chamber
	Six-ton iron ore slab	Meditation Room
Switzerland	World Clock, giving time for each official time zone	General Assembly Hall, reception area
Syria	Replica of 1,800-year-old sculptural relief depicting the Babylonian and Assyrian goddess Ishtar	North-east wall of passage between Conference and General Assembly Buildings, 2nd floor
Thailand	Teak and leather furniture	Delegates' lobby, 2nd floor, north of General Assembly Hall
	Decorated teakwood model of royal barge "Suphannahong"	3rd floor neck area, between Conference and General Assembly Buildings
Tunisia	Third century mosaic mural depicting the yearly cycle	Entrance, delegates' north lounge, Conference Building
Turkey	✓ Copper bas-relief of clay tablet of Kadesh Peace Treaty, the oldest known peace treaty	2nd floor corridor, facing entrance to Security Council Chamber
	Rugs	General Assembly executive offices, 2nd floor, General Assembly Building
Ukraine	Wool carpet, titled "Tree in Blossom", and porcelain vase	Outside delegates' south lounge, Conference Building

(more)

0017

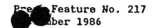

Donor	Description	Location
USSR	Model of first Sputnik, the first space satellite, launched on 4 October 1957	Public lobby, General Assembly Building
	Bronze sculpture, "Let Us Beat Swords into Plowshares", by Evgeny Vuchetich	North garden
United Kingdom	Oak panelling and furniture	Conference Room 8, first basement, General Assembly Building
	Painting, "Vortex", by Stuart Armfield	Outside delegates' south lounge, Conference Building
United States	Four-ounce moon rock and United Nations flag carried on Apollo 11 during its moon landing on 20 July 1969	Public lobby outside Conference Room 4, General Assembly Building
	Mosaic representation of Norman Rockwell painting "The Golden Rule"	North end of Conference Building corridor, 3rd floor
United States (New York City*)	Ornamental fence	Along United Nations Plaza
United States (New York State)	Memorial stairway and flagstaff	North garden
Yugoslavia	Bronze equestrian statue of woman symbolizing peace, by Anton Augustincic	North garden

(more)

---

* New York City has made many other contributions for the completion of the Headquarters and improvement of adjacent areas, including the tunnel carrying First Avenue traffic beneath United Nations Plaza, the widening of East 47th Street between Second Avenue and United Nations Plaza (a block which has been renamed Dag Hammarskjöld Plaza), and the reconstruction of the East 42nd Street approach to Headquarters. In 1980, the small municipal park at the foot of the "Isaiah Wall" and facing the United Nations Secretariat Building across the street was renamed the Ralph J. Bunche Memorial Park by the city. A stainless steel obelisk, "Peace Form One", by Daniel LaRue Johnson, erected there by the Phelps-Stoke Fund, commemorates Mr. Bunche, the late Under-Secretary-General and a Nobel Peace Prize winner.

0018

From Organizations or Individuals

Donor	Description	Location
African Bureau	Bronze bust of Chief Hosea Kutako of Namibia	Exhibit area, 1st floor, General Assembly Building
Muhammad Ali	Painting of United Nations	3rd floor, Conference Building, outside Security Council Chamber
All American Rose Selections, Inc.	1,500 rose bushes	Gardens
American Association for the United Nations	Contribution ($50,000) from United States schoolchildren	For fountain pool, Secretariat plaza
American Needlepoint Guild	"United Nations Peace Rug", depicting national crests of 138 Member States with United Nations seal in centre	Public lobby, General Assembly Building
Anonymous donor	Two murals by Fernand Léger	General Assembly Hall
Association for the Help of Retarded Children	Bronze bust of Eleanor Roosevelt	Exhibit area, 1st floor, General Assembly Building
Austrian Chamber of Commerce	Design and redecoration of Secretary-General's office and dining room; wood panelling and furnishing	38th floor
Jacob Blaustein (United States)	Sculpture, "Single Form", by Barbara Hepworth	Secretariat plaza
Camp Fire Girls Council of Greater New York	Pin oak tree	North garden
Salvador Dali	Painting, "Clasped Hands", by the artist	Postal sales area, General Assembly Building
Marshall Field family	Fresco by Swedish artist Bo Beskow	Meditation Room
Ford Foundation	Dag Hammarskjöld Library building	
	Murals by Bo Beskow ("Composition for a Concave Wall") and Fritz Glarner ("Relational Painting No. 90")	Penthouse and 1st-floor staircase, Library Building
Ford Foundation and Bonniers Swedish Publishing House	Portrait of Dag Hammarskjöld by Bo Beskow	North wall, Secretariat lobby
Friends of Abraham H. Feller	Portrait of the late Mr. Feller, scholar of international law and United Nations General Counsel	Outside Legal Library on 34th floor

(more)

0019

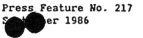

Donor	Description	Location
Friends of the United Nations Meditation Room	Contribution ($12,600) from private contributors	Meditation Room
Friends of U Thant	Portrait of the third Secretary-General by James Fosberg	Secretariat lobby
Guggenheim Foundation	Mural by José Vela Zanetti, "Mankind's Struggle for a Lasting Peace"	3rd floor corridor, Conference Building
Mrs. Albert D. Lasker (United States)	Tapestry of Picasso painting, "Femme sur l'échelle" ("Woman on a Ladder")	Delegates' south lounge, Conference Building
Mrs. Albert D. Lasker and family	170 flowering cherry trees, 25,000 daffodil bulbs, azalea plantings	Gardens
Henry Moore Foundation	Statue by Henry Moore, "Reclining Figure: Hand"	Landscaped area north of Secretariat Building
National Council for United States Art	Three pieces of contemporary American sculpture by Robert Cronbach, Ezio Martinelli and José de Rivera	Lobby of Meditation Room; office of Secretary-General; east exterior wall of General Assembly Building
National Federation of Music Clubs, United States	Steinway Grand Piano	Dag Hammerskjöld Auditorium
Norwegian Friends of Trygve Lie	Portrait of Trygve Lie, by Harald Dal	Secretariat lobby
Public	Contribution ($5,000) for furnishings	Meditation Room
Mrs. Nelson A. Rockefeller	Wool tapestry after Pablo Picasso's La Guernica, on loan	Curved wall on 2nd floor outside Security Council Chamber
Eleanor Roosevelt Memorial Foundation	Granite bench and slab with bas-relief of flame in memory of Mrs. Roosevelt	North garden
Sveriges Stenindustriforbund (Sweden)	Marble floor	Economic and Social Council Chamber
United Nations Association of Japan	Bronze Japanese Peace Bell cast by Chiyogi Nakagawa from coins from more than 60 nations	Landscaped area north-west of Secretariat Building

(more)

0020

Donor	Description	Location
United Nations Association of the United States of America	Portrait of Kurt Waldheim by Raymond Kintsler	Secretariat lobby
United Nations International School building	Bronze bust of Pablo Casals, on loan	Public lobby, General Assembly
United Nations staff and Marc Chagall	Contribution (over $17,000) for Marc Chagall stained-glass panel in memory of Dag Hammarskjöld and those who died with him in 1961	Outside Meditation Room, General Assembly public lobby
United Nations World Youth Assembly	"Light spectrum" oil painting, "Titans", by Lumen Martin Winter	3rd floor neck area, between General Assembly and Conference Buildings
Universal Postal Union	Two-part bronze sculpture	Exhibit area, 1st floor, General Assembly Building
Thomas J. Watson (United States)	Portable stage for concerts	General Assembly Hall
Woodrow Wilson Foundation	Bronze bust of Woodrow Wilson	Woodrow Wilson Reading Room, Library Building
Women's Club of Osaka, Japan	Three Rosashi embroideries	Delegates' dining room entrance
Women's Organizations of the Presbyterian Church in the USA	Ecuadorian rugs	First basement, between General Assembly and Conference Buildings

(more)

0021

Facts and Figures

-- The Headquarters site is owned by the United Nations and is international territory. Under special agreement with the United States, certain privileges and immunities have been granted, but generally the laws of New York City, New York State and the United States apply.

-- The original construction and related costs for the Headquarters buildings were $67,093,290, plus an additional $6,703,567 for the Dag Hammarskjöld Library. Costs for the North Lawn reproduction plant building were $25,600,000; for the new cafeteria annex, $8,690,000. Land for the site was valued at $9,600,000.

-- Some 3,500 meetings are held at Headquarters each year.

-- Signs throughout Headquarters are in English and French, the two working languages of Headquarters.

-- The 5,638 windows at Headquarters require the full-time services of three window-washers.

-- More than 18 miles of carpeting, in strips 27 inches wide, are used throughout Headquarters.

-- There are about 5,000 typewriters in use, with keyboards for typing in the six official languages -- Arabic, Chinese, English, French, Russian and Spanish -- of the Organization. Word processing was introduced in the United Nations in 1977. More than 140 word-processing systems have been installed in various Headquarters locations, with over 600 work stations. Nearly every department uses the equipment for the production of reports, correspondence, statistical tables and other material. Almost half of the word-processing hardware is used by the Department of Conference Services, which has Arabic, English, French, Russian and Spanish stenographic units to handle production of United Nations documents. A computer terminal providing direct access for United Nations translators, revisers and terminologists to a terminology data bank at the Canadian Translation Bureau in Ottawa was a gift of Canada. In exchange for access to data, the United Nations supplies the computer system with its own terminology data.

-- A United Nations Post Office is located in the first basement of the Secretariat Building, providing all the services of a regular post office but selling only United Nations postage stamps which may be used solely for mail posted at Headquarters. A philatelic stamp counter is operated by the United Nations Postal Administration in the concourse (lower) level of the public lobby, General Assembly Building.

-- In 1985, more than 92 million words were sent to or from Headquarters in official United Nations cables. About 55,000 diplomatic mail pouches are sent to some 141 destinations each year. In turn, some 25,000 pouches are received.

(more)

0022

UNITED NATIONS

Press Services
Office of Public Information
United Nations, N.Y.

(FOR USE OF INFORMATION MEDIA — NOT AN OFFICIAL RECORD)

Press Release HQ/244
25 November 1969

WORLD CLOCK PRESENTED BY WATCH-MAKERS OF SWITZERLAND

At a ceremony today the United Nations was presented with a World Clock, the gift of the watch-makers of Switzerland.

The clock was presented by Bernard Turrettini, Permanent Observer of Switzerland to the United Nations, and was received by the Secretary-General, U Thant.

The clock, which has been installed on the east wall of the Secretary-General's conference room on the thirty-eighth floor of United Nations Headquarters, is in the form of a map of the world showing the capitals of all States Members of the United Nations. The official time zones of the world are displayed on the map. At the base is a moving tape which gives the correct time for each zone.

The design also incorporates two large clocks which show the exact time in New York and Geneva.

The World Clock was designed and built by Derby, S.A., of Neuchatel, Switzerland.

* *** *

0023

UNITED NATIONS

Press Services
Office of Public Information
United Nations, N.Y.
(FOR USE OF INFORMATION MEDIA -- NOT AN OFFICIAL RECORD)

Press Release SG/SM/1337
24 September 1970

STATEMENT BY SECRETARY-GENERAL AT PRESENTATION OF GIFT FROM TURKEY TO UNITED NATIONS, 24 SEPTEMBER

I wish to express my very sincere appreciation to the Government of Turkey for this superb gift. It is a particular pleasure to have its presentation to the United Nations made by you personally, Mr. Foreign Minister.

As the repository of numerous international treaties of our own time, the United Nations welcomes the presence of the oldest recorded peace treaty within its walls. As in so many subsequent pacts of a similar nature, the contending leaders - Ramses II, pharaoh of Egypt and Hattusilis III, king of the Hittites - renounce aggression and pledge to bring "good brotherhood and peace between their lands forever". Two major powers of their day are thus shown striving to attain equilibrium and to establish lasting peace. Their treaty should help us to accept the fact that the road to peace is long and arduous. It has been trod by men since the dawn of history.

This pertinent document comes to us from an area of the world which has been of great cultural as well as political importance throughout its long history. Strategically, located at the cross-roads of three continents, the Near East has been a source of material, intellectual and spiritual gifts to human civilization. Its history rings with names of great statesmen, it resounds with those of great prophets, teachers, scholars and artists.

Several versions of the text of this treaty were found recorded in early forms of writing - in cuneiform on the Hittite tablet, in Egyptian hieroglyphs on the walls of the Temple of Karnak and other places. This serves to remind us that the history of man was born with the art of writing. Three thousand

(more)

0024

years have passed since this famous treaty was recorded on stone and clay and silver, but writing remains man's most precious tool for preserving knowledge and for communicating and transmitting his ideas. Literacy remains today the valued attribute of a civilized society.

I understand, Mr. Foreign Minister, that the site of the ancient Hittite capital, where the original clay tablet was found, is only ninety miles from Ankara, the modern capital of your country which is of outstanding archaeological interest. I understand that numerous archaeological excavations are currently being conducted under the auspices of your Government and institutions. The world is deeply indebted to Turkey for its notable encouragement of international co-operation in the cultural sphere. For you have welcomed scholars and scientists of many lands to join you in recovering the past which lies buried beneath your soil. Mankind, as a whole, is thus enriched as the artifacts and records, which comprise its cultural heritage, are brought to light, studied and preserved for the benefit of present and future generations.

Such an historic peace treaty indeed deserves a place of honour in this building, the world centre of contemporary efforts to attain peace. As delegates, officials and visitors gaze upon this monumental rendering of the little clay tablet in the Archaeological Museum in Istanbul, they will gain historical perspective on questions which are of paramount concern to us today.

Would you kindly extend our thanks to your Government, Mr. Foreign Minister, for this generous gift which comes to us on the opportune occasion of the twenty-fifth anniversary of the United Nations.

* *** *

0025

PRESS RELEASE

799 UNITED NATIONS PLAZA
NEW YORK, N. Y. 10017

NOTE TO CORRESPONDENTS

Press Release USUN-75(71)
June 3, 1971

Delegates and staff at the United Nations have a new device to give them instant read out on the precise time in any of the world's 24 time zones.

Ambassador George Bush, United States Representative to the United Nations, on behalf of the United States Government, today presented to Secretary General U Thant an electronic digital Computron clock, developed by the Bulova Watch Company.

The clock, installed at the telephone desk in the main Delegates Lounge, features a miniature keyboard to control electronic read out at the touch of a finger. The new electronic clock has a memory and is programmed like a computer, indicating the precise time and whether it is A.M. or P.M. in any of the world's time zones.

The Secretary General was accompanied by David Vaughan, Assistant Secretary General for Administration. Mr. Harry B. Henshel, President of Bulova Watch Company, explained the operation of the mechanism which combines traditional skills of the watch-maker with modern electronic computer technology.

* * * * * * *

0026

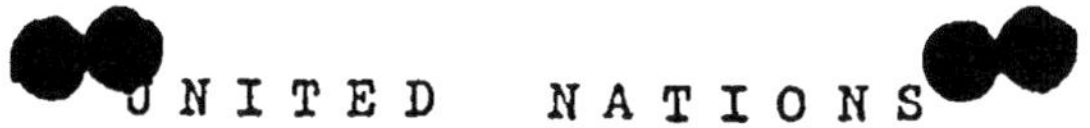

UNITED NATIONS

Press Section
Office of Public Information
United Nations, N.Y.

(FOR USE OF INFORMATION MEDIA -- NOT AN OFFICIAL RECORD)

Note No. 3934
17 September 1975

NOTE TO CORRESPONDENTS

A bronze figure entitled "The Rising Man" ("Die Aufsteigende") was presented to the United Nations this morning by the Foreign Minister of the German Democratic Republic, Oskar Fischer, on behalf of his country. The gift was accepted by Secretary-General Kurt Waldheim at a ceremony held at 10:15 a.m. in the United Nations garden.

The sculpture, created by sculptor Fritz Cremer, depicts a standing male figure, about eight feet tall, and is located at the north end of the garden.

In presenting the gift, Mr. Fischer said the figure symbolized "the rise of man to an awareness of his historic role and shows him wrestling to shake off the fetters of the past". It also embodied the "decades-old struggle of peoples to overcome colonialism and racism, a struggle in which the United Nations has been so successfully engaged". Mr. Fischer added that the gift was presented by the German Democratic Republic in appreciation of the "efforts the United Nations has been making towards peace and détente in the world".

The Secretary-General, accepting the gift on behalf of the United Nations, stated that the "vivid and arresting" statue rightly symbolized the United Nations, which "represents the bondage of the past, the liberation of the present, and the hopes for the future". He added: "Let us resolve to prove worthy of the sacrifices of the past and the aspirations for the future which bind us all together, and which represent our mandate and our task."

(Further details of the sculpture are given in Press Release HQ/341 of 16 September.)

* *** *

0027

United Nations

Press Release

Office of Public Information
Press Section
United Nations, New York

SG/SM/2655
HQ/390
11 December 1978

STATEMENT BY SECRETARY-GENERAL AT PRESENTATION OF GIFT BY FEDERAL REPUBLIC OF GERMANY

Following is the text of a statement made today by Secretary-General Kurt Waldheim at a ceremony held for the presentation of a gift from the Government of the Federal Republic of Germany:

It gives me great pleasure to accept on behalf of the United Nations the gift which the Federal Republic of Germany has made in remodelling the Quiet Room of the Security Council.

One of the main purposes of the Quiet Room will be to serve as a place where members of the Security Council can meet informally to discuss matters of current concern. I believe that the comfortable and relaxed atmosphere which has been created here will do much to facilitate the important work of the members of the Council.

Moreover, the room itself is a significant artistic contribution to the United Nations building and an impressive example of contemporary interior design and creativity. On this occasion, I would like to express a special tribute to Professors Gunter Frahtmrk and Paolo Nestler for their excellent work in designing the new Quiet Room.

It is especially appropriate that today's ceremony should take place at a time when the presidency of the Security Council is, for the second time, held by the Federal Republic of Germany. The Federal Republic has in recent years made an important contribution to the work of the United Nations in the Security Council and in many other areas. Its initiative in proposing an international convention against the taking of hostages and, with other members of the Council, in the efforts to bring about a peaceful solution in Namibia, and its support for the United Nations' peace-keeping operations, are only a few of the instances in which the Federal Republic has played a most significant role.

(more)

0028

UNITED NATIONS

Press Services
Office of Public Information
United Nations, N.Y.

(FOR USE OF INFORMATION MEDIA -- NOT AN OFFICIAL RECORD)

Note No. 3619
11 September 1970

NOTE TO CORRESPONDENTS

A four-ounce rock from the moon, brought to earth by the *Apollo 11* astronauts who landed on the moon on 20 July 1969, will go on display to the public at United Nations Headquarters on Monday, 14 September.

The display, which will be permanent, will also include a small United Nations flag carried to the moon on board *Apollo 11*.

The display will be located in the foyer of the General Assembly building, near the Meditation Room.

The moon rock, irregular in shape and about 1-1/2 inches in diameter, is enclosed in a plexiglass case within a glass case containing the display as a whole.

The moon rock and flag were presented to the United Nations on the first anniversary of the moon landing. The presentation was made to the Secretary-General, U Thant, by Thomas O. Paine, Administrator of the United States National Aeronautics and Space Administration (NASA).

The presentation ceremony at Headquarters on 20 July was attended by the three *Apollo 11* astronauts - Neil A. Armstrong, Edwin E. Aldrin, Jr., and Michael Collins.

(For details of the ceremony, see Note No. 3611 and Press Releases SG/SM/1306 and 1307.)

The moon rock was on display to members of delegations and the Secretariat from 22 to 24 July, prior to preparation of the public exhibit.

* *** *

0029

Press Release

Press Section
United Nations, New York

HQ/432
13 January 1988

SAUDI ARABIA PRESENTS UN WITH CURTAIN OF HOLY KAABA, AS SYMBOL OF CIVILIZATION AND BROTHERHOOD

Saudi Arabia this afternoon presented to the United Nations the curtain of the door of the holy Kaaba in Makkah, formerly known as Mecca.

The presentation was made by Saudi Arabia's Ambassador to the United States, Faisal Alhegelan, to Secretary-General Javier Perez de Cuellar at a special ceremony held in the West Foyer in the United Nations General Assembly building, where the curtain will remain on display.

In presenting the gift on behalf of the King and the people of Saudi Arabia, Mr. Alhegelan said he believed the curtain was an "appropriate gift to the United Nations because of the commonality between the spiritual teachings of Islam and the principles embodied in the Charter" of the world Organization.

He said the gift was "an intricate symbol of human civilization and of the brotherhood of man" and was a "testimony to the profound spiritual values, tradition and achievements" of Moslems all around the world.

Saudi Arabia, as one of the original founders of the United Nations, presented the curtain today, he said, as a reaffirmation of its commitment to the principles of the international Organization. He expressed the hope that those principles would "continue to guide us all in our pursuit of a just and permanent peace for all mankind".

In response, the Secretary-General thanked King Fahd for the "striking demonstration of Saudi Arabia's high regard for the mission and ideals of the United Nations", and said that the sense of unity and of human equality, together with the shared aspiration for peace, allied the people of Islam to the ideals of the Charter of the United Nations.

The gift from Saudi Arabia, he said, was a "particularly appropriate symbol of our common endeavours for peace and international co-operation".

The curtain, a black pure silk cloth embroidered in gold and silver threads, originally hung at the door of the holy Kaaba in Mecca five years ago. It measures 3.20 by 5.20 metres, and is mounted on a frame 4.75 by 7.70 metres large. The embroidery includes verses from the Koran.

Curtains like the one presented to the United Nations today have covered the door of the holy Kaaba for centuries and are periodically changed. They are handcrafted by Saudi Arabian professional artisans in a special workshop in the Holy City of Makkah.

* *** *

5225P

For information media — not an official record

0030

Press Release

Department of Public Information • Press Section • New York

SG/SM/4203
HQ/487
30 September 1988

TEXT OF STATEMENT BY SECRETARY-GENERAL AT UNVEILING OF GIFT FROM LUXEMBOURG

Following is the text of a statement by Secretary-General Javier Perez de Cuellar this morning in unveiling a gift of sculpture from Luxembourg* to the United Nations:

We are here today to unveil a sculpture which we owe to the generosity of the State of Luxembourg and which, I am sure, will not fail to affect everyone who sees it. I am reminded of Gertrude Stein's remark that the essence of truth in art is to combine clarity with energy. The evocative power of this sculpture derives from the fact that it is a striking symbol of non-violence or, more precisely, the rejection and transcending of violence.

The creator of the sculpture, the well-known Swedish artist Carl Fredrik Reuterswärd, who has been kind enough to be with us for this ceremony, has not placed himself in an ideal world from which violence has been banished from the outset. A realist like all true creative individuals, he has had the ingenious idea of taking an ordinary weapon, known and commonly found all around the world, and of tying a knot in the barrel to make it harmless forever.

He thus shows that man is the master of the things he has made, however dangerous they might be. Man has the capability to renounce the use of the weapons which he has fashioned for himself, free not to acquire any more, free even to destroy the weapons he has.

We have recently had proof of this: for the first time, some missiles have been destroyed in the East and in the West, because those who possessed them decided that their security could be based on openness and trust instead of secrecy and fear.

(more)

* For details, see Press Release HQ/486 issued on 28 September.

This is therefore a most opportune time to unveil a sculpture which will symbolize not only the ideal for which mankind is striving but also the initial results of the negotiations that are under way.

I also think that an entirely fitting place has been chosen for this sculpture. Placed as it is in front of the General Assembly building, it will give tangible expression to the continuous concern for disarmament of all Member States of the United Nations.

It remains for me to express to you, Mr. Secretary of State, my most sincere thanks for this outstanding work of art. The United Nations will always be grateful to Luxembourg, one of its founding Members and a country which was a victim in two world wars, for its commitment to the principles and ideals of the Organization and in particular to disarmament. May this sculpture make all who see it pause and reflect, may it arouse in them the desire to reject violence in all its forms, and may it lead them to pursue the goal of security based on mutual understanding and respect.

* *** *

0032

The President of Nicaragua, Her Excellency, Mrs. Violeta de Chamorro presented the Secretary-General of the United Nations with a gift during their meeting this morning at 9:30 a.m.

The gift consists of a destroyed firearm, of the SAR type (self action rifle) that belonged to a member of the Nicaraguan Resistance by the name of Julio Alvarez Pineda, a.k.a."El Picudo". This firearm was received and rendered inoperable by the ONUCA forces in Nicaragua on 5 August 1990, in Region 5, in a place called El Almendro.

The gift by the President of Nicaragua would be on display in the Map room in the 38th floor.

New York 27 September 1990

******

TO THE UNITED NATIONS - 2 UNITED NATIONS PLAZA, NEW YORK, N.Y. 10017 - TEL. (212) 308-7009

PRESS RELEASE

On Friday, February 22, 1991, Her Majesty Queen Margrethe II of Denmark will pay a visit to the United Nations. The Queen and the Prince Consort, His Royal Highness Prince Henrik, are on an official state visit to the United States of America. Today the Queen is being received by President George Bush at The White House. During the visit the Queen is accompanied by the Danish Minister for Foreign Affairs, Mr. Uffe Ellemann-Jensen.

During the visit to the United Nations the Queen and the Prince Consort will have lunch with UN Secretary-General Javier Perez de Cuellar and the Queen will present a special gift to the United Nations. The gift will be received by the Secretary-General at a brief ceremony at 3 pm in the area outside the main entrance to the General Assembly Hall.

The Royal Couple and the Minister for Foreign Affairs will afterwards make a brief tour of the building.

New York, February 20, 1991

0034

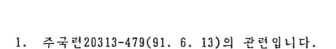

주 국 련 대 표 부

주국련(공) 35260- **509** 1991. 6. 20.

수신 장 관

참조 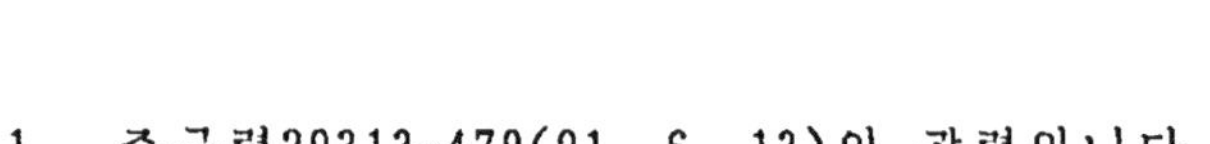국제기구조약국장, 해외공보관장, 문화협력국장, 문화부 문화정책국장

제목 유엔가입(기증품)

1. 주국련20313-479(91. 6. 13)의 관련입니다.

2. 연호관련 1986년이후 1990년까지 유엔이 기증받은 기증품 목록을 추가 송부합니다.

첨 부 : 동 자료 1부. 끝.

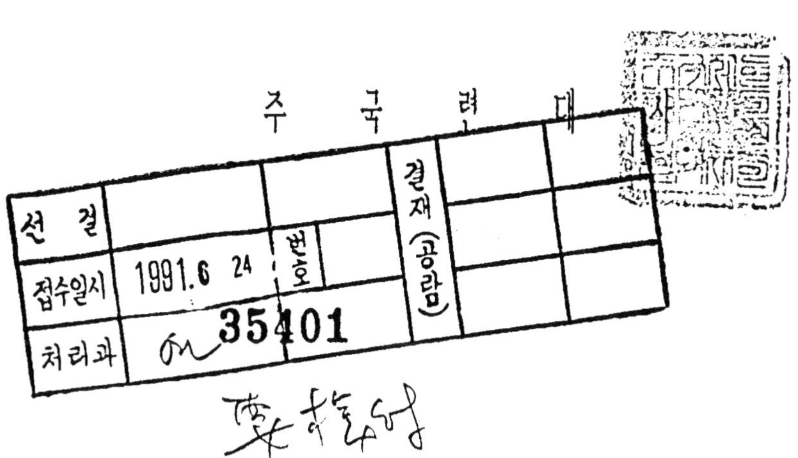
주 국 련 대

선 결			결재 (공람)		
접수일시	1991.6 24	번호			
처리과	35401				

0035

GIFTS DONATED TO THE UNITED NATIONS AFTER 1986

	DONOR	TYPE	TITLE	ARTIST	DESCRIPTION	MATERIAL	SIZE
1.	AFGHANISTAN	RUG	N/A	N/A	ONE MEDIUM SIZE RUG AND 4 SMALL RUGS		
2.	AFGHANISTAN	TABLE			TABLE		
3.	AUSTRIA	PAINTING	"MONOLITH OF PEACE"	FLORIA, HENRIETTE			
4.	COMOROS	PRESERVED FISH			COELACANTH (POORLY PRESERVED)	FISH	
[illegible]	HOLY SEE	PAINTING	"CHRIST CRUCIFIED"	ROUALT, GEORGES	PAINTING		
6.	HONDURAS	SCULPTURE			LARGE MAYAN HEAD		
7.	ITALY	SCULPTURE	"MOTHER AND CHILD"	MANZU, GIACOMO	BRONZE SCULPTURE	BRONZE	25 FEET HIGH
8.	KENYA	PAINTING			WALL-SIZE OIL PAINTING	OIL PAINT.	
9.	KENYA	SCULPTURE			KISII STONE SCULPTURE	STONE	
10.	KOREA	GOLD CROWN			GOLD CROWN		
11.	KUWAIT	REPLICA			REPLICA OF KUWAITI DHOW		
12.	LEBANON				SARCOGHAGUS		
[illegible]	LIBERIA	FIGURE			IVORY FIGURE OF PEACE	IVORY	
14.	LUXEMBOURG	FIGURE	"NON-VIOLENCE"	REUTERSWARD	KNOTTED PISTOL		
15.	MICRONESIA	FIGURE			CARVED WOODEN EEL		
16.	NEPAL				STORED IN FIVE CRATES		
17.	NORWAY	WALL COVERING					
18.	SWEDEN	RUGS			3 RUGS		

GIFTS DONATED TO THE UNITED NATIONS AFTER 1986

DONOR	TYPE	TITLE	ARTIST	DESCRIPTION	MATERIAL	SIZE
19. SWEDEN	RUGS			TWO RUGS		
20. SWEDEN	STATUE	"NEW YORK, NEW YORK"	OLSSON, ARNE	MANHATTAN SKYSCRAPERS		3 METRES HEIGHT
21. TAIWAN	PLAQUE			STONE PLAQUE		
22. TOGO	FIGURE			CARVED WOOD ABSTRACT FIGURE		
TOGO	FIGURES			CAST METAL FIGURES ON TRAVERTINE STONE BASE		
24. UNITED REPUBLIC TANZANIA				AFRICAN ZEBRA HIDE DRUM		
25. USSR	SCULPTURE	GOOD DEFEATS EVIL	TSERETELI, Z.	ST.GEORGE SLAYING DRAGONS(US/USSR MISSILE PARTS)	BRONZE	39 FT.

0037

관리 번호	91 -3835

분류번호	보존기간

발 신 전 보

번 호 : WUN-1659 910611 1609 FO 종별 :

수 신 : 주 유엔 대사. 총영사

발 신 : 장 관 (국연)

제 목 : 유엔가입(기증품)

대 : UNW-1469

연 : WUN-1557

1. 연호, 유엔가입 계기 행사에 관한 관계부처 회의(6.8)시 아국의 기증품에 대하여 큰북(용고) 또는 기타 예술작품을 고려하자는 의견이 제시된 바 있음.

2. 이와 관련 본부는 일단 "용고"가 서울올림픽을 상징하는 기념물로서 부피가 과대하여 유엔내 좋은 장소에 전시되기가 힘들 것으로 보고있음.

3. 따라서 관계부처에 적절한 기증품(안)을 제시 하고자 하니 동 기증품목에 관한 귀견 및 타국의 기증품 목록을 지급 보고 바람. 끝.

예 고 : 1991.12.31. 일반

(국제기구조약국장 문동석)

검 토 필(1991.6.30.)

1991.12.31.에 예고문에 의거 일반문서로 재분류됨

보안 통제	

앙 고 재	91년 6월 11일	유엔과	기안자 성명		과 장		국 장		차 관	장 관

외신과통제

0038

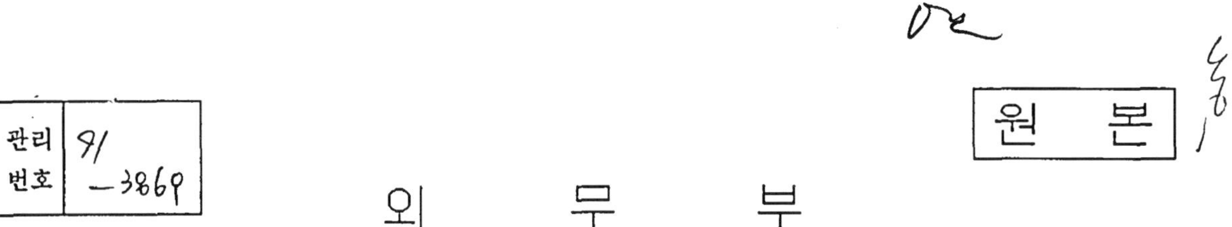

외 무 부

종 별 : 지 급

번 호 : UNW-1549 일 시 : 91 0613 1800

수 신 : 장 관(국연,해기,문정,문일,기정)

발 신 : 주 유엔 대사

제 목 : 유엔가입(기증품)

대:WUN-1659,1668

대호관련 사무총장실등 사무국 관계 요로를 통해 입수한 사항을 우선 중간보고하며 진전사항 추보예정임.

1. 본직은 6.13 사무총장 비서실장 VIRENDRA DAYAL 을 면담, 아국은 유엔가입을 기념하기 위해 기증품을 제공할 의사가 있음을 전달하고 유엔측의 좋은 의견이 있으면 제시해 주도록 요청하였음.

2. 이와관련 DAYAL 비서실장은 아국의 기증품 증정의사에 사의를 우선 표한다면서 기증품은 예술적 조형물과 시설물로 대별할수 있으며 조형물은 ALVARDO DE SOTO/ASST. SECRETARY GENERAL, OFFICE FOR RESEARCH AND THE COLLECTION OF IMFORMATION 에서, 시설물은 J.RICHARD FORAN/ ACTING UNDER-SECRETARY GENERAL, DEPARTMENT OF ADMINISTRATION AND MANAGEMENT 가 담당한다면서 조형물에는 기증한 국가 또는 정부명의를 표시하여 비치되나, 시설물의 경우는 유엔당국으로서는 시설을 제공한 국가 표시를 하지 않고 있으며 예를들면, 서독이 시설.비품등을 제공한 안보리 DELEGATE LOUNGE 와 같이 명칭이 붙여지지 않는 것이 관례이지만, 다만 총회장 주변에 위치한 INDONESIAN LOUNGE 나 CHINESE LOUNGE 의 경우와 같이 비치된 기증품등으로 인해 편의상 통칭되고 있을 뿐 이라고 설명했음.

3. 조형물의 경우는 회원국이 기증의사를 사무총장에게 통보하면 사무총장실 주관 U.N. ART COMMITTEE 를 구성, 기증품의 종류, 규모, 위치할 장소등 관련협의를 하게되며 유엔이 그동안 기증받은 조형물이 많은 관계로 기증품목에 따라서는 아예 전시되지 않거나 전시될때까지 상당기간이 소요되는 사례도 있으므로 (90.12 월 소련이 기증한 미.소 미사일 폐기물로 제작한 조각동상은 설치하는데 3 년이상이 걸렸다함.)

국기국 장관 차관 1차보 2차보 미주국 문협국 분석관 청와대
안기부 문화부 공보처

PAGE 1

91.06.14 08:11
외신 2과 통제관 BS
0039

기증품을 일방적으로 결정제공하기 보다는 유엔관계자와 사전협의하는 것이바람직하다고 말하면서 용고등 아국이 고려하고 있는 조형물 기증에 관해서는 담당책임자 DE SOTO 가 현재 출장중임으로 동인귀임 (7 월초순)후 협의추진토록 하는것이 좋겠다는 의견을 제시했음.

4. 시설물의 경우는 본직면담시 배석한 사무총장실 비서실 담당관 J.PAUL KAVANAGH 로 하여금 시설물담당 DEPARTMENT OF ADMINISTRATION AND MANAGEMENT 와 협의검토후 유엔측의 몇가지 의견을 추후 알려 주겠다고 약속했음.

5. 타국의 기증품 목록은 금주 정파편 송부함. 끝

(대사 노창희-국장, 관장)

예고:91.12.31. 일반

검 토 필(1991.6.30.)

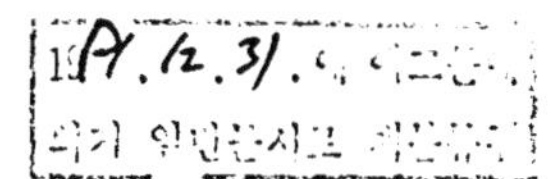

PAGE 2

0040

관리 번호	91-3965

분류번호	보존기간

발 신 전 보

번 호 : WUN-1777 910626 1734 FO 종별 :

수 신 : 주 유엔 대사. 총영사

발 신 : 장 관 (국연)

제 목 : 유엔가입(기증품)

대 : UNW-1549

연 : WUN-1659

연호, 관계부처는 유엔가입기념 기증품 제작에 시일이 많이 소요되므로 가급적 조속히 품목을 선정하여야 한다 하는 바, 사무국측 의견 및 귀견을 조속 회보바람. 끝.

(국제기구조약국장 문동석)

예고 : 91.12.31.일반

검 토 필(1991.6.30.)

1991.12.31.에 예고문에 의거 일반문서로 재분류됨

보안 통제	

앙 고 재	91년 6월 26일	UN 과	기안자 성명		과 장		국 장		차 관	장 관
			송영완				전결			

외신과통제

0041

관리 번호	91 —6052

원 본

외 무 부

종 별 :

번 호 : UNW-1733 일 시 : 91 0705 1600

수 신 : 장관(국연,해기,문정,문일,기정)

발 신 : 주 유엔 대사

제 목 : 유엔가입 (기증품)

대: WUN-1777,1668

연: UNW-1549

1. 신대사는 7.3. 유엔 기증품 (조형물)담당 실무책임자인 ALVARDO DE SOTO 사무차장보를 면담, 대호건 협의한바 요지 아래 보고함.

가. 기증품 접수 및 전시기준

0 기증품 선정은 각국이 자체적으로 결정할 문제이나 다만 사무국으로서는 각국의 기증품이 해당국의 희망대로 설치 또는 전시시킬수 없는 어려움이 있는바 사무국으로서는 시설 또는 장비보다는 조형물을 선호한다고 할수있으며 조형물의 경우에도 예술적 또는 고고학적 가치와 그규모 여하가 주요 고려대상이 되고있음.

0 그간 많은 기증품이 접수되었으나 기증품의 예술적 가치와 전시장소 면에서의 제약으로 인해 현재 30 여개 기증품이 창고에 그대로 보관되어 있는 상태임. (대형목각 제품 또는 수직제품등)

나. 기증절차

0 각국이 기증품을 선정, 사무총장에게 통보하면 상기 차장보가 위원장으로 되어있는 ART COMMITTEE (3 인 전문가로 구성)에서 검토, 접수여부를 결정하게됨.

0 기증품 전달은 총회 기조연설 기간중 간단한 기증식을 통해 행해지는 경우가 많으며 이에는 사무총장등 유엔 고위관계자가 참석하게 됨. 기증국이 희망하는 경우 COUPE DE CHAMPAGNE 을 가질수도 있음.

다. 아측 구상에 대한 견해

1) 용고

동 용고의 상징성에 관한 신대사의 설명에 공감하며 그 의의를 인정하나, 자신의 개인적인 견해는 아래와 같음을 참고바람.

국기국 차관 1차보 문협국 외정실 청와대 안기부 문화부 공보처

PAGE 1 91.07.06 06:12

외신 2과 통제관 CF

0042

0 용고의 크기 (130 CM X 155 CM) 로 보아 건물내 전시는 현실적으로 어려울 것으로 보이며 공식 검토가 있어보아야 알겠으나 옥외전시에도 장소 선정면에서 제약이 많을것으로 보임.

0 동양에서와는 달리 서양에서는 용에 대한 인식이 좋지 않다는 점도 고려되어야 할것임. 90.12 월 소련이 기증한 GOOD DEFEATS EVIL 조각동상의 용 (ST.GEORGE SLAYING DRAGONS-US/USSR MISSILE PARTS) 과 대조적이라는 점도 지적될수있음.

0 옥외전시중 예기치 않게 파손되는 경우도 고려되어야 할것임.

2) 벽 장식물

유엔 건물내 벽화 또는 수직 벽장식물을 추가로 배치할 장소는 거의 없는 실정이고 또 이미 접수한 유사물품도 많아 사무국으로서는 현재 더이상의 벽장식물을 사양 (DISCOURAGE) 하고있는 처지임.

3) 기타 기증품

0 자기생각으로는 전시효과가 큰 좋은위치에 상설 전시되기 위해서는 일반의 관심을 끌수있는 소규모의 역사적 유물 또는 예술작품이 바람직하다고 보며 그 규모는 보관용기를 포함 50 CM(폭) X 170 CM(높이) 를 넘지않는것이 좋으리라고 봄.

0 유사한 예로 에집트는 B.C. 7 세기의 OSIRIS 신상 진품을, 페루는 2-3 천년전 수의를 총회회의장 주변에 전시하고 있는바 진품이라면 더좋겠으나 역사적 가치가 있는 물품이라면 복제품이라도 무방할것으로 봄.

0 옥외시설물로는 안전문제로 그간 폐쇄상태에 있던 구내 어린이 놀이터 전면 보수등도 재미있는 아이디어라고 생각하는바 이들 야외시설물에 관하여는 사무국내 유관부서와 협의해보기 바람.

2. 이와 관련 기증품에 대한 당관의견을 다음 보고하니 동건 검토에 참고바람.

0 용고는 유엔 실무책임자 견해등을 참작, 기증품 대상서 제외하는것이 좋겠음.

0 기증품 대상은 기증후 전시효과, 위치 및 상설전시 등을 우선적으로 고려해야 되기 때문에 유엔측이 선호하는 역사적 유물 또는 예술작품중에서 원칙적으로 선정토록 하는것이 바람직하며 우리문화를 상징성 있게 대표할수 있는 역사적 유물중 선정하는것이 좋겠음.

0 이러한 고려 대상중 신라금관 또는 고려청자를 기증품으로 선정하는것이 좋겠으나, 유엔이 요구하는 폭 50 CM X 높이 170 CM 정도의 소규모 전시품이라는 점을 감안한다면 다른나라의 도자기류와 비교될수 있는 고려청자 보다는 금관 (모조품도

가함)이 적당할 것으로 생각됨. (이경우 지구촌 행사시 기증식을 가질수 있을것임)

0 시설물은 유엔의 관계부서가 제시해오는 의견등을 종합 검토하는것이 바람직하므로 시간적 여유를 가지고 추후 결정하는것이 좋겠음. 끝

(대사 노창희-차관)

예고:91.12.31. 일반

검 토 필(1991.6.30.)

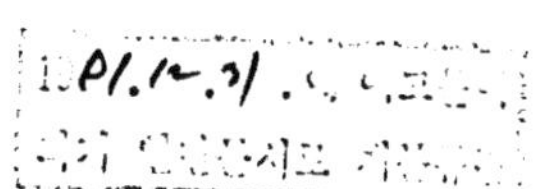

PAGE 3

0044

유엔가입 기증품

1991.7.6.
국제연합과

1. 기증품 접수 및 전시기준

o 유엔사무국은 시설 또는 장비보다는 조형물 선호

o 기증품의 유엔내 전시관련, 예술적 또는 고고학적 가치와 그 규모가 고려대상

- 기증품의 예술적 가치와 전시장소 제약등으로 현재 30여개 기증품을 창고에 보관중

2. 기증절차

o 각국이 기증품을 선정, 사무총장에게 통보하면 Art Committee (De Soto 사무차장보(위원장) 및 3인의 전문가로 구성)에서 접수여부, 전시장소등 결정

o 기증품 전달은 총회 기조연설 기간중 간단한 기증식을 통해 행해지는 경우가 많으며, 사무총장등 유엔 고위관계자 참석

- 기증국 희망시 coupe de champagne 가능

3. 아측구상에 대한 De Soto 사무차장 견해

가. 용 고

o 용고의 크기로 보아 건물내 전시는 어려울 것이며, 옥외전시도 장소선정 면에서 제약 예상

0045

o 서양에서는 용에 대한 인식이 좋지 않음.

- 90.12월 소련이 기증한 조각(God defeats evil)에서 용이 evil로 표현되고 있음.

나. 벽 장식물

o 유엔 건물내 벽화 또는 수직 벽장식물을 추가로 배치할 장소 없음.

다. 기증품 선정에 대한 사무차장보 견해

o 소규모의 역사적 유물 또는 예술작품이 바람직

- 규모는 보관용기를 포함 50cm(폭)×170cm(높이)를 넘지않는 것이 바람직

o 진품이면 더욱 좋으나 역사적 가치가 있는 물품이라면 복제품도 무방

4. 기증품에 대한 주유엔대표부 건의

o 금관 고려

- 고려청자도 고려해볼 수 있으나 타국의 도자기류와 비교될 수 있는 바, 금관은 아국 특유의 문화성을 잘 표현(금관으로 결정시 지구촌 행사기간중 기증식 개최가능)

- 유엔측 견해 고려, 용고는 대상에서 제외함이 바람직

o 시설물(예 : 유엔본부내 어린이공원)은 유엔측이 추후 제시하기로한 의견등을 종합 검토함이 바람직

0046

33281

기안용지

분류기호 문서번호	국연 2031 -	(전화:)	시행상 특별취급	
보존기간	영구·준영구. 10. 5. 3. 1	장	관	
수신처 보존기간				
시행일자	1991. 7. 12.			

보조기관	국 장	전결	협조기관		문서통제
	심의관				검열 1991. 7. 13
	과 장				
기안책임자		황준국			발송인

경 유		발신명의		발송 1991. 7. 13 외무부
수 신	문화부장관			
참 조				

제 목	유엔기증품

참고 : UNW-1733(91.7.5)

~~1.~~ 금년 가을 유엔총회에서 우리의 유엔가입이 실현되는 ~~시 아국이 유엔에 가입할 것으로~~
계기로 유엔에 기증할 기증품은 귀부 사정상
~~예상됨에 따라 귀부도 아시다시피 당부는 유엔에 대한 기증품~~
조속한 시일내 결정해야 할 것으로 사료되오니
~~문제를 적극 검토하고 있습니다.~~

~~2. 당부로서는 동 기증품이 9월 중순으로 예상되는~~
~~대통령의 뉴욕방문시에~~ 유엔측에 전달될 수 있도록 ~~필요한~~
~~조치를 취하는 것이 바람직할 것으로 사료되므로,~~ 귀부에서

0047 /계속/

(2)

이를 유의하여 주시오

~~동 사한을 유념하시어~~ 기증품 선정 및 제작에 대비하여

주시기 바랍니다.

~~3. 현재까지 제반 고려사항을 검토한 결과 당부로서는~~

~~신라금관 모형(순금)이 가장 적합할 것으로 사료되며, 금후~~

~~이와관련된 세부사항을 귀부와 별도로 협의할 예정임을 알려~~

~~드립니다.~~ 끝.

0048

관리 번호	91 -4516

원 본

외 무 부

종 별 :

번 호 : UNW-2047 일 시 : 91 0806 1100

수 신 : 장관 (국연,해기,문정,문일,기정)

발 신 : 주 유엔 대사

제 목 : 유엔가입 (기증품)

연: UNW-1733

1. 연호 관련 지구촌 행사시 기증식을 갖기 위해서는 사무총장실 및 ART COMMITTEE 등 유엔 관계기관과 사전협의를 해야하는바 시일이 촉박하므로 아국 기증품을 조속 선정, 통보바람.

2. 유엔 실무책임자는 아측에서 협의한 용고에 대해서는 전시장소등 이유로부정적 입장에 변함이 없다 하고있음. 끝

(대사 노창희-차관)

예고:91.12.31. 일반

1991.12.31. 에 예고문에 의거 일반문서로 재분류됨

국기국 차관 문협국 안기부 문화부 공보처

PAGE 1

91.08.07 00:59

외신 2과 통제관 FM

0049

長 官 報 告 事 項

報 告 畢

1991. 8. 8.
文化協力局
文化協力1課(6)

題 目 : 我國의 UN 加入 紀念 寄贈品

(文化協力局長과 文化部 文化政策局長間 協議 內容)

1. 品目 選定

가. 選定 計劃

1) 91.8.9(金)중 上部裁可를 받아 決定

2) 가급적 駐 유엔 大使의 建議가 반영되도록 努力

나. 檢討中인 品目

1) 龍鼓: 서울올림픽시 사용한 큰북

2) 月印千江之曲: 國漢文 혼용, 2m x 3m

3) 新羅金冠 및 腰帶: 순금, 實物大

2. 製作 및 傳達計劃

가. 製作期間: 40여일 소요

나. 今秋 UN 總會 期間中 傳達. 끝.

0050

月印千江之曲

1. 부처의 자비로움이 천개의 강(온누리, 중생)에 비춰주기를 기원하는 노래

2. 세종이 왕비(소헌 왕후 심씨)의 명복을 빌기 위하여 지은 부처를 찬송한 것

3. 석보상절을 보고 감흥하여 지은 것으로서 585곡으로 추측

* 석보상절

1) 세종이 소헌 왕후의 명복을 빌기위해 수양대군을 시켜 지은 석가모니의 일대기

2) 한문으로 된 여러 불경을 토대로 하여 한글로 번역

0051

관리번호	91-4697

발 신 전 보

분류번호	보존기간

번 호 : WUN - 2164 910813 1812 DU 종별 : 지급

수 신 : 주 유엔대사 대사. 총영사

발 신 : 장 관 (문정,문일)

제 목 : 유엔가입(기증품)

대: UNW-1733, 2047

1. 문화부는 아국의 유엔가입 기증품으로 전문가들의 회의를 거쳐서 아래와 같이 "월인천강지곡"을 ~~최종~~ 선정예정인바, 아래사항을 참고, ~~하여~~ 유엔당국과 교섭후 그결과를 회보바람.

가. 규격 및 특성

○ 보물 제398호(금속활자본)

○ 한글본

- 원래 한글작품으로 한자로 토를달음

○ 세종어제작품으로 석보상절 다음가는 한글로쓴 최고의 문헌으로 조선초기 서사시의 대표작(1449년 한글금속활자본으로 쿠텐베르크 활자보다 앞섬)

나. 제작방법: 현존 월인천강지곡책자(상)을 펼친상태에서 적당한 크기로 확대하여 동판으로 입체감있게 제작(별도제작된 진열장과 함께 송부예정)

다. 기대효과

○ 우리나라에서 전세계에 자랑할 수 있는 과학적인 발명품은 문화의 기준이 되는 금속활자 뿐임.

○ 한글이 크게 부각되고 한자는 보조표기어로 사용되어 우리의 고유한 문자문화(한글)를 세계인에게 자연스럽게 홍보하는 기회 마련.

○ 아름답게 디자인된 전시기법으로 여러사람을 관심을 끌수 있음.

보안통제	

앙고재	년월일	과	기안자 성명		과 장		국 장		차 관	장 관

외신과통제

0052

	분류번호	보존기간

발 신 전 보

번 호 :

종별 :

수 신 : 주 대사. 총영사

발 신 : 장 관

제 목 :

2. 상기 관련, 유엔측과 협의, 아국 기증품을 전시할 수 있는 space(가로x세로x폭)파악 지급 회보바람.

3. 신라금관도 별도 제작중이니 참고바람.

(문화부 문화정책국장 신현웅)

예고: '91.12.31 일반

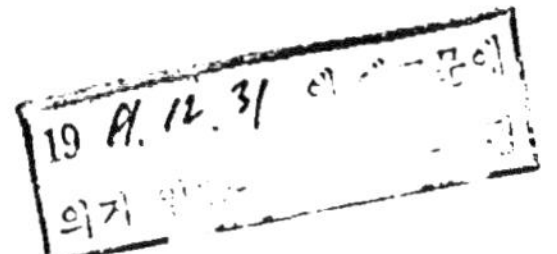

보안 통제	

앙 고 재	년 월 일	과	기안자 성 명		과 장		국 장		차 관	장 관

외신과통제

0053

관리 번호	91 -4142

외 무 부

종 별 :

번 호 : UNW-2139 일 시 : 91 0813 1700

수 신 : 장 관(문일,국연,문정,해기)

발 신 : 주 유엔 대사

제 목 : 유엔가입 (기증품)

대:WUN-2164

연:UNW-1733

1. 대호관련 유엔당국과 협의코자 하니 월인 천강지곡에 관한 영문 설명자료 및 관련 사진등 지급 송부바람.

2. 유엔측은 연호보고 내용과같이 규모가 보관용기 포함 50 CM (넓이) X 170 CM (높이)의 기증품이 바람직하다는 입장인 관계로 규격이 3 M (높이) X 2 M (넓이) X 50 CM (두께)인 월인 천강지곡은 유엔측이 요구하는 기준보다 너무 큰규모임으로 전시장소확보에 문제가 있을것으로 보임.

3. 아국 기증품의 전시장소는 아측에서 기증품을 선정, 유엔사무총장에게 통보한 후 유엔 ART COMMITTEE 에서 협의 결정될 사항으로서 실제전시될때까지는상당한 기간이 요청되는것이 관례인바 현재로서는 아국 기증품의 전시장소를 사전에 파악하는 것은 어려운 실정임.

따라서 아국 기증품이 결정되면 지구촌 행사기간에 우선 전달식을 갖을수있으며 유엔건물내 전시효과가 좋은 위치에 전시될때까지는 상당한 시일이 소요될것으로 생각됨.

4. 1 항관련 자료수령후 유엔당국과의 협의결과는 추보할것임.끝

(대사 노창희-국장)

예고:91.12.31. 일반

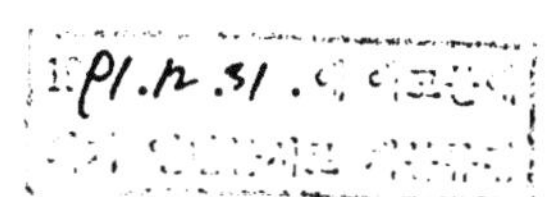

문협국 국기국 문화부 공보처

PAGE 1 91.08.14 07:25

외신 2과 통제관 BS

0054

朝鮮日報

1991. 8. 13. 화, 5면

李圭泰코너

龍鼓

한고조(漢高祖)는 어머니가 꿈속에서 용(龍)과 교합해서 태어난 것으로 돼있다. 고려태조 왕건(王建)도 그의 할아버지가 서해의 용녀(龍女)와 교합해서 태어난 용손(龍孫)이다. 용은 하늘에 계시는 천제(天帝)의 사자(使者)이기에 천제(天帝)의 대행자인 임금은 이 용의 피를 수혈받는 것으로 초인간화(超人間化)해야 할 필요가 있었다. 그래서 임금의 혈통을 용손(龍孫), 임금의 얼굴은 용안(龍顔), 임금의 옷을 곤용포(袞龍袍), 임금이 앉는 자리를 용상(龍床)이라 했음도 그때문이다.

하지만 용이 상서로운 제왕(帝王)이미지로 군림한것은 중국과 한국뿐이다. 이집트의 고대 신화에서 용은 가뭄과 서리를 몰아오는 악령(惡靈)으로 선(善)을 몰아내는 악(惡)의 상징이 되고있다. 이 용이미지가 계승되어 이슬람 세계에서 용이미지는 부정적이다.

기독교 세계에서도 마찬가지다. 「요한계시록」에서 용은 칠두사(七頭蛇)의 괴물로 나오는데 그칠두란 자만-탐욕-질투-분노-나태-호기심-색욕(色欲)의 상징이다. 용이 벌리고 있는 아가리는 지옥의 문이요, 이단(異端)과 사교(邪敎)의 유혹이다. 용이 한국에서 풍작(豊作)을 몰아오는 영물인데 유럽에서는 흉작(凶作)을 몰아오는 흉물이다. 유럽의 축제인 카니발(謝肉祭)에서 용을 퇴치하는 행사가 수반된 것도 바로 이 때문이다.

대천사(大天使) 미카엘의 용퇴치를 비롯, 게르만의 서사시 「니베룽겐의 노래」에 등장하는 영웅 지그프리드도 용과 싸워 이기고 있다. 이처럼 유럽의 정의와 평화는 용을 퇴치함으로써 구제되고 있다.

정부수립이래의 소원이던 유엔가입을 기념하여 당국이 유엔에 선물하는 기념품으로, 처음에 용고(龍鼓)가 선택되었다고 한다. 서울올림픽때 개막을 알렸던 커다란 북으로, 북통에 용그림이 그려져있어 용고다. 이 제의를 받고 유엔측에서는 너무 커서 건물안에 놓을 데가 없으니 건물밖에 설치하려면하되 관리는 당신네들이 맡아 하라는 냉담한 반응이었다는 현지발 보도가 있었다.

사실상 거부를 뜻하는 이 냉담의 저의가 뭣인지는 알수 없으나 그중 용에 대한 부정적이미지가 크게 작용했음직하다.

이세상의 넓은지역에서 흉물이 돼있는 이 용을 평화와 정의의 전당에 들여놓고 싶지 않았을 것이다. 이에 정부에서는 유엔 기념물로 경주백마총에서 출토된 신라금관모조품으로 한다는 보도가 있었다. 우리 찬란한 고대문화를 과시하는데는 십상인지 모르지만 그것이 전시된 곳이 민주-평화-정의의 전당인 유엔이고보면 제왕(帝王)-곧 전제군주의 상징인 금관도 알맞지않고 또 반갑지 않은 선택이라고 본다. 더욱이 3백50개의 금제영락이 나풀거리는 이 모조금관을 만드는데 적지않이 6천7백여만원이 든다하니 기념품치고 과람하다는 생각이 든다.

0055

世界日報
1991. 8. 14. 수, 2면

유엔에 「月印千江之曲」 금속활자 판틀 기증

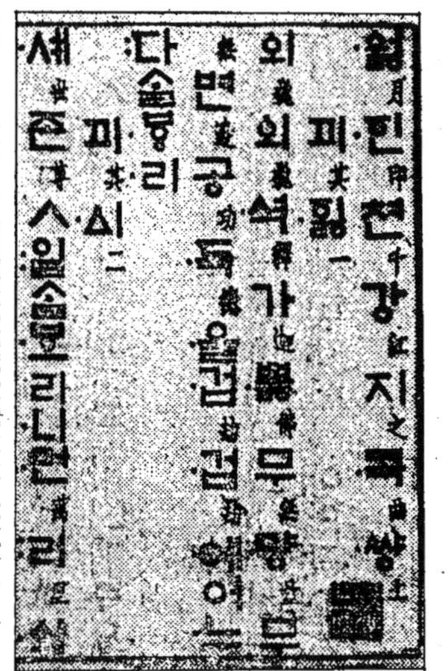

◇정부가 유엔가입을 기념해 금속활자판으로 만들어 기증할 보물 제398호 「月印千江之曲」의 처음 부분。

盧대통령 방문때 직접전달
인간문화재 김근수씨 제작

정부는 유엔가입 기념품으로 세종대왕의 「月印千江之曲」을 인쇄한 금속활자판틀과 영인본및 그 장식품을 유엔본부에 기증키로 13일 확정했다.

盧泰愚대통령은 오는 9월 유엔방문때 이를 직접전달할 계획이며 이문화선물은 유엔본부의 전시실에 상설전시된다.

문화부가 이들을 문화선물로 선정한 것은 우리나라 금속활자인쇄가 세계에서 가장 앞선 것으로 국제적으로 공인됐으며 (「고금상정예문」1234년,「직지심경」1377년) 특히 「월인천강지곡」은 우리의 글자인 한글의 字體가 금속활자로 인쇄된 최초의 실물로서 이또한 구텐베르크의 금속활자인쇄(1450년)보다 앞섰기 때문이다.

문화부는 그동안 문화선물 후보품목으로 백자 龍鼓 자수병풍 신라금관등을 검토했으나 유엔본부의 전시공간사정과 한국문화의 상징성, 해외에서의 희소가치등을 감안해 「월인천강지곡」으로 결정했다.

이 금속활자판의 주조는 인간문화재 77호인 안성유기匠 김근수씨가 제작키로 했다.

0056

朝鮮日報 1991. 8. 14. 수, 2면

유엔가입 기념 문화선물 선정

월인천강지곡 인쇄字版등 기증키로

문화부는 13일 유엔가입을 계기로 유엔본부에 기증할 기념품으로 월인천강지곡(月印千江之曲)을 인쇄한 금속활자판틀과 영인본및 장식품을 선정했다.

문화부가 금속활자판등을 문화선물로 택한 것은 금속활자인쇄문화에서 우리나라가 세계 어느나라보다도 앞섰다는 사실을 알리기 위한 것이다.

활자판은 인간문화재 77호인 안성유기장 김근수씨가 제작한다.

이 문화선물은 남북한의 유엔가입후 유엔본부에 기증돼 다른 회원국들의 선물과 함께 전시된다.

韓國日報 1991. 8. 14. 수, 2면

「月印千江之曲 금속활자틀」 기증

유엔가입 기념품…「인쇄문화 우수성」알려

문화부는 13일 유엔 가입 기념품으로 세종대왕의 月印千江之曲을 인쇄한 금속활자틀과 월인천강지곡 영인본및 인쇄된 한 판을 확대한 장식품 한세트를 선물하기로 최종 확정했다.

문화부는 당초 신라금관을 선물하기로 잠정 결정했었으나 우리나라 금속활자가 서양최초의 금속활자인쇄보다 2백여년 앞선 사실을 감안, 활자문화의 우수성을 알리는 의미에서 한글의 字體가 금속활자로 처음 인쇄된 월인천강지곡 활자틀을 선물하기로 했다.

인간문화재77호로 지정된 안성 유기장 金根洙씨(76)가 제작을 맡을 이문화선물은 오는9월 유엔가입을 계기로 유엔본부에 기증되며 유엔 사무처에서는 다른 회원국의 선물과 함께 유엔본부전시실에 전시할 예정이다.

0057

中央日報

1991. 8. 14. 수, 2면

月印千江之曲 유엔에 기증

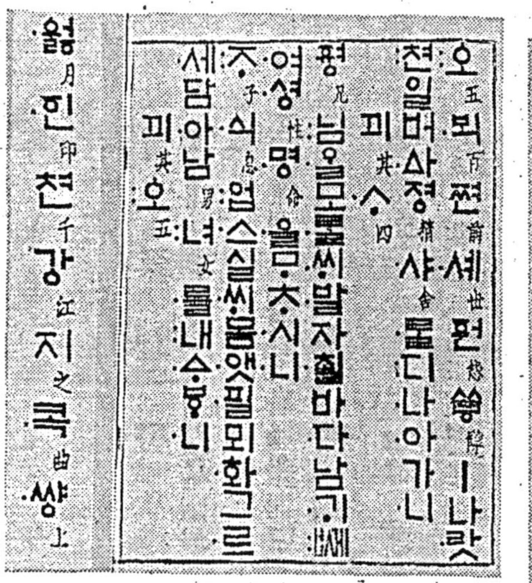

월인천강지곡 상 (月印千江之曲 上)

오뵉쪈셰원쓯ㅣ나랏
쳔일버ᅀᅡ졍샤ᄅᆞᆯ디나아가니
끵ᄉᆞ
평님ᄋᆞᆯ모ᄅᆞᆯᄊᆡ발자ᄀᆞᆯ바다남기ᄢᅦ
여셩명ᄋᆞᆯᄆᆞᄎᆞ시니
ᄌᆞ식업스실ᄊᆡ몸앳필뫼화그르
세담아남녀ᄅᆞᆯ내ᅀᆞᄫᆞ니
끵오

유엔가입기념 문화선물로 선정된「月印千江之曲」금속활자인쇄본(보물 제398호). 이 인쇄본의 확대사진과 금속활자 일부가 함께 기증된다.

중앙 2면 8.14

盧대통령 9월 방문때

인쇄문화 우수성 세계에 과시

龍鼓·자수병풍은 전달 않기로

정부는 유엔가입 기념품으로 世宗大王의「月印千江之曲」을 인쇄한 금속활자판들과 영인본·관련 장식품을 유엔본부에 기증키로 13일 확정했다.

이 기념품은 盧泰愚대통령이 다음달 24일 유엔본부를 방문할때 기증할 예정이며 유엔본부내 전시실에서 상설 전시된다.

문화부가 이 기념품을 문화선물로 선정한 이유는 우리의 금속활자 인쇄기술이 서구 최초인 구텐베르크 금속활자인쇄보다 2백년이상 앞선데다「月印千江之曲」은 한글 창제후 금속활자로 인쇄한 최초의 실물이기 때문이다.

문화부는 그동안 문화선물로 백자·금관·자수병풍·龍鼓등을 검토했었으나 유엔본부 전시공간사정과 우리문화의 독창성, 해외에서의 희소가치등을 감안해「月印千江之曲」을 결정한 것으로 알려졌다.

이 금속활자판의 주조는 인간문화재 77호인 성유기匠 金근수씨가 제작키로 했다.

東亞日報

1991. 8. 14. 수, 2면

月印千江之曲 금속활자를 유엔가입기념품으로 기증

우리 인쇄文化 우수성 알리기로

오는9월 유엔정기총회에서 유엔가입이 확실시됨에따라 정부는 유엔본부에 한국을 효과적으로 알릴수있는 상징적인 선물로 세종대왕의「月印千江之曲」을 인쇄한 금속활자판들과 영인본을 선정했다.

문화부는 유엔가입을 계기로 우리나라가 세계최초의 금속활자를 발명, 인쇄문화에서 가장 앞선 문화국임을 상징하는 기념품을 증정하기로 했다고 14일 밝혔다.

「月印千江之曲」은 세종31년 세종이 손수 지은 문헌으로 조선초기 서사시의 대표작으로 인정받고있으며 그 내용은 세종이 석가의 공덕을 찬양하는 것으로 돼있다.

이번 선물은 우리의 글자인 한글 자체가 금속활자로 인쇄된 최초의 실물이면서 서양최초의 금속인쇄인 구텐베르크성서보다 앞섰다는 점에서 우리의 인쇄문화와 고유글자를 세계에 알릴수 있는 선물로 평가된다.

0058

관리 번호	91 -4659

외 무 부

종 별 :

번 호 : UNW-2154 일 시 : 91 0814 1900

수 신 : 장관(문일,국연,문정,해기)

발 신 : 주 유엔 대사

제 목 : 유엔가입(기증품)

대:WUN-2180,2164

. 1. 대호관련 유엔기증품(조형물) 담당책임자 ALVARDO DE SOTO 사무차장보 및 실무담당 사무총장실 보좌관 LISA BUTTENHEIM 이 현재 출장중으로 8.19 귀임예정임.

2. 이와관련 SOTO 사무차장보가 귀임하는 8.19 중 면담, 동협의결과 회신예정임.다만 대호크기 (높이 3 M X 넓이 2 M) 의 기증품은 아측의 희망하는 장소에 전시는 어려울것으로 보임을 우선 참고바람. 끝

(대사 노창희-국장)

예고:91.12.31. 일반

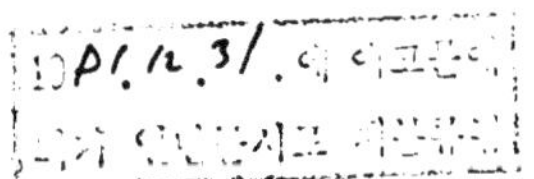

문협국 국기국 문화부 공보처

PAGE 1

91.08.15 08:03

외신 2과 통제관 DO

0059

외 무 부

번 호: WUNF-0127 910817 1918 FO 년월일: 시간:

수 신: 주 유엔 대사(~~총영사~~)

발 신: 외무부장관(문 일)

제 목: 月印千江之曲

보 안 통 제	725
외신과 통 제	

총 4 매 (표지포함)

0060

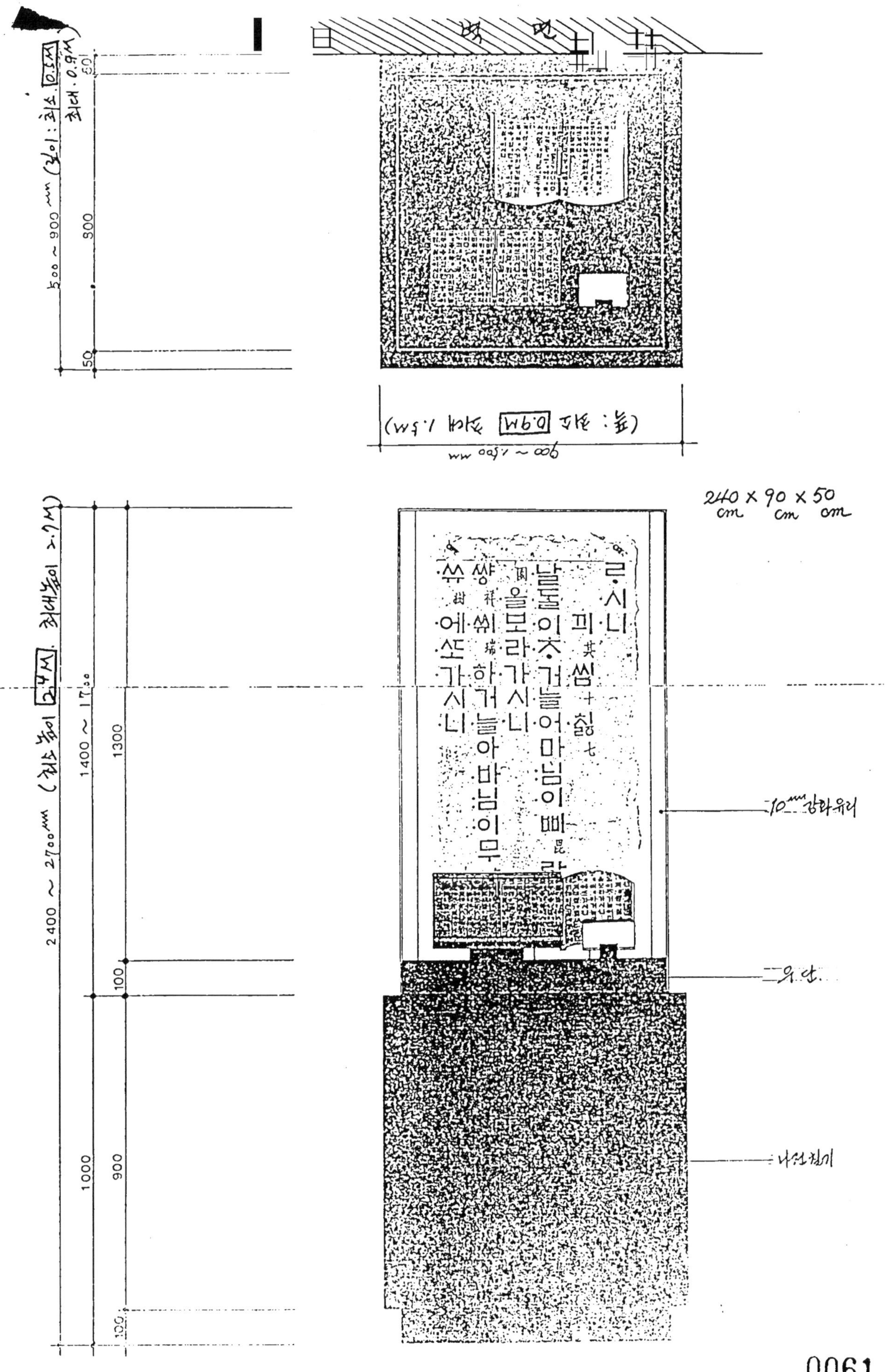

0061

<80 ~ 134 cm>

(월인천강지곡 영인본)

-인쇄할 한지 견본-

<130cm ~ 163cm>

0062

月印千江之曲

※적당한 크기의 동판으로 제작.

○ 規格 및 特性

– 寶物 第398号 (金屬·木板 活字本)

– 한글·漢文混用

∘元來 한글作品으로 漢字 挿入 形態

– 世宗 御製作品으로 龍飛御天歌 다음가는 最高의 文獻으로 朝鮮初期 敍事詩의 代表作 (世宗 31年(1449) 刊行)

○ 現所在地 : 大韓教科書株式會社 (作家 : 김근수(人間文化財))

○ 期待效果

– 구텐베르크의 活字보다 앞선 우리의 金屬活字 (1449) 紹介

– 한글이 크게 부각되고 漢字는 補助表記語로 使用되어 우리의 固有한 文字文化(한글)를 世界人에게 自然스럽게 弘報하는 機會마련

○ 問題点

– 外國의 膳物作品과 比較할 때 華麗함에서 뒤떨어져 觀覽客의 視線을 끌지 못할 憂慮

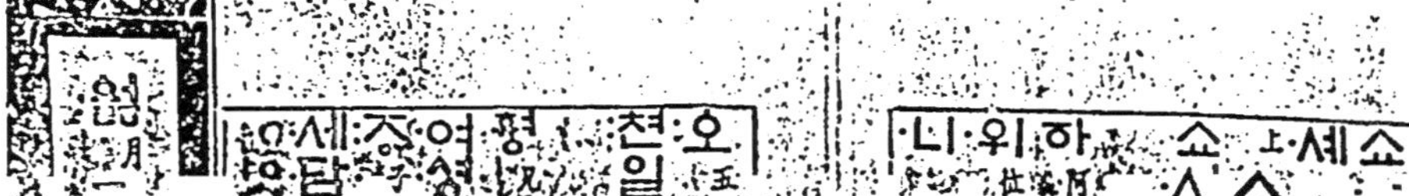

0063

初期 敍事詩의 代表作 (世宗 31年(1449) 刊行)

○ 現所在地 : 大韓教科書株式會社 〔作家 : 김근수(人間文化財)〕

○ 期待效果

- 구텐베르크의 活字보다 앞선 우리의 金屬活字(1449) 紹介
- 한글이 크게 부각되고 漢字는 補助表記語로 使用되어 우리의 固有한 文字文化(한글)를 世界人에게 自然스럽게 弘報하는 機會마련

○ 問題点

- 外國의 膳物作品과 比較할 때 華麗함에서 뒤떨어져 觀覽客의 視線을 끌지 못할 憂慮

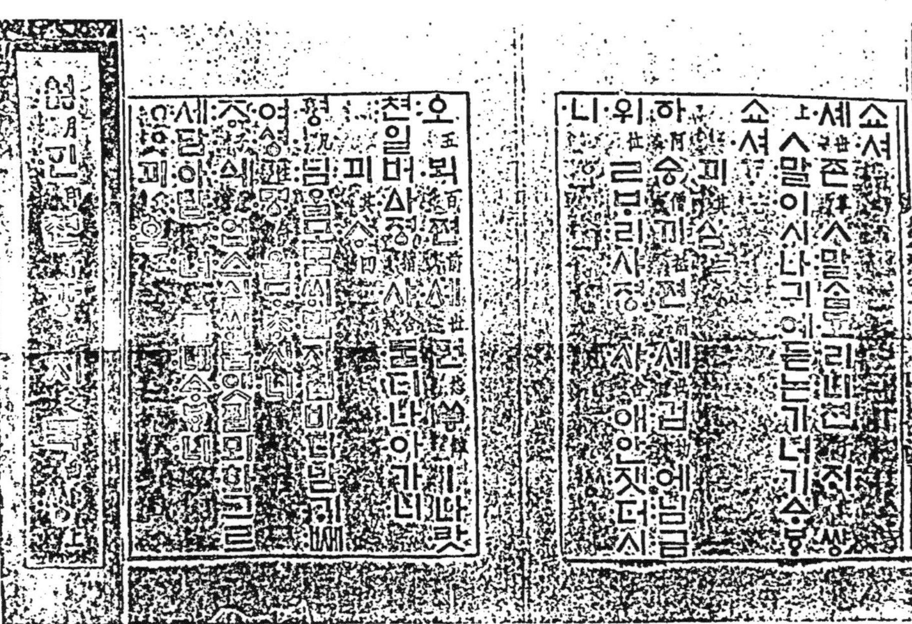

0064

쇼·셔

·셰世존尊ㅅ ·말 ᄉᆞᆯᄫᅩ·리·니 쳔千·ᄌᆡ載·썅上ㅅ

·말·이·시·나 ·귀·예 듣·논·가 너·기ᅀᆞᄫᆞ

쇼·셔

끠其삼三

하阿숭僧끼祇 쪈前·셰世겁劫에 님금

·위位ㄹ ᄇᆞ·리·샤 ·졍精·샤舍애 안잿·더·시

·니

:오五·ᄇᆡᆨ百 쪈前·셰世 ·ᅙᅯᆫ怨쓤讐ㅣ 나랏

:쳔 일버ᅀᅡ ·졍精·샤舍ᄅᆞᆯ 디·나·아 가·니

끠其ᄉᆞ四

훵兄님·을 모ᄅᆞᆯᄊᆡ ·발자·쵤 바·다 남·ᄀᆡ ᄢᅦ

·여 ·셩性·명命을 ᄆᆞ·ᄎᆞ·시·니

ᄌᆞ:子·식息 :업스실·씨 :몸앳 ·필 뫼·화 그르

·세 담·아 남男녀女ᄅᆞᆯ ·내ᅀᆞᄫᆞ·니

끠其ᅌᅩ五

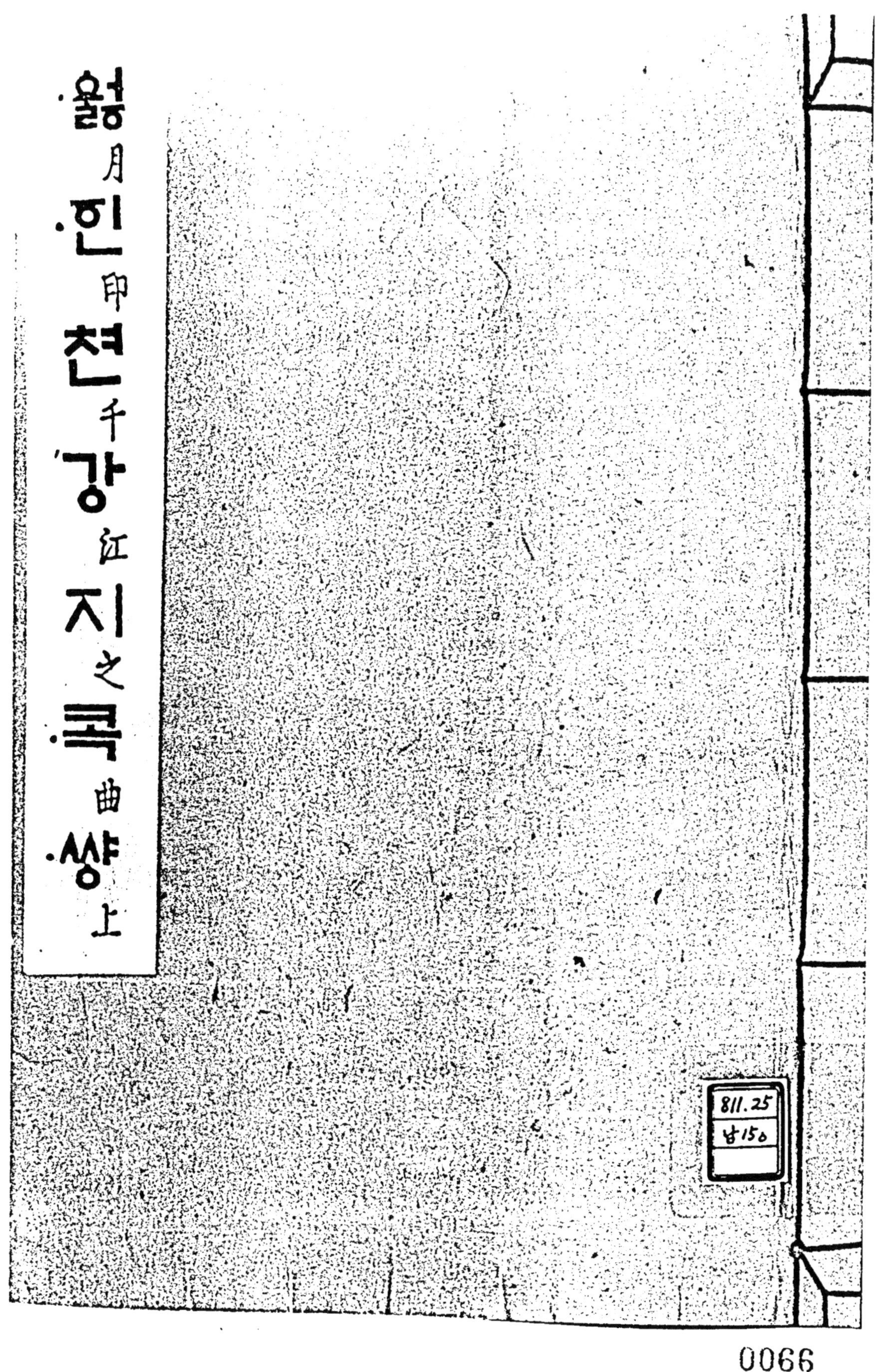
웛月힌印천千강江지之콕曲샹上

I. 寄贈品 展示

1. 槪要

가. 諸元

1) 規格: 높이 240Cm, 폭 93Cm, 두께 53Cm

2) 重量: 220Kg 및 274Kg의 2種 製作, 현지 상황에 따라 擇一 설치

나. 構成

1) 影印本 月印千江之曲 上卷

2) 月印千江之曲을 인쇄한 금속활자판 틀과 낱개 활자

3) 인쇄된 2面을 확대한 韓紙

4) 칠기 받침대

5) 10mm 강화 유리틀

다. 特徵

1) 보물 第398號(목판 금속활자본)의 複製品

2) 金屬活字로 인쇄된 最初의 한글 作品

3) 한글은 크게 부각, 漢字는 補助表記

4) 구텐베르크의 금속활자 인쇄(1450)보다 1年 앞선 世宗 31年(1449) 御製

5) 世宗이 王妃(소헌왕후)의 명복을 빌기 위해 지은 作品으로 부처의 慈悲와 功德이 온 누리에 가득함을 찬송하는 內容

0067

2. 品目 選定 經緯

가. 91.5月부터 他國의 유엔가입 紀念物 寄贈慣行 및 品目調査

나. 91.6월 후보품목 提示, 展示場所 交涉

1) 龍鼓: '88 서울올림픽 開·閉會式에 사용한 큰북

o 展示空間 確保 困難

o 서양인의 龍에 대한 이미지가 좋지 않음

2) 벽 장식물: 대형자수 作品등

o 유엔에 寄贈된 벽 장식물 다수가 창고에 산적

3) 新羅金冠 또는 高麗靑瓷

o 駐유엔 代表部 建議 品目

다. 月印千江之曲 選定

1) 文化財委員, 考古學者, 美術家, 建築디자이너등 관계 專門家 會議에서 檢討, 選定

2) 우리 傳統文化 및 한글의 우수성을 널리 알릴수 있고, 금관이나 도자기에 비해 희소가치가 있는 品目

- 2 -

0068

라. 91.8.19 유엔당국에 品目 通報, 寄贈節次 協議

1) Alvardo de Soto 寄贈品擔當 사무차장보(위원장) 및 3人의 專門家로 구성된 藝術委員會에서 檢討, 接受與否 決定

2) 展示 및 管理에 따른 費用은 전액 기증국 負擔

3. 製作 및 展示

가. 製作者

1) 總 指揮: 韓 道龍(홍익대 美大 教授)

2) 활자판 주조: 金 根洙(인간문화재 77호, 安城 鍮器匠)

3) 판형 製作: 孫 寶基(단국대 教授, 古活字 硏究 權威者)

4) 組立 및 接合: 東洋企業社

나. 包裝 및 運送

1) 寄贈品을 分解, 대형 나무상자 4개로 包裝

2) 9.11(水) 정파편 駐유엔 代表部로 송부

ㅇ 9.12(木) 10:00 KE-026편 김포공항 出發,
11:10 뉴욕 JFK공항 到着

3) 駐유엔 代表部에서 引受, 保管

4) 91.9.15(日) 專門家 2名 現地到着, 設置 作業

다. 寄贈 및 展示

1) 場　　所: 유엔本部 2층 Delegate Lounge와 總會長 入口 사이 복도

2) 除幕日時: 9.23(月) 18:00경(유엔 事務總長 面談後 傳達式 擧行)

0070

유엔 사무총장 면담 및 기증품 전달식

가. 시간.장소 : 9.23(월) 17:30-18:10
- 면담 : 유엔 사무총장실(S 3800)
- 기증품 기증식 : 2층 전시장

나. 참석범위
- 아측 (4명) : 외무부장관, 주유엔대사, 외교안보보좌관, 이정하비서관
- 유엔측(2명): 사무총장비서실장

다. 복 장 : 평복

라. 취 재 : 풀

마. 절 차

17:10 · 면담 배석자, 승차대기

17:12 1) 대통령, 거실출발

17:15 2) 대통령, 호텔출발

17:30 3) 대통령, 유엔사무국 현관 도착
- Teymour 의전장, 하차선 영접
- Cuellar 사무총장, 현관 영접

4) 기념촬영 (사무국 1층로비)

5) 사무총장실 (38층)로 이동

6) 기념촬영

7) 면담

8) 승강기편, 기증품 전시장(사무국 2층) 으로 이동

9) 대통령, 사무총장에게 기증품 설명, 기념촬영

18:10 10) 대통령, 유엔본부 출발
- 사무총장, 회의장 현관 전송
- Teymour 의전장, 승차선 전송

18:25 11) 대통령, 숙소도착

마. 준비 및 확인사항
- 좌석배치
- 기증품 사전 전시
- 의장용 태극기, 유엔기 규격

0071

月印千江之曲

◦ **規格 및 特性**

– 宝物 第 398号 (金屬 · 木板 活字本)

– 한글 · 漢文 混用

· 元來 한글作品으로 漢字 挿入 形態

– 世宗 御製作品으로 龍飛御天歌 다음가는 最古의 文獻으로 朝鮮初期 敍事詩의 代表作 (世宗 31年 (1449) 刊行)

– 內 容 : 世宗이 釋迦의 功德을 讚揚하여 지은 노래를 실은 冊임
(上·中·下 3卷中 上卷만 現存)

◦ **製作方法** : 現存 月印千江之曲 冊子(上)를 펼친 狀態에서 適當한 크기로 擴大하여 銅板으로 立体感있게 製作

◦ **期待效果**

– 우리나라에서 全世界에 자랑할 수 있는 科學的인 發明品은 金屬活字(1449) 뿐임.

– 한글이 크게 부각되고 漢字는 補助表記語로 使用되어 우리의 固有한 文字文化 (한글)를 世界人에게 自然스럽게 弘報하는 機會마련

◦ **問題点**

– 外國의 膳物作品과 比較할 때 華麗함에서 뒤떨어져 觀覽客의 視線을 끌지 못할 憂慮

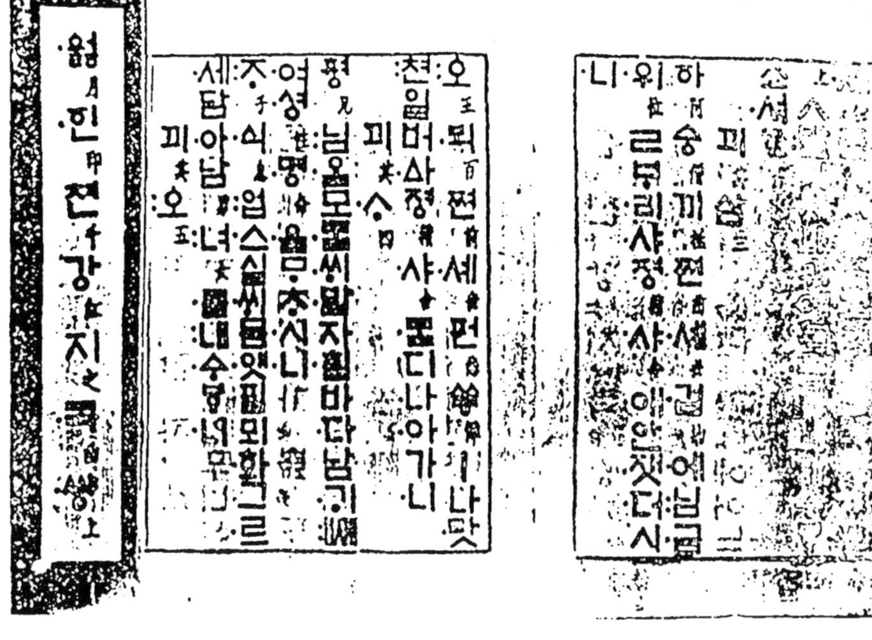

0072

WOL-IN-CHON-KANG-JI-KOK(The Moon Shining on All the Rivers of the Earth)

Korea began making books using mulberry paper and wood blocks as early as the 8th century. The Mukujungkwang-Dharani Sutra , one of the earliest volumes, is housed in the National Museum of Korea. Wood block printing gave way to the advent of the movable metalic type printing at the begining of the 13th century. It is recorded that the first book printed by movable metal type was published in 1232 and again in 1234, 200 years earlier than that made by Johannes Gutenberg of Germany.

The oldest movable metal type printed book in the world is Jikji-Shimche Yojul (A Gist of Enlightenment) which was published in Chongju, Chungbuk Province in 1377 and later taken to France, where it is currently housed in the National Library in Paris. The development of metal type continued till the 19th century.

King Sejong of the Choson Dynasty invented the Korean alphabet called hangul in 1446, in which he wrote a long epic poem called "Wol-In-Chon Kang-Ji Kok." The poem was first printed by the metal type, called Kapinja , cast in 1434. In 1447, another metal type was cast and the poem was printed again with the new type.

The special significance of this book lies in the fact that the long epic poem is the very first one written in hangul and printed by the first movable metal type the world has ever known.

What is exhibited here is a photocopy of "Wol-In-Chon-Kang-Ji-Kok," and a movable metal typeset frame, and an enlarged copy of one page of the book, made of hanji (Korean mulberry paper) which are known to last for as long as a thousand years. The exhibits are designed so that they blend in with the surrounding in which they are exhibited.

0073

02 송

관리번호	91-4722

외 무 부

종 별 : 긴 급

번 호 : UNW-2186 일 시 : 91 0819 1900

수 신 : 장 관(문일,국연,문정,해기,기정)

발 신 : 주 유엔 대사

제 목 : 유엔가입(기증품)

대:WUN-2209,2219

연:UNW-2154

1. 신대사는 8.19 오전 유엔기증품담당 책임자 ALVARDO DE SOTO 사무차장보를 면담, 아국정부가 월인천강지곡을 기증품으로 선정하였음을 알린후 월인천강지곡의 역사적, 문화사적 의의, 동 기증품의 소재및 크기등관련 설명하고 이에대한 유엔측의 적극적 협조를 당부한바 동요지 아래보고함.

가. 동인은 우선 월인천강지곡이 호의적인 반응을 얻을것으로 본다함.

나. 동 기증품의 크기와관련, 동인은 사견임을 전제로 최소규모 (높이 240 CM X 폭 90 CM) 라면 비교적 희망하는 장소에 전시하는데 큰 어려움은 없을것으로 생각되나 최대규모(높이 270 CM X 폭 150 CM)로서는 아측 희망장소에 전시되기에는 여전히 문제가 있을것으로 보며 확정적인 입장을 사무총장실 및 ART COMMITTEE 위원들과 협의해 본후 알려주겠다함. 동 협의를 위해서는 동 기증품의 총 중량이 어느정도인지 필요하니 지급확인 통보하여 주길 바란다함.

다. 동인은 이어 전시후보장소 관련 아측에서 대표단만이 이용하는 2 층 (유엔 총회의장입구, DELEGATE LOUNGE, 2 층 복도) 또는 일반관광객이 방문하는 장소 (1 층 VISITOR'S ENTRANCE, 3 층 복도등)중 어느편에 전시되길 희망하는지를 조속 알려주길 바란다함.

라. 또한 동인은 지구촌 행사기간에 전시될수 있기 위해서는 아측 기증품이최소한 행사개최 10 일 이전에 유엔측에 전달되어야 준비에 차질이 없을 것이라는 바, 제작에 참고바람.

2. 상기 나항 기증품의 총 중량을 지급 알려주시고 다항 전시장소 관련 당관으로서는 홍보효과를 위해서는 일반관광객 출입이 가능한 장소에 전시하는것이더

문협국 장관 차관 1차보 국기국 청와대 안기부 문화부 공보처

PAGE 1 91.08.20 08:01

외신 2과 통제관 BS

0074

좋지 않을까 생각되는바, 본부입장 회보바람. 끝.

(대사 노창희-국장)

예고:91.12.31. 일반

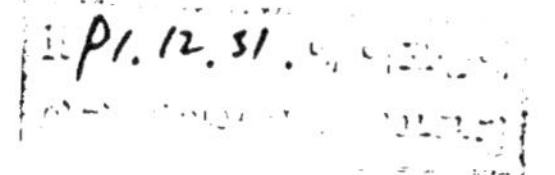

관리 번호	91-4246

외 무 부

종 별 :

번 호 : UNW-2203　　　　일 시 : 91 0820 1700

수 신 : 장 관(문일,국연,문정,해기,기정)

발 신 : 주 유엔 대사

제 목 : 유엔가입(기증품)

대:WUN-2243

1. 대호관련 신대사는 8.20 오전 ALVARO DE SOTO 사무차장보를 방문, 확정된 아국 기증품의 규모, 중량및 전달시기등에 관해 설명하고 동 기증품이 2 층 DELEGATE LOUNGE 에 전시될수 있도록 적극 협조해 줄것을 요청했음.

2. 동인은 아국기증품 크기라면 유엔측이 수용할수있는 규모라면서 2 층에 있는 여러개의 LOUNGE 중의 하나에 전시되도록 노력하겠으나 NORTH DELEGATE LOUNGE 또는 총회의장 입구등 장소에의 전시 가능여부는 유엔건물 관리사무소등 전시 관계자들과 협의해 보아야겠다고 하면서 그결과를 8 월말까지는 알려주겠다고약속했음. 또한 동인은 기증품 전시 및 관리에따른 일체 비용은 기증국가에서 부담한다는 점에 주의를 환기한바, 별전관련 규정 참고바람.

3. 이와관련 당관은 아국기증품이 2 층 DELEGATE LOUNGE 의 아측희망장소에 전시되도록 최대한 교섭위계이며 지구촌 기간중 기증품관련 행사 진전사항은 사무총장실등과 협의후 추보예정임.끝.

첨부:FAX 2 매:UNW(F)-438 끝

(대사 노창희-국장)

예고:91.12.31. 일반

91.12.31.

문협국	장관	차관	1차보	2차보	국기국	청와대	안기부	문화부
공보처								

PAGE 1　　　　91.08.21 08:25

외신 2과 통제관 BS

0076

#별첨

유엔(기)-438 1982 1700
(문일. 국연. 문정. 해기. 기청.) 총2매

United Nations

Finance manual

Section 10.00 - 10.01
Page 1 of 2
Rev. 1
Date 22/6/83

10.00 PROCUREMENT, MANAGEMENT AND DISPOSAL OF PROPERTY

10.01 PROPERTY

.011 Definition of property. Property consists of supplies, equipment, buildings and land belonging to or entrusted to the charge of the United Nations, whether acquired by purchase, rental, loan, donation or other means.

.012 Categories of property. There are three categories of property.

(a) Expendable property is movable property with an original cost of less than $500 a unit or with an original cost exceeding $500 a unit but with a serviceable life of less than five years. Property records and controls are not required to be maintained for expendable property except for items considered to be of an attractive nature (e.g., cameras, recording equipment, technical equipment, silver tableware). For administrative purposes property records are, however, maintained for special items (e.g., office equipment and furniture). In accordance with financial rule 110.25(b), the Under-Secretary-General for Administration, Finance and Management (USG/AFM) determines the items for which records are maintained.

2-1

0077

United Nations 

Finance manual

Section 10.00 - 10.01
Page 2 of 2
Rev. 1
Date 22/6/83

(b) Non-expendable property consists of movable items of equipment valued at $500 or more a unit, exclusive of additional charges such as freight and insurance, and with a serviceable life of at least five years. Property records and controls are maintained for such items.

(c) Real property is non-movable property. It consists of land, buildings and built-in fixtures.

.013 Gifts and loans of property. Offers of gifts and loans of property to the United Nations (not including land and buildings which require the approval of the General Assembly) are extended to the Secretary-General, who in the case of works of art may seek the advice of the Art Committee prior to acceptance. The policy of the United Nations is to require that the donor of the gift or loan accept complete financial responsibility for its installation and maintenance. Each gift or loan of property accepted by the United Nations is entered in the property records of the Organization by the Office of General Services.

2-2

0078

관리 번호	91 -4655

외 무 부

종 별 : 지 급

번 호 : UNW-2459 일 시 : 91 0905 1900

수 신 : 장관(문일,국연,의전,해기)

발 신 : 주 유엔 대사

제 목 : 유엔가입(기증품)

대 : WUN-2512

1. 대호 관련 유엔 건물관리 사무국 기증품 담당관 NICHOLAS SARDEGNA(CHIEF, UN BUILDING MANAGEMENT SERVICE)는 2 층 전시물의 중량관련 건물관리 규정상 1 SQ. FEET(30.48 CM X 30.48 CM929.03 SQ.CM)당 100 POUND(45.359 KG)로 제한되어 있다면서 아국기증품 규모가 90CM X 50 CM(4500 SQ.CM)인 경우 484 POUND(219.54 KG)을 초과치 않도록 제작함이 바람직 하다는 의견을 제시해 온바, 총중량이 300 KG 정도가 될 경우 2 층 전시에 어려움이 있지 않을까 염려됨. 유엔측에 공식 통보하기전에 지금이라도 중량 감축이 어느정도 가능한지를 우선 참고로 회보 바람

2. 전시장소는 ALVARO DE SOTO 사무차장보가 해외 출장중으로 9.10 귀임 즉시 동인과 최종 협의 동결과를 보고 위계이며, 기증식 행사내용도 전시장소 확정후 추보 예정임

3. 기증품 도착 일시, 항공편을 통보 바라며, 운반을 위한 특수차량등 사전준비 사항도 아울러 통보 바람. 끝

(대사 노창희-국장)

예고 91.12.31 일반

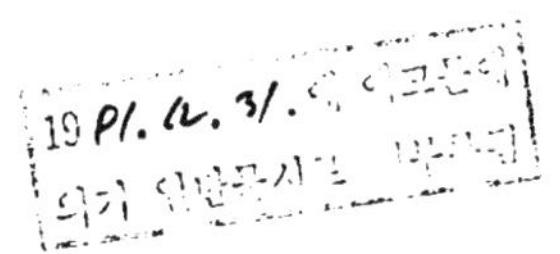

문협국 공보처	장관	차관	1차보	2차보	의전장	국기국	청와대	안기부

PAGE 1 91.09.06 09:33

외신 2과 통제관 BW

0079

長官報告事項

報告畢

1991. 9. 6.
文化協力局
文化協力1課(13)

題 目 : 유엔加入 寄贈品 製作 및 運送

1. 寄贈品 重量: 유엔당국의 制限重量인 219.54kg 이내로 製作

o 유리: 140kg

o 한지 및 서적: 5kg

o 활자들: 10kg

o 받침: 5kg

o 칠기: 50kg

계: 210kg

2. 措置事項

가. 包裝 및 發送(文化部에서 經費負擔)

o 91.9.7(토) 부터 文書擔當官室에서 包裝

o 91.9.11(수) 外交貨物로 發送

나. 專門家 2名 派遣

o 現地 設置作業 支援

o 美國 入國査證 申請中, 91.9.12경 出國豫定. 끝.

0080

관리번호	91-4789

외 무 부

종 별 :

번 호 : UNW-2562 일 시 : 91 0910 1940

수 신 : 장 관(의전,국연,해기)

발 신 : 주 유엔 대사

제 목 : 지구촌(기증품)

대:WUN-2636,2640

연:UNW-2494,2459

1. 신대사는 9.10 ALVARO DE SOTO 사무차장보를 면담 전시장소 관련 협의한바, 선발대 당지 방문시 아측이 제시한 2 층 DELEGATE LOUNGE 엘리베이터 정면우측 장소를 아국 기증품 전시장소로 제공키로 유엔 ART COMMITTEE, 건물관리 사무국및 경호실측과 합의되었다고 알려주면서 자신으로서도 대통령의 역사적인 유엔방문의 의의에 비춰 아측에서 요청한 장소가 확보된것을 매우 다행스럽게 생각한다 하였음.

2. 전달식은 세부절차 관련 연호 보고 내용과 같이 시간 제약등으로 사무총장 면담후 2 층 전시장으로 사무총장과 함께 이동, 대통령께서 기증품에 관해 간단히 설명하시면 사무총장의 사의표명에 이어 기념 촬영순으로 진행토록하며,(약5 분 정도 소요), 유엔측에서는 사무총장, 비서실장, 의전장, DE SOTO 사무차장보등 유엔 고위관리들이 참석할 것이라하며, 세부 절차사항은 사무총장 면담 일정 확정후 추보함

3. 기증품 설치, 제막을 위한 장식은 기증품 도착후 아측 전문가와 협의, 조치하고자 하는바, 대호 전문가는 내주초 당지 도착케 하면 될것으로 생각되니적의 조치 바람. 끝

(대사 노창희-의전장)

예고 91.12.31 일반

1991.12.31.에 예고문에 의거 일반문서로 재분류됨

의전장	장관	차관	국기국	청와대	청와대	청와대	안기부	공보처

PAGE 1

91.09.11 09:08

외신 2과 통제관 BS

0081

유엔가입 기증품 설치 및 기증식 거행

1. 기증품 설치

가. 전문가 파견: 9.15(日) 10:00 KE 026편 김포공항 출발

10:30 뉴욕 JFK 공항 도착

나. 인계 및 설치

1) 9.16 오전중 유엔 건물관리 사무국에 기증품 인계

2) 주유엔 대표부, 유엔당국 및 전문가간에 설치작업 가능시기 협의

2. 기증식 거행

가. 일시 및 장소: 91.9.23(月) 11:30경, 유엔본부 2층 Delegate Lounge

입구 승강기 정면 우측

나. 진행순서(약 5분정도 소요)

1) 대통령, 사무총장 면담후 전시장으로 이동

2) 대통령께서 기증품에 관해 간단히 설명

3) 사무총장의 사의 표명

4) 기념촬영

5) 견본 및 설명서 배포

0082

유엔 사무총장 면담 및 기증품 전달식

가. 시간.장소 : 9.23(월) 17:30-18:10
- · 면담 : 유엔 사무총장실(S 3800)
- · 기증품 기증식 : 2층 전시장

나. 참석범위
- 아측 (4명) : 외무부장관, 주유엔대사,
  외교안보보좌관, 이정하비서관
- 유엔측(2명): 사무총장비서실장

다. 복 장 : 평복

라. 취 재 : 풀

마. 절 차

17:10 · 면담 배석자, 승차대기
17:12 1) 대통령, 거실출발
17:15 2) 대통령, 호텔출발
17:30 3) 대통령, 유엔사무국 현관 도착
- Teymour 의전장, 하차선 영접
- Cuellar 사무총장, 현관 영접
4) 기념촬영 (사무국 1층로비)
5) 사무총장실 (38층)로 이동
6) 기념촬영
7) 면담
8) 승강기편, 기증품 전시장(사무국 2층)으로 이동
9) 대통령, 사무총장에게 기증품 설명, 기념촬영
18:10 10) 대통령, 유엔본부 출발
· 사무총장, 회의장 현관 전송
· Teymour 의전장, 승차선 전송
18:25 11) 대통령, 숙소도착

마. 준비 및 확인사항
- · 좌석배치
- · 기증품 사전 전시
- · 의장용 태극기, 유엔기 규격

0083

문화 '91-
1991.9 .

문화부 공보실 ● 720-9671 / 736-7946-9(220)
내용문의: 720-4037(조사과)

UN 가입계기 문화선물 보내

- 세계최초의 금속활자 발명 사실을 알리는 활자판틀과 영인본 및 장식품 -

문화부는 UN 가입을 계기로 UN 본부에 기증할 문화선물로 한국의 옛 금속활자와 그 인쇄본인 月印千江之曲의 제작을 완료하여 외무부에 전달하였으며, 이 선물은 9월 12일(목) 현지로 송부될 예정이다.

문화선물은 월인천강지곡 인쇄에 사용되었던 금속활자를 인간문화재 김근수씨가 재현·제작한 금속활자판틀과 월인천강지곡 영인본 및 인쇄된 한 판을 한지에 확대 인쇄한 장식품으로 구성되어 있으며, 재현된 금속활자판은 가로 45Cm, 세로 33Cm, 두께 4Cm 이고 전시물의 전체크기는 높이 240Cm, 가로 90Cm, 폭 50Cm 이다.

이 선물은 문화재위원, 고고학자, 미술가, 건축디자이너 등 관계전문가들로 구성된 회의에서 검토되어 선정된 것이며 이 제작 과정에도 관계전문가들이 참여하였다.

월인천강지곡은 우리 고유의 문자인 한글의 자체(字體)가 금속활자로 인쇄된 최초의 실물로서 우리나라의 인쇄문화와 문자문화(한글)를 전세계에 알릴 수 있는 좋은 계기가 될 것이다.

이 문화선물은 오는 9월 23일경 유엔사무국에 기증되어 전시될 예정이다.

본 문화방에 관한 구체적인 자료와 내용은 문화정책국 (조사과)에서 제공합니다. (☎ 720 - 4037)

0084

	분류번호	보존기간

발 신 전 보

번 호 : WUN-4001 911120 1506 BE 종별 : 암호송신

수 신 : 주 유엔 대사. 총영사

발 신 : 장 관 (문정, 문일)

제 목 : "일인천강지곡" 사후관리

1. 유엔본부에 기증한 "월인천강지곡"의 관리에 참고코자 하니, 아래 사항 회보바람.

가. 사무국내 관리부서 및 관리자 성명 (영문 포함)

나. 현재의 진열상태

다. 유엔관계자 및 일반관객의 반응

2. 상기 관리에 따른 문제는 수시로 본부와 협의바람.

(문화부 문화정책국장 신 현 웅)

보안통제	725

앙고재	91년 11월 20일	문일 1과	기안자 성명	담당	과 장	심의관	국 장		차 관	장 관
				박인주	725	28	전결			書

외신과통제

0085

2

주 국 련 대 표 부

주국련(공)35260- 012 1991. 12 . 31 .

수신 장관

참조 문화협력국장, 해외공보관장

제목 "월인천강지곡" 사후관리

1. WUN - 4001의 관련입니다.

2. 대호 문의사항에 대하여 다음과 같이 보고합니다.

가. 사무국내 관리부서 및 관리자의 직성명

1) 유엔사무총장실 기증품 담당보좌관

o 성명 : Ms. Lisa Buttenheim

o 직함 : Senior Officer

Executive Office of the Secretary General

2) 청사관리 전반

o 성명 : Mr. Nicholas J. Sardegna

o 직함 : Chief, Buildings Management Service

Department of Adminstration and Mangement

3) 관리 및 보수담당

o 성명 : Mr. Martin Bender

o 직함 : Chief, Maintenance & Operations Section

Department of Adminstration and Mangement

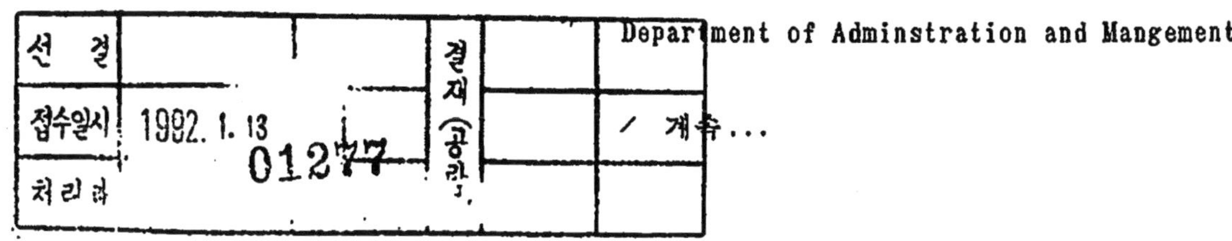

선 결		결재(공람)		
접수일시	1992. 1. 13			
처리과	012??			

/ 계속...

0086

나. 현재의 진열상태

1) 동 기증품은 총회회의장, 안보리등 유엔 주요기구 회의장 건물 및 유엔 사무국 건물과 연결되는 주통로에 있는 엘리베이터 옆 시계탑 하단에 위치하고 있어 유엔에 출입하는 각국대표단 및 사무국 직원들이 일상적으로 접할수 있는 최상의 위치에 진열 되어 있음.

2) 또한 조명등 동 기증품의 전시상태는 양호하며, "Gift from Republic of Korea 24 October 1991"라는 Name Plate 를 유엔 관리부서에서 제작, 기증품 진열관옆에 부착했음.

다. 유엔 관계자 및 일반관객의 반응

1) 관련부서 담당자들은 동 기증품이 한국의 발달된 고유문화를 소개하는 문화적 가치가 높은 전시품으로써 전시기법도 훌륭 하다는 평가와 함께, 유엔측이 희망했던 선정기준에 부합되는 기증품이라고 환영한다고 말했음.

2) 일반 관광객들은 금속활자 사용이 구텐베르크보다 200년이나 앞선 한국의 문화적 유산에 대한 인식을 새롭게 갖게되는 계기 였다는 반응이며, 특히 동 기증품을 관람한 뉴욕 교민들은 우리 문화에 대한 자긍심을 가지게 되었다고 함.

첨 부 : 관련사진 및 DWB 기사 각 1매. 끝.

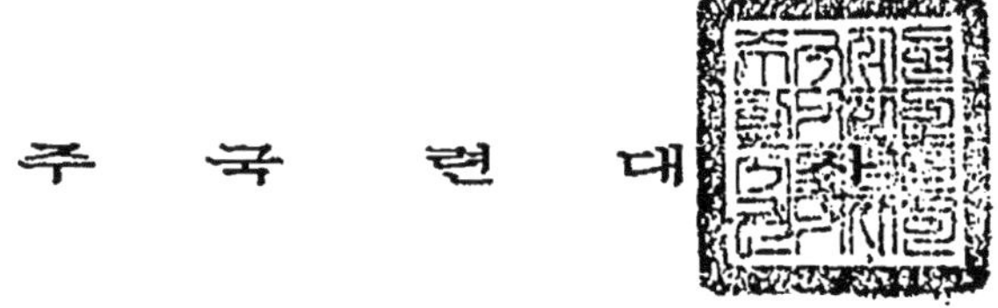

주 국 련 대

0087

발 신 전 보

분류번호	보존기간

번 호 :

종별 :

수 신 : 주국련 대사. 총영사

주미대사

발 신 : 장 관 (문일)

제 목 : "월인천강지곡" 관리

대: 주국련(공) 35260 - 012(91.12.31)

연: WUN - 2640(91.9.10)

주 유엔 대표부에 송부한 "월인천강지곡" 2조 가운데 유엔본부에 기증·전시하고 남은 1조는 활자판만 보충하면 완성품으로의 조립이 가능하므로 이를 대표부 또는 대사관저에 전시하는 방안을 검토하였으나 뉴욕 시내에 동일 품목을 전시하는 것은 홍보효과를 저하시킬 것이라는 의견이 있어 미주대륙 발견 500주년 기념선물로 워싱턴 소재 미주기구 본부에 기증·전시하는 방안을 관계부처와 협의코자 하니, 이에 대한 귀견을 보고 바람. 끝.

(문화협력국장 이 해순)

보안통제	

앙고재	92년 1월 20일	문협1과	기안자 성명		과 장	심의관	국 장		차 관	장 관
			오동일				전결			보류

외신과통제

0088

외 무 부

110-760 서울 종로구 세종로 77번지 / (02)720-2220 / (02)738-9515

문서번호 문일 20521-

시행일자 1992. 1.23.( )

수신 문화부장관
사본 : 공보처장관, 한국국제교류재단 이사장
참조

취급		장 관
보존		보류
국 장	전결	
심의관		
과 장		
기안	오 동일	협조

제목 "월인천강지곡" 관리

1. 주 유엔 대사는 별첨 공문과 같이, 우리 정부가 유엔본부에 기증한 "월인천강지곡"의 진열위치 및 전시상태가 양호하고 유엔 관계자 및 일반의 반응이 좋을 뿐만 아니라 교민들의 문화적 자긍심을 고취시키고 있다고 보고하여 왔습니다.

2. 주 유엔 대표부에 보관중인 나머지 1조도 주 유엔 대표부 또는 대사관저에 전시하는 ~~등 활용 방안을 강구함이~~ 등의 방안도 좋을 것으로 사료되나, 뉴욕 시내에 동일 품목을 전시하는 것은 홍보효과를 저하시킬 것이라는 의견이 있~~어 미주대륙 발견 500주년 기념선물로 워싱턴 소재 미주기구 본부~~으므로 적절한 다처에 기증·전시하는 방안~~에~~을 강구함이 ~~대한 주미대사관 및 주유엔 대사의 의견을 청취코자 하니~~ 더욱 바람직할 것으로 사료되는 바, 이에 대한 귀부의 검토의견을 회보하여 주시기 바랍니다.

첨부: 상기 공문 사본 1부. 끝.

0089

외 무 부

110-760 서울 종로구 세종로 77번지 / (02)720-2220 / (02)738-9515

문서번호 문일 20521- 61

시행일자 1992. 1.31.( )

수신 문화부장관(사본: 공보처장관, 한국국제교류재단 이사장)

참조

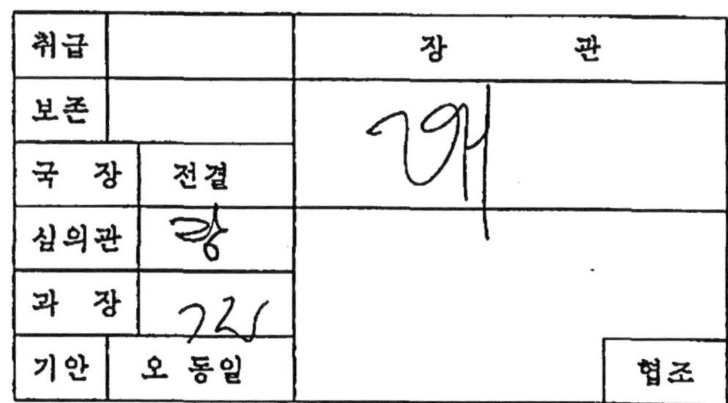

취급		장 관
보존		
국 장	전결	
심의관		
과 장		
기안	오 동일	협조

제목 "월인천강지곡" 관리

1. 주 유엔 대사는 별첨 공문과 같이, 우리 정부가 유엔본부에 기증한 "월인천강지곡"의 진열위치 및 전시상태가 양호하고 유엔 관계자 및 일반의 반응이 좋을 뿐만 아니라 교민들의 문화적 자긍심을 고취시키고 있다고 보고하여 왔습니다.

2. 주 유엔 대표부에 보관중인 나머지 1조도 주 유엔 대표부 또는 대사관저에 전시하는등의 방안도 좋을 것으로 사료되나, 뉴욕 시내에 동일 품목을 전시하는 것은 홍보효과를 저하시킬 것이라는 의견이 있으므로 적절한 타처에 기증·전시하는 방안을 강구함이 더욱 바람직할 것으로 사료되는바, 이에 대한 귀부의 검토의견을 회보하여 주시기 바랍니다.

검열 1992 2 0 3 통제관

첨부: 상기 공문 사본 1부. 끝.

0090

외 무 부

110-760 서울 종로구 세종로 77번지 / (02)720-2220 / (02)738-9515

문서번호 문일 20521-123
시행일자 1992. 3. 3. ( )

수신 문화부장관
참조

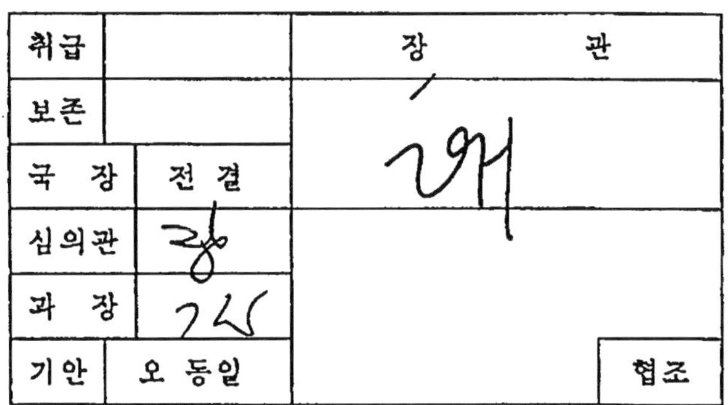

취급		장 관
보존		
국 장	전 결	
심의관		
과 장		
기안	오 동일	협조

제목 "월인천강지곡" 활용

대: 국교 35104 - 102(92.2.13)

현재 주 유엔대표부에 보관중인 "월인천강지곡" 진열장은 우리나라의 유엔 가입을 기념하여 유엔본부에 기증한 상징성과 운반 및 조립에 소요될 경비등에 비추어, 내용물을 동일품목으로 완성하여 타처에 기증·전시하는 것보다는 뉴욕 시내에서 여타 문화재를 전시하는데 활용함이 적절할 것으로 사료됩니다. 끝.

0091

((

문 화 부

우110-050 서울 종로구 세종로 82-1 / 전화 (02)720-4038 / 전송 736-8513

문서번호 국교 35104-102
시행일자 1992.02.13

수신 외무부장관
참조 문화협력국장

선결			지시		
접수	일자 시간	92.2.14	결재·공람		
	번호	5206			
처리과					
담당자		2			

제목 "월인천강지곡" 관리

1. 귀부 문일 20521-61('92.2.6) 관련입니다.

2. '91.9 UN가입과 관련, 문화부가 주UN대표부와 협조하여 UN본부 사무국에 기증한 "월인천강지곡"은 현재 상당한 문화적 전시효과를 거두고 있는 실정입니다.

3. 미국지역에 대한 문화적 홍보효과의 극대화를 위하여 현재 주유엔대표부에서 보관중인 나머지 1조를 미국 지성의 전당이며 국가대표도서관인 미국립의회도서관에 기증하는 방안을 적극 검토, 협의중에 있음을 알려드리오니 적의 참고하시기 바랍니다. 끝.

문화부 전문 타전 요청(2.14)하였다가 철회(2.15)

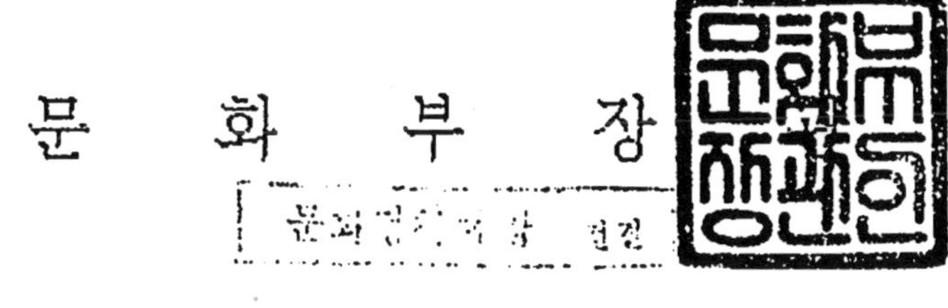

0092

문 화 부

우110-703 서울 종로구 세종로 82-1 / 전화 (02)720-4038 / 전송 736-8513

문서번호 국교 35104-207
시행일자 1992.03.21

수신 외무부장관
참조 문화협력국장

선결			지시		
접수	일자 시간	92. 3. 23	결재·공람		
	번호	9828			
처리과					
담당자					

제목 "월인천강지곡" 사후관리

1. 문화부 국교 35104-102('92.2.13) 및 귀부 문일 20521-61('92.2.1) 및 문일 20521-123('92.3.5) 관련입니다.

2. 현재 주UN대표부에서 보관중인 월인천강지곡의 나머지 한세트(유리전시장 포함)의 활용방안은 우리부에서 별도 검토중인바, 조치계획 통보시까지는 UN본부이외 기타지역에서 전시 및 활용되지 않도록하고 보관.관리에 철저를 기하여 주시기 바랍니다. 끝.

문 화 부
문화정책국장 전결

0093

외교문서 비밀해제: 남북한 유엔 가입 11

남북한 유엔 가입 결의안 채택 및 대응 2

초판인쇄 2024년 03월 15일
초판발행 2024년 03월 15일

지은이 한국학술정보(주)
펴낸이 채종준
펴낸곳 한국학술정보(주)
주 소 경기도 파주시 회동길 230(문발동)
전 화 031-908-3181(대표)
팩 스 031-908-3189
홈페이지 http://ebook.kstudy.com
E-mail 출판사업부 publish@kstudy.com
등 록 제일산-115호(2000. 6. 19)

ISBN 979-11-6983-954-9 94340
979-11-6983-945-7 94340 (set)